Critics and Criticism

Critics
and
Criticism

A. G. GEORGE

ASIA PUBLISHING HOUSE
BOMBAY · CALCUTTA · NEW DELHI · MADRAS
LUCKNOW · BANGALORE · LONDON · NEW YORK

Copyright © 1971 A. G. George
Arapara Ghevarghese **George** (1928)

ISBN 0.210.22347.2

PRINTED IN INDIA
AT ANANDA PRESS, LUCKNOW, AND PUBLISHED BY
P. S. JAYASINGHE, ASIA PUBLISHING HOUSE, BOMBAY

PREFACE

This book contains detailed studies of some important literary critics and some modern movements in criticism.

One of my main concerns here has been to clarify and elucidate many of the central concepts in criticism and poetic theory. Thus the critics who have been included here are those in whose writings we find the first formulations of these concepts. They are Plato, Aristotle, Sidney, Dryden, Wordsworth, Coleridge, Arnold, T. S. Eliot, T. E. Hulme, I. A. Richards, F. R. Leavis, and Yvor Winters. Special care has been taken to give as far a detailed treatment as possible to the masterworks of these critics, elucidating their historical importance and explaining their particular contributions. I have been chiefly concerned with the task of simplification and clarification, and therefore no claim for originality of contribution is made. On the contrary, I gratefully acknowledge my indebtedness to specialized authorities on each of these critics.

Delhi, May 1969   A. G. GEORGE

v

CONTENTS

CHAPTER ONE

INTRODUCTORY

On the Nature and Function of Criticism

One sometimes wonders why there are controversies on the nature and function of criticism, because the problems involved appear to be simple enough. The nature of criticism seems easy enough to understand. It is an activity of the human mind, distinct from the creative activity which results in works of art.

And the function of criticism seems even more simple to understand. Its function is to criticise a work of art, bring out its excellences, point out the defects, and thus finally judge its artistic qualities. In other words criticism must interpret and elucidate in order to judge. Thus far it is simple. The critical activity is directed towards arts and artists. But complications arise from unexpected quarters. And what appeared to be simple enough proves to be too complex to be explained in easily understandable terms. In the explanation given above it was assumed that we all know what art and poetry are, what are the specific details needing interpretation, and what are the criteria of excellence.

Now, a critical theory is built on a literary theory. The idea of what criticism is varies in accordance with the idea of literature. Thus neo-classical criticism derives from neo-classical literary theory, and to take a modern example, existential criticism is the product of existential literary theory or theories. We are not certainly making rigid demarcation between critical and literary theories. Often they blend into one. But the close dependence of critical theories on literary theories cannot be overlooked.

Now no philosopher or literary thinker has been able to produce a universally acceptable theory of poetry. On the contrary, there are a large number of poetic theories dealing with the origin, nature, and function of poetry. Corresponding to each of these we have a theory of criticism and its function.

1

Furthermore, a literary theory again takes its origin in a given philosophy of life. The interpretations of life vary, and these variations in turn affect our views of poetry, and these views further determine critical theories. Thus arises the complexity in the problem of the nature and function of criticism.

Any simple statement on criticism can be compared to an iceberg. The simple critical statement is only one part of a whole complex of attitudes in the critic's mind which lies submerged. I am not supporting critical relativism or critical determinism. But for the critic of criticism this is an essential fact. He cannot overlook criticism's direct dependence on, and relation to, the critic's own larger intellectual pre-occupations. No criticism is possible without a philosophy of life, even a philosophy which rejects all philosophies. Let us take some statements on the nature and function of criticism.

To set up as a critic is to set up as a judge of values.

I. A. RICHARDS

Criticism is a disinterested endeavour to learn and propagate the best that is known and thought in the world.

MATTHEW ARNOLD

To feel the virtue of the poet or the painter, to disengage it, to set it forth, are the three stages of the critic's duty.

WALTER PATER

According to Victor Hugo:

Is the work good or bad ? That is criticism's domain.

J. E. Spingarn (borrowing from Croce) makes the sole task of criticism to answer three questions :

What has the artist tried to express ? How has he succeeded in expressing it ? Was it worth expressing ?

Carlyle's conception of criticism is of a piece with his idealism. The critic must enquire :

Whether and how far this aim (the aim of the poet) this task of his accorded not with us . . . but with human nature, and with the nature of things at large ; with the universal principles of poetic beauty . . . as it stands written in the hearts and imagination of all men.

We notice that in ancient days the function of criticism had not become so problematical. Neither Plato nor Aristotle troubled themselves much about the nature of the critical function. For Dryden and Dr. Johnson, criticism was the art of judgement. For Wordsworth, criticism was essentially interpretation. And according to Coleridge, criticism must formulate the principles of poetic composition. On account of the Victorian pre-occupation with the criticism of life, literary criticism was brought into close affinity with discussions on contemporary problems in thought and belief. Arnold's critical writings show this widening of the sphere of critical enquiry. The impressionists of the early 20th century restricted criticism to the formulation of subjective impressions.

Serious and detailed enquiries in the 20th century into the nature of the critical function and process begin with T. S. Eliot's essays in *The Sacred Wood*. Eliot, while conceding that literary criticism is not autotelic, mainly restricts himself to comparison and analysis in criticism. With the New Critics the status of criticism becomes equal to that of creative literature itself. The special service rendered by New Criticism lies in responding to a widely-felt demand, in contemporary thought, for intellectual discipline, the craving for standards, the revolt from confusion, and the impatient quest for an acceptable hierarchy of values.

Some of the New Critics are acutely aware of this question of the function of criticism. Yvor Winters, for instance, examines this in *The Function of Criticism* and in "Preliminary Problems" (See the 12th Problem). He sees in criticism an actual union of the act of analysis and the act of evaluation. In one sense, according to him, criticism will be informative, since some basic biographical and historical facts are preliminaries of the critical operation. The next steps in criticism are analytic in character, having to do with the understanding of the literary theory involved, the paraphrasable content, and then the style or technique.

The final stage of the critical act consists in "receiving from the poet his own final and unique judgement in the judging of that judgement" on the basis (previously defined) of "the accuracy of his rational understanding and of his intuition and upon the accuracy of their interaction upon each". Winters maintains (in *The Function of Criticism*) that art is the evaluation of human experience by means of technique which renders possible an evaluation more precise than any other.

When we turn to another modern critic Austin Warren (see his "Rage for Order"), we see that the critic's function becomes a search for order. The critic should discover the poet's "systematic vision of the World". Second, as he says, the critic should define the spiritual cosmos of the writer and the specifically literary structure which corresponds to it.

It thus becomes clear that, whatever the type of criticism we examine, most, if not all, of the critics consider interpretation and judgement as the two functions of literary criticism. But in interpreting the process of interpretation and the object of interpretation they disagree.

But we may look upon the function of literary criticism from another angle. The critical process is the process of reflection upon an immediate poetic (or literary) experience. Through literary criticism we arrive at the total meaning of a poem. Criticism also should concern itself with the study of a given work in relation to the tradition to which it belongs, and also analyse the likenesses and differences it has in relation to other works, its effects not only on the aesthetic faculty of man, but also in shaping our attitudes to life, the formal qualities of a work of art, and its historical circumstances.

Thus stated, we are including a large number of functions for criticism, and this, it may be objected, tends to eclipse its most important aesthetic function, that of assessing an aesthetic experience or judging a work of art. It is true that this particular judicial function is considered only one among the many functions. To restrict the function of criticism to interpretation and judgement is to deprive it of its *very raison d' etre*. Although the final verdict we expect from criticism is the answer to the question "Is this (or is this not) a good poem?", the essential function of criticism is not the formulation of this answer alone. Even before the judicial verdict "this is a good poem", criticism should show how appreciation (or understanding or interpretation) finally leads to this verdict.

Our conception of the function of criticism outlined above is a composite one. Thus criticism is the verbal structure embodying the rational reflections on the total meanings of a work of art. This view of criticism holds even when the poem is its own meaning. Indeed, all the great poets who have been also critics never restricted the function of criticism as some of the practitioners of criticism (in the narrow sense of the word) have done. Wordsworth, Coleridge, Arnold, T. S. Eliot, (to take only a few important names from English Literary History) all so much widened the scope of literary criticism.

T. S. Eliot in fact goes to the extent of maintaining that the distinction between creative ages and critical ages should vanish, and criticism is as much a valuable activity as creation. According to him, it is one of criticism's supreme function to assist creation, and the best part of creation itself is criticism. He does not of course concede the converse that the best part of criticism is creation. He says:

The critical activity finds its highest, its true fulfilment in a kind of union with creation in the labour of the artist.

The Scope of Criticism in the Modern Age

Criticism in the twentieth century has widened its scope of enquiry and has appropriated to itself several areas of intellectual enquiry. In thus establishing itself as a major intellectual discipline of the modern age, in dealing with fundamental questions, criticism is partly tending to assert its own autonomy and independence of the creative activity. Criticism today has discovered that it is impossible to deal with creative literature, either with a view to explication or evaluation, unless it deals also at the same time with the larger problems of life.

Consequently, the development of social sciences and psychological disciplines and the growth of the history of ideas have in turn influenced criticism redefining the nature and function of the critical process. Thus we have criticism which is related to the history of ideas, or criticism which uses psychological, sociological, and cultural concepts. Such schools of criticism may be designated on the whole by the name "Extrinsic Criticism". At the same time there are critical movements which ignore these extrinsic data, and assuming that a "literary work" has an ontological status of its own, consider explication of the text as the sole function of the critical endeavour. These as we have seen above are the "Ontological Critics" or the "New Critics". The function of the critical process has been enlarged as the scope of the critical activity has widened.

The scope of criticism today is co-extensive with that of the humanities. This is a conclusion which will be supported even by the psychological or sociological critics. Nonthrop Frye in his *Anatomy of Criticism* (Princeton, 1957) points out the different functions of four types of criticism, i.e., Historical Criticism, Ethical Criticism, Archetypal Criticism, and Rhetorical Criticism. In his conclusion he refers to the fact that modern theories of criticism embrace the humanities in their educational aspects. Literary criticism today has to concern itself with the problems of education also. Well in a wider sense, this was what Matthew Arnold too had thought of as the function of criticism. As the scope of the critical enquiry widens, its function too becomes proportionately complex and diversified. And in any given literary situation this function can be determined only in relation to what is then thought to be criticism's scope.

CHAPTER TWO

CRITICISM IN ANCIENT GREECE

1. Judicial Criticism before Plato. 2. Plato : Art as Imitation

Judicial Criticism before Plato

Systematic poetical theory and literary criticism emerge in ancient Greece almost at the same time as creative writing. In fact the very concept of poetics is a Greek invention. We generally take it for granted that criticism follows (rather than precedes) the making of literature. But with the Greeks criticism makes its appearance almost simultaneously.

Pre-Platonic Greek criticism of antiquity is contained in many pronouncements which imply literary standards and principles. We find such remarks in ancient epic poetry, lyric, drama, philosophy, and oratory. For instance, the principle of poetic inspiration is to be found in Homer's *Iliad* II. Pindar too shows a concern with the permanent problem of inspiration versus technique. Philosophers like Heraclitus and Xenophanes bring moral problems to the consideration of literature. We see Thucydides pronouncing strictures on his predecessors. These judgements of poets and writers show a highly developed sensitivity to the standards of their craft. But these preconceptions were not organised into critical theories dealing with clearly formulated poetical problems. One has to wait till Plato's time for such formulations.

But before the beginning of theoretical criticism judicial criticism existed in ancient Greece. This is an interesting fact because one normally expects theoretical criticism to precede judicial criticism. Final judgement and evaluation is the goal towards which critical theories are directed.

It is with Aristophanes the Greek comic dramatist that the judicial criticism of the Greek tragic poets becomes a distinct activity. To say this is not to argue that there was no criticism at all in Greece before Aristophanes. It is only to make it explicitly clear that criticism emerges from obscurity with Aristophanes.

Aristophanes, (*circa* 448-380 B. C.), the great Athenian comic poet, was concerned with criticising the evils of his time. Eleven of his tragedies have come down to us. He criticized the Peloponnesian War for which the contemporary demagogues were chiefly responsible. He attacked the educational system introduced by the Sophists. He inveighs against the tragic poets, especially against Euripides. Aristophanes was against the modernist movements in his time. Euripides was a modernist among poets. He had taken the burning problems of his time as the subject matter of his dramas. He took women, lame men, beggars, and ordinary human beings as the central figures in his dramas. He rejected the poetic diction of Aeschylus and Sophocles, holding that poetry should use the language of common speech.

Aristophanes opposed these innovations and accused Euripides of demeaning the language of poetry, of dealing with unworthy subjects and of indulging in cheap sentimentalism. This criticism is especially to be found in the comedy of Aristophanes entitled *Frogs*. This was produced in Athens about the year 405 B. C. The title of the play is taken from a chorus of frogs who sings while Charon is ferrying Dionysus over the marsh after his death. The scene is in Hades.

Aeschylus and Euripides were dead. And Sophocles had just died. Dionysus masquerades as Hercules and goes to Hades to bring back to earth one of the tragic poets. Dionysus finds in Hades a contest between Aeschylus and Euripides for the throne of tragedy, and is called upon by Plato to decide the contest. The tragedians attack each others plays. Friendly Aeschylus is chosen because his poetry "weighs more". To quote from the play :

Dionysus :   Now then each repeat a verse.
Euripides :   "I wish that Argo with her woven wings".
Aeschylus :   "O streams of Spercheius, and ye pastured plains".
Dionysus :   Let go ! See now—this slab outweighs that other very considerably.

This of course is not serious criticism. But here we have the beginning. We find also for the first time in Euripides the general theoretical assumption of both Plato and Aristotle that the poet is a teacher, that poetry should teach wisdom and should be useful to the state. In the *Frogs* Aristophanes makes Aeschylus ask :

Pray tell me on what particular ground should a poet claim admiration ?

Aristophanes makes Euripides reply :

If his art is true, and his counsel sound ; and if he brings help to the nation. By making men better in some respect.

These have been the major theoretical concerns of Greek criticism.

Plato : Art as Imitation

If, as A. N. Whitehead said that the history of European thought is essentially a series of footnotes to Plato's philosophy, the history of literary criticism may also be likewise considered a series of footnotes to Plato's observations on beauty, art, and poetry. Plato had formulated in his dialogues many of the burning problems in philosophical aesthetics. But sometimes his formulations have been characterised by a rigour of analysis leading him to aesthetic theories unfriendly to poets and rhapsodists. But it must not be forgotten that it was Plato who gave genuine philosophical formulation to aesthetic and critical problems. It is true that Plato's observations on poets and poetry are unfriendly. He denounces poets and poetry. In spite of this, to consider Plato as an enemy of poetry and art in general will not be correct.[1] It is a strange fact that Plato himself was a supreme stylist. His prose is poetic. His *Dialogues* are dramatic. He has an idealist conception of Beauty and Love.

Plato's aesthetic theory is not our immediate concern. These are

[1] See the analysis of Plato's aesthetic theory by J. W. H. ATKINS in his *Literary Criticism in Antiquity*, Vol. I., (London : Methuen & Co. Ltd., 1952). See also J. G. Warry : *Greek Aesthetic Theory* (New York, Barnes & Noble Inc., 1962).

to be found in his Dialogues entitled *Hippias Major*, *Phaedrus Philebus*, and *Symposium*.

Let us now turn to Plato's critical theories. And for this purpose we have to consider the two dialogues the *Ion* and the *Republic*. (In the last dialogue *Laws*, we find the same objections restated). Thus we may concentrate on the *Ion* and the *Republic*. When we read these dialogues we must remember that Plato's main concerns were those essentially stated by Aristophanes, namely the relation between art and truth, and the wisdom to be obtained from poetry, and the moral and educational purpose which poetry can impart to the citizens of a state or a nation.

The *Ion* is a debate between Ion the reciter of Homer's poetry and Socrates. Socrates's main contention is that the art of the poet as well as that of the rhapsode who recites, poetry is the result of a sort of "madness", "frenzy" or "inspiration". In *Ion* we have Socrates commenting as follows:

> For the poet is a light and winged and holy thing, and there is no inventions in him until he has been inspired and is out of his senses, and the mind is no longer in him : when he has not attained to this state, he is powerless and unable to utter his oracles.[2]

According to this dialogue neither poetry nor criticism results from art and knowledge. A rhapsode like Ion has no rational technique which can be applied to all poetry. Here we find the theory of poetic inspiration directly adumbrated. In other words poetry is not a species of knowledge. And no knowledge or science is required in the criticism of poetry. Poetic inspiration is thus critically rejected by Plato.

It is in his *Republic* that we have Plato's theory of imitation fully stated. It is not possible to summarise the brilliance of Plato's *Dialogue*.

In the 10th Chapter of the *Republic* the debate is between Socrates and Glaucon. The main points at issue debated by Socrates and Glaucon are : the nature of poetic activity, the doctrine of imitation, explained on the analogy of the bed, the

---

[2] Unless otherwise stated all quotations are from *Plato's Dialogues* translated by Benjamin Jowett, edition of 1892.

function of the poet in an ideal state, and the practical (social and moral) uses of poetry.

From the ideal Republic, the imitative tribe has been excluded. Socrates explains to Glaucon the nature of imitation, and Plato thus introduces his theory of ideas. Briefly it is as follows.

Whenever a number of individuals have a common name, it is assumed that there is a corresponding idea or form. For instance, there are beds and tables in the world. But there is only one idea or form corresponding to all the tables, and another idea or form corresponding to all the beds in the world. Let us call the idea of the bed, the "ideal" bed and the beds in the world the actual beds.

When a carpenter makes a bed, he imitates or copies the idea of a bed or the ideal bed. But no artificer or carpenter can make the idea of the bed. This idea can only be made by God. It exists in the world of supersensible realities.

Plato further attacks poetry because the productions of the imitative arts are bastard and illegitimate. The poets imitate contradictory qualities. Poetry is at variance with the exhortations of philosophy. Poets recall trouble and sorrow and poetry ministers in an inferior manner, to an inferior principle in the soul. Poetry may be attractive but not true. Poets encourage weakness. Their teachings differ from the exhortations of philosophy. They merely recall trouble and sorrow and inculcate no useful moral.

Plato further asks : Is it morally right to sympathize with the sorrows of poetry? Moral training demands that we should restrain ourselves from over-sympathizing with the sorrows of real life. For a sentimental pity soon creates a real weakness. Likewise the love of comedy may turn a man into a buffoon. These in sum are Plato's main arguments against poets and poetry.

From the point of view of literary men, it is easy to criticize Plato's views. But no criticism of Plato's poetic theory is possible unless at the same time we attack Plato's philosophy in general. The essence of his argument is that poetry is a form of imitation, and is thus a *representation* of the actual and the contingent and not of the ideal and the essential. For us, poetry is a creative activity and so we tend to value poetic activity.

There are three important poetical concepts which Plato dealt with in detail in the dialogues. These are : poetry as education, poetry as imitation, and poetry as inspiration.

As a philosopher, Plato's chief concern was the application of philosophy to personal and social problems. And education was for Plato the realization of the ultimate values, the Good, the Beautiful, and the True. And because of this bias, Plato believed that poetry should subserve individuals and social morality, and when poetry fails to do this, poetry produces a corrupting influence. The state must protect the citizens against the corrupting influence of meritricious poetry. More important than this criticism of the immorality of poetry is the charge that poetry is inevitably trivial. This conclusion is reached through his theory of ideas.

According to this theory the created world is an imperfect imitation of a divine archetype. And poetry is explained in the *Republic* as an imitative art, using as its models the objects and actions which the poet sees in the created world. Poetry is therefore "an imitation of an imitation" more false than that which it imitates". Thus poetry leads away from the true rather than toward it. Poetry has no concern with serious things and it is a form of trivial amusement. Aristotle has dealt with this problem in the *Poetics*.

But the most important conceptions which Plato developed (in the *Ion*) is the conception of poetic inspiration. In the *Ion*, a rhapsodist is satirized who could not explain the nature of his ability to recite poetry. Socrates jokingly explains that both poets and rhapsodists must be under the influence of a divine power while composing poetry and speaking about it. This idea was lately developed as the idea of poetic inspirations or "furor poeticus". When a poet is "inspired", he has a superhuman ability by which he is able to have a glimpse of the ultimate nature of things, their eternal forms, and their divine archetypes. The Platonic theory of divine inspiration is often cited to prove that Plato was not opposed to poetry. The Renaissance psychology of poetic composition had for its basis the notion of poetic inspiration. But Plato had, however, wanted to prove that poetry was not the product of knowledge and wisdom. The best criticism of Plato's theories is contained in the *Poetics* of Aristotle.

CHAPTER THREE

ARISTOTLE ON THE ART OF POETRY

The Importance of the Poetics

Aristotle's *poetics* is the first important document in the history of Western Criticism. The *Poetics* (written about 330 B. C.) is a small treatise on tragic poetry. Although written in the distant past, no modern student of literature can afford to ignore it. Many fundamental problems relating to literary and aesthetic criticism are advanced in it for the first time. Even today it is not possible to improve upon the formulation of some Aristotelian doctrines. In short the *Poetics* is a seminal work in literary criticism.

The text of the *Poetics* has not come down to us in a complete form. It is fragmentary and incomplete. Its twenty six short chapters are not always coherent. There are even repetitions and contradictions. Accordingly, the most important difficulty which a modern student faces is a textual one. But this can only be overcome through caution, and through a conscientious adherence to the contextual importance of all statements of Aristotle.

The Historical Background of the Poetics

The *Poetics* contains many doctrines which to a modern reader

13

of criticism may appear strange unless we take into account the tradition of thought behind it and also the literary tradition on which the critical generalizations of Aristotle are based.

It is evident that Aristotle had Plato's denunciation of the arts in mind as he developed his own theory. Plato had, in several important works, (*The Laws, The Republic,* and *Ion*) maintained that poetry is unreal, harmful, and socially speaking, wasteful. In the tenth Book of the *Republic,* he completes his burning denunciation of poetry as one false siren, the imitator of things which themselves are shadows, the ally of all that is low and weak in the soul against that which is high and strong. He attacks the poets and their art from several quarters. But his most important criticism is based on a metaphysics of art and poetry. Poetry was unreal, was remote from truth and reality. Having its origin in the imitative activity of man, poetry exists in the world of illusion and not in the world of truth, in the world of sensible reality and not in the sphere of ultimate reality. He proceeds by comparing poetry and painting. The painter paints an actual object, say, a bed (to take Plato's own example). The actual bed, which we know through our senses (what we called the sensible reality) is only a copy of an Ideal bed or the Real bed or the Essential bed which exists above and beyond the sensible world. This is the true bed, and not the actual bed. And the actual bed itself is at two removes from the real bed. And further, the painter paints a copy of the actual bed, a doubly unreal activity. The picture of the bed is thus at three removes from the real bed. All paintings are thus far separated from truth. Likewise poetry too. Plato generalizes and concludes that all artistic objects are mere copies of reality.

Plato proceeds from first principles. He enquires into the nature of poetry according to certain dogmatic attitudes. It is difficult to concede Plato's arguments.

Plato has other arguments against poetry also. The activity of imitation is the womb and matrix of all the arts. But imitation leads not to utility, but to pleasure. Plato the puritan disliked pleasure, and pleasure-giving arts. Furthermore, poets generally spread bad morals and theology. Consider the theology in Homer. He makes the gods all too human. The gods in the *Iliad* fight; they quarrel, take sides in human events, and have most of man's frail characteristics. This was blasphemy to Plato.

When the collective welfare of an ideal republic is taken into consideration, poetry can produce the most disastrous consequences. "Has poetry ever helped in the making of a good general?", he asks. The formative influence of poetry, especially tragic poetry, is debilitating on man's moral character. Tragedy, by arousing the emotions of pity and compassion undermines courage, and makes men unfit to bear the trials of life as they happen to come. In the *Republic* he asks a basic question :

Are we not taught to be patient under misfortunes and not to give way to emotions ? If so, then, why should we weep and express pity at the poetic representation of tragedy ?

The answer to this question and many another was given by Aristotle in the *Poetics*. Unlike Plato, Aristotle is not dogmatic. His method of approach is historical, comparative, and analytical. He formulates his theories on the basis of a thorough knowledge of the ancient Greek tragedies. We have to know their essential characteristics and the differences between ancient and modern tragedy before we begin our study of the *Poetics*.

Greek Tragedy—Greek Theatre—Greek Life

In the modern tragic conception, the individual and the psychology of his motivation play a dominant part. Shakespeare is more praised as a delineator of character than as a creator of plot. But this tragic conception is inconsistent with Aristotle's theory that characters emerge out of action and are dependent on action. To understand fully Aristotle's statements on character we have to remember the salient features of ancient Greek tragedy. The ancient tragedians, Aeschylus, Sophocles and Euripides worked within the framework of a theatrical and dramatic convention in which there was little scope for elaborate character portrayal. Their plays were written for actual performance in the theatre during dramatic festivals. The limitations of the theatre severely restricted the freedom of character portrayal.

The ancient theatre was a semi-circular, curved bank of seats. The size of the theatre was incredibly large by modern standards. The theatre at Athens could provide seats for 17,000 persons.

At the centre of the theatre was a circular area called the orchestra (literally, the dancing place) and at the centre of the orchestra was an altar. A part of the dramatic action (the manoeuvres and dances performed by the chorus) took place in the orchestra.

Beyond the circular orchestra lay the scene building which in most cases represented the facade of a house, palace or temple. Various devices were developed to denote to the audience the nature of the building or the general background which the scene was supposed to provide. This is the essential structure of the Greek theatre.

This large open-air theatre imposed a limitation upon the playwright in the choice of scenes and characters. The absence of realism made it impossible for the poet to bring out on the stage internal motivation of characters.

The prevailing attitudes to life of the Greece of the fifth century B.C. also tended to minimise the importance of the individual. Human life was at the mercy of fortune and misfortune, accident and fate. There was no system of social justice. The tyrants came into being, they fell and disappeared or were destroyed by other rising tyrants. (The sudden and unexpected fall of might is a recurring theme in Greek tragedy). Thus the conception of Fate as an active agent in the disposition of human fortune was quite familiar to the ancient Greek mind. Moral responsibility in the shape of individual decisions and motives was unknown.

The nature of the Greek religions, too influenced Greek drama. Drama had its origin in the ritual performance. The performance of ritual was the only form of appeasing the Olympian Gods. (Aristotle points out that the origin of drama lay in ritual ceremonies). Thus the Greek drama is more of a ritual performance than a representation of character in action.

To the modern reader the creation of characters seems the most important element in imaginative writing. But the circumstances explained above made the portrayal of character in Greek tragedy extremely difficult. Other facts also rendered characters subordinate to action. The myths which were the raw materials of Greek tragedy showed man in relation to universe, and in relation to the unseen powers (the gods of mythology) behind it. The dramatic plots, based on myths, did not reveal significant differences between human beings. The myths were concerned with divine purpose and not human motives. Interest in character for its own sake in the processes and struggles of the human souls and the mysterious quality of the personality is a late growth.

Characters in Greek tragedy possessed only such obvious traits as the mechanism of the story requires. Most of the figures in Aeschylian tragedy are presented with the minimum of characterisation. They are reduced to the requirements of plot. We know little of the motivation of Aeschylus's Agamemnon or Clytaemnestra, or Orestes, or Aegisthus. They are people caught in the movement of larger forces. Their individual dispositions are really given by the story. But the story does not depend on their motivation. The characters of Aeschylus are heroes and god-like figures.

The best example of this subordination of character to action is in Sophocles's *Oedipus Triology*. Consider the first play, *Oedipus the King*. Aristotle uses this tragedy more than any other play to illustrate his various critical theories. *Oedipus the King* has frequently been called a tragedy of fate in which the characters are caught in a web of circumstances from which they try in vain to extricate themselves.

Oedipus the King deals with the destruction of Oedipus, the King of Thebes. But those events are slowly revealed to us during the course of the play. The events of the story, antecedent to the opening of the play, are as follows:

Laius, the father of Oedipus was told by an oracle that a son would be born to him, and that this son would slay him. In spite of the oracle, Laius begot Oedipus. To thwart the oracle Oedipus was exposed to die, but was rescued and reared by Polybus and Merope, King and Queen of Corinth. The boy regarded them as reaching his manhood, Oedipus, in ignorance, slew Laius, came to his parents. On Thebes, solved the riddle of the sphinx, was made king, and married the recently widowed-queen Jocasta who actually was his own mother. Soon after a plague started, and virtually destroyed the city.

Sophocles begins his tragedy at this point in the story. A group of subjects appeals to their king Oedipus to help them in their desolation. The action of the play reveals how Oedipus gradually comes to learn how he had actually killed his father and married his own mother.

Oedipus sends his brother-in-law Creon to the oracle to find out what sin brought this plague on the Thebans. The oracle declares that the plague is due to the presence of the murderer of Laius in

Thebes. Oedipus pledges himself to discover this criminal and punish him. The blind seer Tiresias is sent for. Tiresias accuses him; but Oedipus dismisses him angrily.

Next follows an angry scene between Oedipus and his brother-in-law Creon. Jocasta interrupts this angry scene. She tries to pacify Oedipus and remove all his anxiety by describing the place and manner in which her former husband Laius was killed by robbers (at a place where three highways meet). This is the most critical moment of the tragedy. Oedipus is aghast. The description of the murder tallies with his own memory of killing a wayfarer years ago.

At this moment a messenger from Corinth arrives to announce the death of Polybus whom Oedipus thinks to be his father and from whose presence he had departed in order that another oracle might not be fulfilled.

The sequence of terrible events in the tragedy slowly reveals to Oedipus the horrible truth that Oedipus is the murderer of his own father Laius. When exposed to die, Oedipus was found as a child by a shepherd and reared by Polybus as a son. Jocasta too realises the grim tragedy. She commits suicide. Oedipus, in inner agony, blinds himself and prepares to leave the city as the play comes to an end.

It is easily seen by a careful study of this tragedy that the Fate of the tragic hero depends on pre-determined events. It is not Oedipus's character that has brought about his destiny. No doubt his own character was part of the set of dark forces slowly enveloping him in destruction. From this play primarily, Aristotle derived his famous definition of the Tragic Hero given in the *Poetics*.

An Analytical Summary of the Important Chapters of the Poetics

(It may be mentioned here that instead of reading through the whole of the *Poetics*, it will be more advantageous for the beginner to select the various chapters which deal with important problems and study them thoroughly).

Synoptically and briefly we may present the principal themes of the *Poetics* as:

(1) The origin of Tragedy; (2) The definition of Tragedy;

(3) The various parts of Tragedy: Plot, Character, Diction, Thought, Spectacle, Melody; (4) Plot and its supreme importance; (5) The various types of Plots: Simple and Complex; (6) The parts of Plot: Peripety (or Reversal), Discovery, and Suffering. (7) Tragic Hero and his qualities; (8) The tragic emotions of Pity and Fear and their *catharsis*; (9) The nature of the Tragic Flaw; (10) Comparison between the Epic Form and the Tragic Form.

Chapters 1-3: All forms of poetry originate in imitation. But these forms of poetry differ from one another according to the means, the objects and the manner of imitation. Language is the means employed by the poets. But, for this kind of imitative art (using language) whether in prose or verse, there is no common name. (Aristotle is referring to the fact that there did not exist, in his day, in Greek, any word equivalent to "literature".). Thus Aristotle is the first critic to recognise the distinctive characteristic of the literary arts. Poetry is not merely metrical language. Even if a theory of medicine or physical philosophy be put forth in a metrical form, it will not constitute a poem.

All the arts, the arts of painting, music and dancing, imitate life, as literature does. We distinguish the imitative arts from one another by the various means employed. A second basis of distinction is the nature of the objects represented. The object may be rendered better than what it actually is (idealised), or rendered worse (caricatured), or realistically presented as it actually is. Tragedy idealizes the characters, and comedy caricatures them. Thirdly, the arts may be distinguished according to the mode of imitation. Thus a poet may imitate life by the method of narration as epic poets do, or through actual representation of an action as the dramatic poets do. In the drama, the poet never speaks through the medium of his own personality.

Chapters 4-5: Aristotle traces the origin of poetry. He accounts for the origin of poetry in terms of three causes: (1) the human instinct for imitation; (2) man's instinctive pleasure in recognizing imitation; (3) the instinctive pleasure in harmony and form.

Unlike Plato, Aristotle recognised "imitation" or (mimesis) as much a part of human nature as "doing" or "acting", This instinct, on the one hand, makes us imitate life, and create poetry and the arts. On the other hand, the very recognition of an imitation gives man pleasure. We have thus the aesthetic response in this instinct.(See Section 5 for this theory of imitation).

Aristotle traces the historical evolution of tragedy. Originating in the Dionysian hymns and developing through the Homeric epic, tragedy reaches its perfection in the Greek Tragedy of the fifth century B.C. (We need not consider Aristotle's historical treatment of the evolution of the tragedy very seriously. Modern scholarship disagrees with Aristotle). The most important point advanced by Aristotle here is the relation between epic poetry and tragedy.

In Chapter five, Aristotle distinguishes the characteristics of the Epic and the Tragedy. This comparison between Epic and Tragedy is continued in Chapters 23, 24 and 26. Epic and Tragedy are similar except for two things. They differ from each other (1) in that the epic is in narrative form, and (2) in its length, which is due to its action having no fixed limit of time. But tragedy endeavours to keep within a single revolution of the sun. This statement of Aristotle has given rise to the doctrine of the 'unity of time'. But Aristotle's is not a dogmatic statement. When he observes that tragic action is confined to one revolution of the sun, he merely compares Tragedy and Epic. (There is an incidental reference to comedy and the nature of the comic in these chapters. But these references are not developed further. Probably Aristotle wrote a second book on comedy, but it has not come down to us).

Chapter 6 : This is the most important chapter of the *Poetics* where a definition of tragedy is given. In fact, the remaining chapters of the book only bring out the implications of this definition of tragedy. The essential points of the definition are the following : (1) Tragedy is essentially an imitation in language ornamented with various devices such as rhythm and melody. (2) It imitates an action which is serious, and which has a certain appropriate magnitude (neither too large nor too small), and which is complete. (3) The imitation is not in the form of narration, but in the form of drama. (4) Pity and fear are the appropriate tragic emotions. (5) The function of tragedy is to effect a catharsis of these emotions.

There are six parts in a tragedy. They are : Fable or Plot, Characters, Diction, Thought, Spectacle and Melody. Of these the important elements are Plot, Character and Thought. (The rest may be omitted for the time being). And plot is the most important part of tragedy. Character comes only in the second place. This is a very controversial doctrine. It is contrary to our modern post-renaissance conception of a tragic poet as primarily a creator of characters. For instance, it is commonly held that Shakespeare's excellence lies in the creation of his tragic characters. And Shakespeare is seldom praised as the contriver of the plots of his tragedy. How are we to interpret Aristotle's remarks? Can we reject his view as wrong? Or, is his theory relevant only to Greek tragedy? These are important questions whose answers require more elaborate treatment than the space here will allow. But it may be noted here initially that this view is consistent with Aristotle's philosophy of life. As he explains :

> Tragedy is essentially an imitation not of persons but of action and life, of happiness and misery. All human happiness or misery takes the form of action ; the end for which we live is a certain kind of activity, not a quality. Character gives us qualities, but it is in our action—what we do—that we are happy or the reverse.[1]

Further he endeavours to substantiate his doctrine by various arguments. First, a tragedy is impossible without action, but there may be one without character. Second, a beginner may more easily succeed in the creation of characters, than in the creation of plots. Third, the most important elements of attraction in tragedy —Reversals (or Peripeties) and Discoveries—belong not to characterization, but to plots. Plot in tragedy corresponds to the shape or design in painting, and there cannot be a picture without a shape or design. Similarly there cannot be a tragedy without a plot. (Except for Chapter 15, all chapters up to the 22nd discuss the various aspects of the plot).

Chapter 7 : Aristotle discusses the question of the magnitude of a tragic play. It must be a whole story, and not a collection of incidents. There must be organic unity in the action. This further implies that the action must have a beginning, a middle, and an end. And in order that we may be able to apprehend this organic unity, and the proportion of the several parts to the whole, the tragic play should be neither too long, nor too short.

Chapters 8-9 : Contain comments upon the phrase "complete in

---

[1] The *Poetics*, vi., Tr. Ingram Bywater. All quotations used in this monograph are from Bywater, unless otherwise stated.

itself" in the definition of tragedy. In other words, we have here
what is meant by the unity of action. The doctrine of the unity of
action is introduced here.

The plot or story must have a unity of form, and it must be a
single whole. This unity is not an external one. The various
incidents which happen to one man need not have a coherent unity.
Instead, there should be an internal unity, in a series of incident,
so that the removal or transposition of a single incident will
effect the structure of the whole series of incidents. This further
implies that the chain of events constituting a tragic plot should be
connected either by the laws of probability or by the laws of
psychological causation. Thus the poet's function is to describe not
the thing that has happened (that is the work of the historian), but
to describe the kind of thing which might happen, that is, what is
possible as being probable or necessary. History deals with the
actual. But poetry deals with the universal. Hence poetry is more
philosophic than history. (We must remember the context of this
statement. This applies to epic and dramatic poetry in general,
but not to lyric poetry).

Poetic truth is different from the truth of history. Poetic truth
is the law of universal becoming. Thus a poet need not always
conform to historical data (or borrow names, places, or incidents
from history). He may create his own plots, and his characters so
long as the laws of probability are not violated.

Chapter 10-12: Various kinds of plots and their constituent
elements. Plots are either simple or complex. In simple plots, we
have a straightforward story without any complications. In complex plots, we have complications in incidents, and a reversal or
peripety in the fortunes of the hero is brought about. The reversal
takes place as the result of discoveries. Thus Reversals and Discoveries are the essential parts of a plot. And every good tragic play
must have a complex plot having both discovery and reversal. In
the best plays the discovery and the reversal coincide. For
example, in *Oedipus the King* the discovery of the personal identity
of Oedipus as Laius's son brings about a reversal of his fortunes.

(Chapter 12 is probably an interpolation):

Chapters 13-14 : The cathartic function of tragedy. These are
very important chapters. Aristotle discusses the nature of tragic
pity and fear. But the discussion involves the qualities of a typical
tragic hero, and the nature of tragic suffering. Suffering is the third

part of the action or plot in tragedy. The three parts of tragic action therefore are Peripety or Reversal, Discovery, and Suffering.

Tragedy can arouse pity and fear only when the tragic hero is reduced to a state of suffering. But not all kinds of suffering evoke pity and fear. The unmerited suffering of a wholly virtuous man never arouses pity, but provokes indignation. The sufferings merited by a plain criminal or a bad character, too, never make us pity him. Thus the tragic emotions of pity and fear depend upon some specific qualities in the tragic hero. To quote Aristotle's own words :

> There remains, then, the intermediate kind of person, a man not pre-eminently virtuous and just, whose misfortune, however, is brought upon him not by vice and depravity but by some error of judgement, he being one of these who enjoy great reputation and prosperity . . . .

What is the nature of this error ? Is this *hubris* or pride ? Or, is it ignorance ? Whatever the nature of this tragic flaw, it must not be external, but must be inherent in the psychological make up of the character.

Chapter 15 : Elaborates the problem further. In the delineation of characters, the poet must make them see to it that ; (1) the characters are good ; (2) they are appropriate, and (3) are like the reality, and (4) are consistent and the same throughout.

The third requirement of the tragic character is ambiguous. Professor Butcher translates the passage as follows :

> Thirdly, a character must be true of life . . . .

Chapters 16-18 : Sum up the previous discussions. No new points are introduced in these chapters. (This is a part of the textual difficulty which we pointed out at the very beginning).

(Chapters 19-22 : deal with style and diction. Here again, the treatment is cursory, incoherent, and not systematic. They may also be omitted without much loss.)

Chapters 23-24 : Aristotle reverts to the nature of epic poetry, and discusses the epic in relation to tragic poetry. He refers to this topic in the fifth chapter to point out that Tragedy and Epic both have the same origin. More accurately, tragedy has evolved out of epic poetry. In these two chapters the art of drama and that of epic poetry are further compared. In epic, as in drama, the unity of story is of capital importance. The epic story, too, must have unity of action, must have a beginning, a middle, and an end. The epic plots may be simple or complex. The constituent elements of an epic are the same as those of a drama except the Spectacle.

But an epic poem does not have unity of time, as its action is much longer than that of a drama. Since it is in the form of narration, it can present simultaneous actions taking place at several places, and also marvels, which cannot be staged. Of course, the epic metre is different from that of the drama. Epic metre is the 'heroic hexameter'. Aristotle takes Homer as the supreme model of artistic unity.

Homer's superiority lies in the field of creating "fiction, *i.e.*, the art of telling lies in the right way." The effect of fiction depends upon illusion. A great poet must be a master of the art of creating this poetic illusion. Poetic credibility is not achieved by merely keeping to incidents which might have happened, if the presentation is not convincing. He says:

A likely impossibility is always preferable to an unconvincing possibility.

(Chapter 25 is again probably an interpolation : It deals with some superficialities of literary criticism. It may be omitted).

The last chapter (No. 26) takes up the comparison of epic and dramatic poetry. Aristotle's aim is to show that tragedy is superior as an art-form to epic. His theory is that the historically later form (tragedy) is nearer to perfection than the earlier (the epic).

Tragedy is criticised by some because it can appeal to the vulgar, and because acting can degenerate into monkey tricks. But Aristotle maintains that this is not an inherent defect of tragedy. Neither is epic free from such defects. Besides, acting is not essential to the appreciation of tragedy. On the other hand, tragedy is superior to epic, because it contains all the pleasure-giving elements with music and spectacle in addition. Its emotional effect is stronger because it is more concentrated and because it is shorter. It has greater unity.

These, in brief, are the most important theories advanced by Aristotle in the *Poetics*.

The Concept of Imitation or Mimesis

According to Aristotle (the *Poetics*, Chapter IV) imitation is a fundamental human instinct. It is an intellectual instinct and poetry is one manifestation of the instinct. But he has re-defined imitation or (*mimesis*) to mean not the counterfeiting of the sensible reality but the presentation of the universals. The Aristotelian universals are not like the Platonic ideas, abstract metaphysical entities. They are the permanent modes of human thought and action. The poet can represent these universals through the faculty of imitation, and the reader of poetry can grasp them. Tragic poetry (like epic poetry) is imitation of an action. The element of imitation is lodged in the plot (and not in the characters) of the poem. By plot Aristotle means not only a sequence of events, but an organic *structure* of events which would be a valid representation of the actions of men according to the laws of probability and necessity.

Thus the central conception in Aristotle's theory is the new theory of *poetic structure* which is evolved from a re-definition of the concept of imitation not as a copying of ordinary reality but as a generator of idealized rendering of character in action. This is the essence of the Aristotelian conception of poetic *mimesis*. Thus as against Plato's theory of imitation as representation, we have the Aristotelian *mimesis*, the act of creating a poetic structure. But is this new concept of imitation a purely aesthetic faculty or part of the general faculty for learning which man is endowed with? Is the pleasure derived from poetry the result of a distinct aesthetic experience or part of an intellectual experience? Modern critics of Aristotle have attempted to analyse this problem.

According to Professor Butcher, it is Aristotle who recognizes imitation as an aesthetic faculty.[2] We find the concept of imitation in Greek thought before Aristotle. Plato uses it in his discussion of poetry and the arts. But Plato dismisses the activity of imitation instead of according to it an aesthetic status. To the Greek mind, all human activity was either doing things or making things. In doing things the action itself was to be judged, in making things the action was to be judged by what it made—the tangible object which it brought into existence. It was in the latter case that activity was an art. The value of the art was easily judged when

[2] *Aristotle's Theory of Poetry and Fine Art*, 4th edition, Dover Publications.

the thing it produced was a shoe or a pot. But when human activity produces a picture or a poem, how was judgement possible? In this case, the value of a thing did not consist in its material nor even in the arrangement of its material; it consisted in the way the material and its arrangement stood for something. The Greeks before Aristotle said that the value of such an object consisted in the way that object imitated something. In this sense the meaning of the word is vague. And they vaguely explained away the existence of what we call art as imitation.

The inevitable result of this notion was that art imitates nature. Art then is the skilled copying of the objects of nature. This was the popular way of arguing, and it was also Plato's way. It enabled him, in accordance with his theory of ideas, to disparage poetry and art in general. Aristotle was no doubt in the early part of his *Poetics* concerned with Plato's attack on imitative nature of poetry. He meets this charge by giving a completely different interpretation of the whole notion of imitation in poetry. As a direct consequence of this, the distinction between the fine arts and the useful arts emerge.

But there is another difficulty. The word "imitation" occurs in other works of Aristotle. (In *Physics*, and in *De Mundo*) in the sense of emulation. That is to say, imitation with a view to learning. There is the famous statement of Aristotle in the *Physics* that art imitates nature. Through the arts we learn from nature. Thus the art of cooking is a close imitation of the natural process of digestion. Except in the *Poetics*, Aristotle never uses imitation as an aesthetic term. Imitation leads to utility, to learning from nature. It does not give pleasure. If this is the interpretation of imitation, then the *Poetics* is not a defence of fine arts. Indeed there are critics who maintain this view. R. G. Collingwood observes:

The Poetics is, therefore, in no sense a Defence of Poetry[3].

But this is an extreme view which we need not subscribe to. This view is partly the result of a textual confusion at the beginning of the fourth chapter. Aristotle here gives us two causes of the origin of poetry: (1) the instinct for imitation, and (2) the pleasure we derive from recognizing imitation. A little later he adds "to be learning is the greatest of pleasure." Thus are we to understand the pleasure

[3] *The Principles of Art*, (Oxford, 1955), p. 51.

deriving from imitation as an aesthetic pleasure or as the pleasure deriving from knowledge ? In the latter case the fine arts will be a form of knowledge. Thus a certain confusion in the use of the idea of imitation in the *Poetics* is unavoidable.

But Aristotelian scholars (while recognizing the difficulty in the mimetic vocabulary of Aristotle) endeavour to remove the confusion as follows :

Both meanings of the word "imitation" or "mimesis" are present in the *Poetics*. But the aesthetic meaning of the term is more relevant. The precise aesthetic meaning of imitation (or mimesis) is "portrayal". But by portrayal is not meant literal copying of the world of reality. This is clear from the fact that Aristotle points out that the artist may imitate things as they ought to be. There can never be a literal transcript of things as they ought to be. Nor does art attempt to embody the objective reality of things, but their sensible reality. Thus according to Prof. Butcher, art in the Aristotelian theory is not a symbol, but a semblance of reality.

The work of imitative art is an image of the impressions made by an independent reality upon the mind of the artist.[4]

The reality thus reflected deals with the facts of human life and nature. From Chapter 9 we learn that poetry imitates the universal elements in human life. Imitation thus reveals the universal beneath the individual. Imitation imitates not the created nature, but the creative nature. The aesthetic faculty of imitation neither draws lessons from nature, nor produces a copy of reality. But it produces a higher form of reality, an ideal or formal reality, suitable for "sensible" appreciation.

It is in this sense that Aristotle uses the concept of imitation. By aesthetic imitation the artist seizes the universal and reproduces it in simple and sensuous forms.

Aristotle's Conception of Plot in Tragedy

Aristotle explains his conception of plot in the sixth chapter of

[4] See Butcher. Op. Cit., J. G. Warry, *Greek Aesthetic Theory*, London, 1962 ; Prof. Else. *Aristotle's Poetics : The Argument*, Harvard, 1957.

the *Poetics* where he calls it the arrangement of the incidents. The purpose of the plot is to represent one complete action. Plot, then, "is the first principle, and, as it were, the soul of tragedy". He thus introduces the organic metaphor in the analysis of a work of art. By soul Aristotle (who was a biologist) means the formative principle in any living thing—whether man, animal, or plant. Professor Else (in *Aristotle's Poetics : The Argument*) says : "For Plot is the structure of the play, and around which the material parts are laid, just as the soul is the structure of a man" (p.242). Butcher comments on this : "Plot in the drama . . . is the artistic equivalents of 'action' in real life" (p.333). The Plot, then, contains the kernel of the 'action' which it is the business of tragedy to represent.

About the plot of a tragedy, Aristotle makes three general observations : (1) it must be of a certain size ; (2) it must be of a certain structure, and (3) it is the most important thing—the soul of a drama. As Humphry House points out, the difference between a plot and a story must be borne in mind. The story is there, but the plot is something the poet makes. "Aristotle's famous statement that a tragedy must have a beginning, middle and an end is thus related to his whole view of the scope of the poet as maker.

Parts of the plot : In Chapter 12, he lists the quantitative parts of tragedy : prologue, episode, exode, and choric song. (This section probably is an interpolation). He explains the organic parts of the plot (in Chapter II). By "the organic parts" are meant those parts which represent the tragic action and which produces the specifically tragic effect. They are Reversal or Peripety, Recognition or Discovery, Pathos or the scene of Suffering. These should be inherent in the basic structure of the plot.

Reversal is a change by which action veers round to its opposite. Thus in *Oedipus the King,* the messenger comes to cheer Oedipus and free him from his qualms about his mother, but by revealing who he is, he produces the opposite effect. Recognition is a change from ignorance to knowledge. Oedipus's change from ignorance to knowledge occurs as he cross-questions the messenger, and then the old shepherd. By plotting this crucial moment in this way, Sophocles has, as it were, spread out before our eyes the whole turn of Oedipus's inner being, from the triumph which seems just ahead to utter despair. The tremendous excitement of this passage is due to the fact that what he "recognizes" is the reversal. The best form of recognition is coincident with a Reversal of the situation as in *Oedipus the King* (11.2). Aristotle has little to say about the scene of Suffering. What little he has to say in this context is related to his idea of the tragic character.

Aristotle's Criticism of Greek Dramatists in the Poetics

He shows little sympathy with Aeschylus. His few references to that poet are either purely historical or rather faint praise, or even censure. In this, Aristotle has the support of his contemporaries who seem to have completely shelved Aeschylus in favour of his two rivals. To the average critic elevation of thought needed impeccable style for its communication; and Aeschylus failed to please the later Greeks. The Greeks never fully appreciated in those days a poet who was neither rhetorical nor sententious.

Aeschylus was further eclipsed as a playwright. Here Aristotle is speaking as a craftsman, as a critic of plays. So the high poetry of Aeschylus is of small importance. In technique, Aeschylus was plainly out of date. It might be thought that the author of the *Agamemnon* would have satisfied the Aristotelian desire for pity and fear.

Aristotle's own canonic artist (Sophocles) alone fulfilled the law of the Mean, which is so conspicuously Aristotelian that we are to forget its universality in Greek thought. Although Aristotle does not, in so many words apply his favourite doctrine to Sophocles, the application is implicit. In addition, that poet was always recognised as standing between the "pomp" of Aeschylus and the "quibbling" of Euripides. Again in technical construction, Aristotle prefers his use of the chorus to that of Euripides and, of course, to that of Aeschylus, who in this respect was quite out of fashion; the part played by the chorus in his *Supplices* or even in the *Eumenides* was too overpowering. Still more important, Sophocles, above all, provided the perfect plot, and hence Aristotle's preference for the *Oedipus Tyrannus*. Further, the Theban story is a fine example for drawing out pity and fear; for its, "Reversal" (whether this term is to be understood as meaning a simple reversal of fortune, or as the effect of a blinded human action ironically recoiling on the agent's head); for the type of its hero, and for the

skill with which the "irrational" element is kept outside the
action. In fine, *Oedipus* gives Aristotle the standard to which none
other can attain. Modern judgement backed by the experience so
completely bears out this claim.

Euripides, on the other hand, had been steadily gaining ground
in public estimation between the publication of the *Frogs* and the
Poetics. In Aristotle's own time, Eupripides was regarded as the
greatest dramatist. But Aristotle himself personally disagreed. He
was biased by the old moralistic standards. Euripidean characters
were not good according to the Aristotelian standards.

So, he objects to the character of Menelaus as needlessly bad,
while Melanippe is too sophistic, and Iphigenia (in *Aulis*) is
inconsistent. On grounds of construction, he finds several faults in
the Euripidean chorus, and objects to the misuse of the *deus ex
machina* (in *Medea*) and to the handling of the "irrational" in the
same play, where the appearance of Aegeus has neither probability
nor dramatic use. But the *Medea* was rightly held to be a master-
piece, and the Stoic Chrysippus paid tribute to it. In the light of
these, Aristotle's "criticisms" of its technique, in which Euripides
"manages badly", have a special interest. But Aristotle allows that
the *Cresphontes* and *Imphigenia in Tauris* are well-made plays, a true
judgement.

The broader issues involved in the Euripidean drama are hardly
mentioned. Although Aristotle is still so far under the influence of
morals as to prefer the "nobler" types of Sophoclean character, he
nowhere blames Euripides for realism. Provided that the characters
are not needlessly bad, he seems to regard tragedy as having no
less right to imitate "men as they are" than to aim at portraying
them "as they should be"—whether the word "should" is to be
explained as aesthetic or moral obligation. Nor does he express
any opinion on other innovations which Aristophanes had noticed
and condemned, such as his beggar-kings, his women in love, and
above all, the questioning and argumentative spirit of the new
school, which was turning the drama of heroic action into a debate
analogous to a modern "discussion-play." To Aristotle, Euripides
has faults, but they are almots entirely the faults of the playwright. But he has one great redeeming merit, he is "the most
tragic of poets." This statement of course refers to his doctrine of
pity and fear.

If we agree with Aristotle, that pity and fear are the emotions purged by tragedy, it follows that these emotions must not be weakened by a happy ending. Even if we do not agree with the above doctrine, we must still admit that sentimentality—the "weakness of the audience"—is the ruin of the really tragic play, as it ruins many novels. The essence of the tragic hero lies not in his death (which happens even to the most unheroic), but in the fact that after a certain crisis in his life, we cannot imagine its continuance to be tolerable or thinkable. This principle holds good even if the play does not end in actual death. Aristotle is content with "a change from good to evil fortune" and *Oedipus Tyranus* does not require its hero to die. What the play does require is that Oedipus should henceforth be dead in the sense that tragically matters—dead not merely to the world (that, perhaps may be of great moment), but to himself. His true life is done. He may still be the cause of pity and fear in his physical death (as shown in the later play *Oedipus at Colonus*), but the drama is not so much a true tragedy as a religious mystery. It may prove that there was a purpose in his life, but it starts from the point at which that life is really finished. The truth of Aristotle's great pronouncement on the tragic ending is perhaps too obvious to need illustration. See *Hamlet, Macbeth,* or *St. Joan.*

The Function of Tragedy : Catharsis

Aristotle spoke of catharsis through pity and fear. The general meaning of the statement has been well established. The basic idea of catharsis is certainly borrowed from medicine—purgation, not purification that is primarily intended. The latter meaning is not totally excluded, since purge is also a means of purification. In ancient medicine when blood was drawn the rest was purified. Behind all this there lies the primitive conception of homoeopathy. Tragedy is viewed as arousing certain emotions (which would be deleterious if allowed to remain dormant) in order to quell these disturbing elements in the soul by their violent discharge. Aristotle's general meaning is made clear by his analogy from music. This, he says, is to be studied for education, purgation, intellectual employment and relaxation (See *Politics*).

Pity and fear are united in Aristotelian psychology. He coordinates the two by holding that "what we fear for ourselves, we pity in others". Both have to be equally modified by purgation. But we confront the difficulty that pity and fear are not homogeneous. Pity is good, though fear is not. Aristotle seems, however, to have reduced them to a single psychological unit, so that the same purgation can be applied with equal effect to unhomogeneous parts. Aristotle had really to meet Plato's difficulty that the satisfaction of tragedy is mixed with pain—people weep when they are taking pleasure and the pressing problem is therefore to explain how this pain is only apparent. His solution seems to be that, in tragic pleasure, the element of pain (which we should feel in real life) is expelled by purging. On the stage, calamities are viewed without the excess either of pity or of fear so that the Peripatetic doctrine of the Mean is preserved.

Historically, then, Aristotle's position is clear. Pity and fear had been accepted by his predecessors as the chief emotions concerned, in some way, with the effect of tragedy. He explained how their working could be harmonized with the leisure of dramatic art. Nevertheless, Aristotle's solution is only partially satisfactory. I. A. Richards bases his partial defence of Aristotle on the Hegelian doctrine that tragedy is a reconciliation of opposite or discordant qualities, "Pity, the impulse to approach, and Terror, the impulse to retreat, are brought in Tragedy to a reconciliation which they find nowhere else . . . ." (I. A. Richards, *Principles*). Their union in an ordered single response is the catharsis by which tragedy is recognised. F. L. Lucas in *Tragedy* criticises this theory.

Modern criticism views this theory with scepticism. The most serious objection lies in the theory of purgation of pity and fear. To treat the function of tragedy as a purge may serve as a metaphor, but this cannot be elevated to the dignity of a true doctrine. It has now been called a "vaccination theory", and vaccination is no pleasure. The pleasure of tragedy is both immediate and positive, something more than simply prudential and medicinal. As W. M. Divon, in *Tragedy* (p.127) observes : "Aristotle would have this medicine restore us to the normal, to health, but surely it is an elixir, not a remedy, and the function of tragic drama is to exalt, not to cure us". C. E. Montague in *A Writer on his Trade* (p. 221) is interesting on this point. In fact, if a medical metaphor is to serve at all, tragedy must be more than a sedative ; it should be a tonic and a stimulant. Its value is certainly an enlargement of our experience, the learning that our work-a-day philosophies do not always dream of all things in heaven and earth, the recognition that character may triumph over circumstances. So, "O the pity—or the terror—of it" is not the final word. In seeing a great tragedy, we can perhaps find a stimulus that may produce exultation—a sense of triumph in realizing that pain and death may have more than a physical bearing, even in a world that may seem unintelligible.

Like all Greek critics, Aristotle was confronted with the difficulty of explaining the pleasure derived from the contemplation of the ugly, for pain and death are obviously ugly, yet their "imitation" is a source of pleasure. A solution of this thoory was attempted by Timocles, a writer of the Middle comedy, who suggest that the spectator forgets his own troubles, in contemplating the far sadder fate of a Tantulus or a Niobe, and so, "thrilled" by another's misfortune, he goes away with both pleasure and instruction. This, of course, is no answer. Longinus is nearer the truth when he says, even if tragedy has its "own" pleasure, this specific pleasure belongs to the more comprehensive satisfaction of all great poetry, and indeed of all great creative literature. To some extent Aristotle too emphasized this when he emphasized that the aesthetic value was based on recognition. The poet like any other artists expresses his intuition of life, not otherwise revealed to our normal existence. The tragic poet has imitated life. He has shown us life, as exhibited us to his consciousness, and our own perceptions have been broadened (Scott-James). In the end, it is precisely this poetic experience that gives the highest value to the great tragedies of the world. The argument of *Agamemnon* or *Macbeth* is, in itself, a sordid matter for the newspaper. It remains for the poet to describe not only the ugliness of the particular facts in their relation to human life, but their deeper, more universal significance in the art of living.

Aristotle on the Parts of Tragedy

Aristotle's pronouncements on the six parts of tragedy have also aroused much speculation. Of these his ideas on the chorus, action and character need special examination.

Was the chorus a help or hindrance in the fully developed theatre? The hindrance arises from the mere presence of a group, more or less remote from the main action, which may often require secrecy, and this constitutes a severe strain both on the ingenuity of the dramatist and the credulity of the audience. But it can also be a help in the hands of a master. During the major pauses of the plot (afterwards marked by the "Acts") the "relief" of choric odes is patent enough; but this relief is no less needed in those places where the plot is being developed at its most tense and emotional stages. A Greek chorus, uttering the tritest sentiments in a couple of lines between the passionate or closely-reasoned speeches of the chief persons, often strikes the *reader* as a tiresome interruption. But *on the stage* the effect is very different. A continuous flow of essential dialogue cannot be followed without some mental pause of less tension. Failing comic "relaxation", the chorus gives this breathing-space with a break which can be really welcome and indeed necessary.

Aristotle himself being mainly interested in the actors, especially in the hero, does not deal with these psychological and technical problems. The chorus was a well-established tradition, and his object was simply to determine its proper place in the economy of the play. Obviously its members performed a double function, firstly as dancers and singers and secondly as participants in the action, and they had to be considered in both capacities. He does not minimise the pleasure of music; but in this respect, he regards the chorus as an accessory (like scenic effects) rather than as a vital part of tragedy.

What is important is to consider their relation to the plot, as managed by the actors technically so called. Here Aristotle is quite definite. "The chorus should be regarded as one of the actors and as a part of the whole and should share in the action, not in the manner of Euripides but of Sophocles." He does not fully discuss Aeschylus, for the simple reason that Aeschylus is considered only as a stepping stone to the goal of Sophoclean perfection. The earliest extent play of Aeschylus (*Supplices*) in which the chorus is really the protagonist, discloses the dramatic restrictions involved in the use of only two actors and the introduction of a third in his later plays was borrowed from Sophocles himself. Probably Aristotle holds that a play like the *Eumenides* laid too much stress on the chorus of Furies, who may be said to divide with Orestes the honours of the protagonist. But if Aeschylus here shows the excess of the Mean, Euripides is no less an example of its defect. But it is not easy to understand his definite preference for Sophocles in this respect. As far as we can judge from his surviving works, he gives much of the same importance to the chorus, both in the proportion of lines assigned to their part, and in their relation to the plot. Both equally satisfy the requirement of "participation", as needed to preserve the unity and coherence of the drama, and the typical chorus of Euripides is not more separated from the action than, for example, the chorus of the *Ajax*. But it is sometimes argued that the choral odes of Sophocles are more relevant to the plot than are many Euripidean lyrics. But Aristotle, however, does not expressly state this. Here his interest in the chorus ends.

Aristotle nowhere expands his views on the precise link between chorus and actors, nor between chorus and audience. Modern criticism of the Greek chorus has taken a curious turn. W. M. Dixon in *Tragedy* calls it a "deliberate sentry against realism, to exclude verisimilitude, to forbid the illusion that we are witnessing a scene from real life" (p.53). But the practical usefulness of the chorus lay in the opposite direction—how to give verisimilitude to a body of semi-actors whose presence is so often unconvincing. A Greek play had other types of such "sentries" against verisimilitude, masks, buskins, language, metre and conventional scenery. But Dixon is correct in pointing out that the chorus acted as a bridge between the stage and the audience. This is his historical function. It has sometimes been called a body of ideal spectators. Often they are the vehicle of expressing the poet's own views, which may by no means coincide with popular opinion. But chiefly their parts is that of simple average humanity, a foil to the superhuman persons of the plot; and it is here that they mediate between the stage and the audience.

The problem of the relation between plot and characters as formulated by Aristotle can be approached through an analysis of the function of the chorus. The problem of communication does not concern Aristotle. This is not within the scope of psychology. Here he starts with the relation of chorus to action. In his own words "tragedy is essentially an imitation not of persons, but of action and life, of happiness and of misery....."

Aristotle is here at grips with the very essence of drama, independent of time and circumstance. What justification for this emphasis on action ? Historically, there is plenty of justification. Greek tragedy was originally a piece of ritual in which the characters or the participants counted for little or nothing. At this stage, *mimesis* or (impersonation) is simply to take the place of somebody. It is the re-enactment of action. But Aristotle based his preference for action on his philosophy. His teleology is there evident. The *End* is the chief concern of art as of life and, the plot being the end of tragedy, is logically prior to character. The essence of tragedy is to exhibit men in action.

But a moment's reflection will show all kinds of men "in action" do not constitute action. (Carlyle said that every death-bed is not the fifth act of a tragedy. A railway accident is not tragedy, nor is burglary). Events or "actions" can only become tragic in relation to the character of its victims. But Aristotle admits that there are several types of tragedy one of which is "ethical"—the drama of character. He clearly allows that character may be as prominent as action. He might have well instanced the *Prometheus Vinctus* where there is really no action in the physical sense from the beginning to end. We have, later, Dryden warning us against holding "nothing to be an action till the players came to blows". Even *Philocletes* of Sophocles shows that the character can be as important as plot. But Aristotle is ever eager to stretch the existing tragedies to a philosophical theory he lays down.

His insistence on the plot may, in fact be regarded as a protest against a common tendency to subordinate action to character (see M. MacGregor, *Leave of Hellas*, p.138). He finds Oedipus precisely illustrating his theory. Here we have one of the most complicated of Greek dramatic plots, and the character is subservient to action. Unlike Shakespeare's *Hamlet*, the plot of *Oedipus* would have been equally effective, if attached to a person of quite different psychology and morality. In fine, we can understand Aristotle's statement only in relation to the history of Greek drama. Here characters are typical and not individual as in Shakespeare. The use of the mask itself suggests it. As A. C. Bradley in *Oxford Lectures on Poetry* suggests :

"We are interested in the personality of Orestes and Antigone, but chiefly as it shows itself in one respect, as identifying itself with a certain ethical relation..."

The classical drama excluded free will. If the action was entirely directed by an external cause the persons of the play would be automata, so that the plot would become not only the main but the sole consideration. It would seem that Greek tragedy is simply predestinarian. Sophocles appears to send the innocent to death because such is the will of higher powers. Antigone, and Oedipus himself are to our mind innocent.

The Aesthetic Philosophy of Plato and Aristotle

Plato's attack on poets in its developed form is both ethical and metaphysical. The *Ion* is the first Socratic dialogue concerning poetry. Here he advances the doctrine of phrenzy (consult *Ion*, *Republic* and *Laws*). In general, the strongest of Plato's attacks are based on metaphysical grounds, on the prior questions of the nature of poetry. As a literary term, *mimesis* is first found in Plato. The Greeks did not regard the poet as an imaginative creator—a maker—but as a specialised workman in material language. It was this notion that was behind Plato's disparagement of the poet as a mere imitator of sensible things. He objects to *mimesis* or Impersonation. He assumes that art impersonates life, but as life is itself teleological, the artist should have a moral purpose.

Metaphysically, Aristotle had rejected the theory of Ideas in his model of the universe, substituting the ideas of *Becoming* in place of the Platonic *Being*. This principle not only explained the nature of poetry, but gave it a high philosophic status. As knowledge of the universal could only be obtained by a study of particulars, it followed that all process of *Becoming*, must be observed, whether in the physical world or in the spiritual life of man.

Aristotle prefers poetry to history because it is more universal. Such universals have a real existence as concrete and objective things in the world. They are common to many individuals and are therefore, worthy of philosophic study. History itself may be treated by the poet in a universal sense, for the philosophic reason that "that there is nothing to prevent some events which have actually happened from conforming to probability and inevitability". Agamemnon was a real person. The poet, however, does not report his words on a given occasion, but gives the words and actions typical of the persons. The type is essential to poetry and here Aristotle draws the logical conclusions from his theory of universals but correctly interprets the genius of Greek epic and drama—the two standards of Aristotle's poetry.

This is how he counters the Platonic view about the source of poetry, that is, ecstasy or phrenzy and makes it the product of natural ability. The poetic "mania" is no temporary enthusiasm, but permanent and conscious ability.

The main defects of the *Poetics* derive from Aristotle's theoretical position. Aristotle's view of art is too circumscribed and anthropocentric. In his insistence on the formula of poetry—representing men in action—he appears to have excluded all internal nature. Further, he limited even the proper study of mankind as a poetic motive to "universal" man, so dismissing, in theory at least—the personal impulse in lyrical poetry.

Next, his genius was entirely systematic and comprehensive so that he does not confine himself to one poem, one drama, or even to one author. His notable enthusiasm for Oedipus did not lead him to analyse the whole works of Sophocles. Again, he lacks enthusiasm essential to the critic of poetry. His view of poetry is intellectualist.

To Aristotle, man is a political animal. Ethics is branch of Politics. Art is therefore not regarded so much as the expression of a rare individuality as a form of giving delight to the whole community. Art must be universal in its range, because only the universal can find a response in the whole body politic to which it should appeal. It must shun the bizarre, the outrageous and the excessive, and cling to the mean, which is perfect sanity.

Can a state of sanity, or perfect self-control (as opposed to phrenzy or inspiration) express that intensity which is usually considered to be essential to poetic creation ? Can poetry be produced by skill, by acquired ability, as Aristotle seems to suggest ? A universally applicable conclusion is difficult to arrive at. There are the examples of Homer and Sophocles who combined genius with enthusiasm, as far as we know, without putting themselves in a state of phrenzy.

The Doctrine of The Three Unities

The Renaissance critics of Italy in the sixteenth century deduced from Aristotle's *Poetics* their famous doctrine of the three unities. By the Unity of Place they meant that the action of the play should be confined to one place. There should be no change of scene. Aristotle mentioned no such unity in the *Poetics*. The Unity of Place is derived by the Italian critics from the Unity of Time, occasionally referred to in the *Poetics*.

By the Unity of Time is meant the correspondence between the dramatic time of representation and the actual time of the incidents comprising the plot. This doctrine demands that the period of time imagined to lapse in the play should exactly correspond with the time taken in the production. The only reference of time in Aristotle's *Poetics* is in the fifth chapter where Aristotle is comparing epic action and dramatic action. The only unity stressed by Aristotle in the *Poetics* is the Unity of Action. He places on this the strongest emphasis. Before we consider the Unity of Action let us examine the other two Unities—Unity of Time and Unity of Place.

Aristotle points out that epic poetry and tragedy differ in their lengths, for tragedy endeavours to confine itself to a single revolution of the sun. But the epic action has no limits of time. This observation of Aristotle has been formulated by the later neo-classical critics into a doctrine. But Aristotle gives us only the rough generalization as to the practice of the Greek stage. The practice was not always uniformly maintained. This is not explained as an inviolable doctrine. Even in ancient tragedy there are conspicuous examples of the disregard of the Unity of Time. In *Eumenides*, years lapse between the opening of the play and the next scene. The *Supplices* of Euripides afforded another striking incident. In *Agamemnon* there is no correspondence between dramatic time and real time.

The doctrine of the Unity of Place was first formulated by Castelvetro in his edition of the *Poetics* in 1570. Before Castelvetro, Julius Caesar Scaliger (*Poetics*, 1561) had identified the time of action with that of representation. Through Sir Philip Sidney (*Apologie for Poetrie*, 1595) the doctrine of the Three Unities entered into the English literary criticism. Ben Jonson had borrowed the doctrine and made it the basis of his dramatic theory. In France, Corneille (1606-84) in his *Three Discourses on Tragedy*, upheld the same doctrine. In short, during the Renaissance, the doctrine of the Three Unities became an important rule for the epic poet and the dramatist.

The Unity of Place was generally supposed to be a corollary of the Unity of Time. The French critics did not derive their dramatic rules directly from the Greek models or from the *Poetics* of Aristotle. They were influenced more by the Roman tragedians. Having learnt the doctrine of the Unity from Roman writers, they wanted to discover sufficient authority for this doctrine in Aristotle. There was an even greater error in the Italian critics. They subordinated the Unity of Action to the other Unities of Time and Place. They considered the Unity of Action to be derived from the Unity of Place and Time. The efforts of the French dramatist of the seventeenth century to obey the rules strictly resulted in restricting the scope of their tragedies and comedies.

The most important requirement of tragic action according to Aristotle is Unity. By Unity of Action, Aristotle does not mean the unity of the hero, or the unity of the incidents, or even mere outward unity inherent in a series of incidents. Unity in Aristotle is the principle by means of which an object retains its identity. Without unity no entity can exist. Thus a drama in order to be effective must contain unity. The greater the unity, the nearer it will be to perfection.

The Unity of Action is not a mechanical, superimposed unity. It is organic unity. As Prof. Butcher rightly observes, "The idea of Unity is not opposed to the idea of manifoldedness and variety". This principle demands that the several constituent elements of a dramatic action should form an integral structure so related that no part can be removed without affecting the tragedy as a whole. The successive incidents in dramatic action are connected together by the inward and causal bound by the law of necessary and probable sequence.

In the eighth chapter of *Poetics*, Aristotle explains at length what is meant by the Unity of Plot. The incidents selected for the plot of the drama must be such that each leads on to the next so that they form a coherent whole. This unity of form is attained by making the contents of the story universal. The poet, whether in epic or in drama, shows the inevitable or the probable sequence of events. It is this inevitable or the probable sequence of cause and effect which arouses the emotions appropriate to a tragedy. The mere accident does not arouse fear and pity as a disaster which is in the sequence of events.

Speaking in the context of the dramatic criticism, it is important to point out that in this chapter of *Poetics*, Aristotle praises Homer, the epic poet, for the Unity of Action. We thus gather that the Unity of Action was advanced by Aristotle as a fundamental requirement of aesthetic creation. It will be difficult to point out any good tragedy which does not obey the Unity of Action, though there are instances where the Unities of Time and Place are disregarded without advantage.

The close connexion between dramatic action and dramatic character makes it imperative that we should discuss the Aristotelian notion of tragic character. Aristotle's definition of the tragedy and the requirements of the tragic character laid down by him, have become the most controversial part of his *Poetics*. The chief characteristics of the tragic character are : (1) A tragic character must be good, (2) appropriate, and (3) consistent.

In other words the tragic hero must be especially of common humanity. At the same time he must be above the common level. Though not a paragon of virtue, he must yet be a man of high moral reputation.

The tragic hero must fall from prosperity into misfortune. This transition must be effected not through any vice and villainy which may justify the disaster. It must be through an error. This error, commonly called as the tragic flaw, must cooperate with the malignity of fate. Thus though the tragic hero does not deserve his fall, yet his own mistake reinforces the tragic disaster.

These are the essential characteristics of the tragic hero which Aristotle lays down. No doubt Aristotle's generalisation about the tragic hero are based on Greek tragedy, especially on Sophocles's *Oedipus Triology*. He refers to Oedipus the King as a perfect hero.

The first point of disagreement between the Aristotelian and the post-Renaissance conception of tragic character lies in the relative importance of the tragic hero in a drama. In the Greek tragedy, the tragic hero chiefly suffered under the impact of an external fate. Consequently the plot was more important, as Aristotle points out, in a typical character tragedy. Aristotle's statements on the tragic hero have to be interpreted bearing in mind his subordination of the tragic character to the tragic plot.

According to Aristotle the suffering of the tragic hero must be such as those which can produce the typical tragic emotions—pity and fear. Thus any discussion of the definition of the tragic hero given by Aristotle in the *Poetics* must be understood with reference to his conception of the plot and his conception about the tragic pleasure. If we accept these two basic theories then Aristotle is right in describing a tragic hero as "the intermediate kind of person, a man not pre-eminently virtuous and just, whose misfortune, however, is brought upon him not by vice and depravity, but by some error of judgement, he being one of those who enjoy great reputation and prosperity for example, Oedipus, Thyestes and the men of note belonging to noble families."

The serious objections which modern critics level against this definition are based upon tragic characters in modern tragedy. In the modern tragedy (post-Renaissance), character has come to occupy the most important place, and the plot, the second. It is doubtful whether pity and fear are the only emotions evoked by modern tragedy, because our tragic conception has altered. The characteristics of the ideal tragic hero also appear different to us. Aristotle's doctrine of *Hamartia* or tragic flaw does not apply to Shakespeare's *Tempest* or to Arthur Miller's *The Death of a Salesman*. Indeed, one need not multiply instances. The Aristotelian idea of tragic hero neatly fits in with Aristotle's theory of plot and his theory of tragic pleasure. The fact that Antigone is a tragic character who does not conform to Aristotle's definition, need not invalidate his generalisations. But then Shakespearean tragedies are also different from the Greek tragedies. It is doubtful if pity and fear are the only emotions appropriate to Shakespearean tragedy. Further, in a typical Shakespearean tragedy the plot is subordinate to character. Here character replaces fate, and in a Shakespearean tragic catastrophe, we do not see the operation of an inevitable fate, but rather an individual through his own inner psychological motivations coming to a catastrophic end. Thus a Shakespearean tragedy produces its effect by the revelation of subtle psychological motives. A typical Shakespearean tragic hero, Lear, or Hamlet, or Timon of Athens, is cast in a different mould.

CHAPTER FOUR

SIR PHILIP SIDNEY: THE DEFENCE OF POESY

1. Renaissance Poetics. 2. The Defence of Poesy.

Renaissance Poetics

The Renaissance is characterized by a new attitude towards the arts of poetry, painting, and sculpture, and a new confidence in human powers along with a belief in the observation of physical nature. Many of the medieval theories in aesthetics and poetics have been abandoned, and the beginnings of new doctrines can be detected. Yet we must remember that no serious discontinuity of thought, or a complete reversal of the directions in thinking did take place. Renaissance poetical theories (especially in England) constitute a compromise between the old and the new.

Thus in spite of the conflict between the theological outlook of the priests and the theologians, and the new secular outlook of the humanists, the sense of medieval piety and religiosity lived on in the new reformers and poets. The Bible continued to be still an authority, although the Greek and Roman classics were gaining prestige and popularity. Paradoxically the very arguments of St. Augustine were used by the new humanists in the new defence of poetry and art as Plato is cited as a friend of the poets and poetry by Sir Philip Sidney in his *Defence of Poesie*. It is not necessary to labour this point. A careful study of the *Defence of Poesie* by Sidney alone can make it clear that many of the medieval ideas continued to exist in the new schools of criticism.

Literary theory and criticism received a new emphasis in Italy during the 16th century. One reason for this was the discovery and the rising popularity of the *Poetics* of Aristotle which had almost been ignored. It had lain almost unknown in Latin translations of the abridged Arabic versions. But in Venice in 1498, we have the first Latin translation of the whole text, and this gave a fresh impetus to critical activity in Italy. One of the main problems of the Renaissance critic and theorist was that of defending imaginative literature which was being attacked on moral and social grounds.

In contrast to Italy, England was not fertile in critical writing. Literary criticism occurs incidentally in other writings, and such criticism is not of a systematic nature. For instance, Sir Thomas Elyot's *The Book Named the Governour* (1531) contains critical fragments, but the main purpose of the book is to give advice to train youth in politcal life. Elyot's theory is wholly didactic, and he recommends the study of poetry for the moral instruction it can give, and points out the "commendable sentences and wise counsels" to be found in poets. Critical remarks too are to be found in the works of rhetorics. The theory of rhetorics was a popular one in the Elizabethan age, and poetry was referred to by writers on rhetoric such as Thomas Wilson (*Art of Rhetoric*, 1553), and Roger Ascham (*Schoolmaster*, 1570) for its power to teach allegorically.

Indirectly, however, the study of poetical and critical theories received fresh impetus on account of the attacks on poetry by the puritans of the time. Stephen Gosson (1554-1624) attacked poets and players in his *The Schoole of Abuse*. Sir Philip Sidney's *Defence of Poesy* (published posthumously in 1595; another edition of the same work in the same year bore the title *Apology for Poetry*) came as a reply to Gosson. This is the only critical work of the first rank in England comparable with similar works of the Italian critics to be found in the 16th century. In it we find qualities and ideas derived from Sir Thomas Elyot and the classical spirit of Roger Ascham strongly supported by a diligent study of the Italian critics of the Renaissance.

The Defence of Poesy

The *Defence of Poesy* is a methodical examination of the art of poetry and a critical discussion of the state of the contemporary English poetry. Starting with the essential nature of poetry, the art of imitation or representation, the author classifies various kinds of poetry, discusses their relation to philosophy and history, the objections that have been raised to poetry, and English poetry from Chaucer onwards. He then concerns himself with the principles that should be observed in tragedy and comedy. He laments the poverty of English lyrical poetry, and the artificiality and the affectation of the current style. He also deals with prosody in its relation to English language.

Sidney's arguments for the defence may be synoptically summarized as follows : The first argument in favour of poetry is its antiquity. The earliest philosophers were poets. Likewise the earliest historians were poets. Among the Romans a poet was called *Vates* which means a "diviner, fore-seer, or prophet". The prophetic character of poetry is illustrated by this name. There are further illustrations of the divine nature of poetry. The Psalms of David are a divine poem. The Greek word "poet" expresses the creative power by which poetry is exalted above all branches of knowledge which deal with the world as it is.

Next he deals with the functions of poetry. The poet's function is to improve upon nature. "Only the poet...lifted with the vigour of his own invention, does grow, in effect, into another nature, in making things either better than nature brings forth, or, quite new forms such as never were in nature, as the heroes, demigods, cyclops, chimeras, furies, and such like; so he goes hand in hand with nature, not enclosed within the narrow warrant of her gifts, but freely ranging only within the zodiac of his own wit. Nature never set forth the earth in so rich a tapestry as divers poets have done...."

Poetry is defined to be an art of imitation. Of this art there are three kinds : sacred poetry, philosophical poetry, and poetry in the strict sense of the Greek term. In the promotion of the final goal of all knowledge, poetry may be shown to be superior to all sciences. The final goal of poetry is "to lead and draw us to as high a perfection as our degenerate soul, made worse by their clayey lodgings, can be capable of." Philosophy claims to be the best teacher of virtue, and history, on certain grounds, claims to be superior to philosophy. But the pre-eminence claimed by philosophy and history as a teacher of wisdom really belongs to poetry. Because philosophy gives precepts, history gives examples, but poetry gives both. It gives perfect pictures of virtue which are far more effective than the mere definitions of philosophy. (Here Sidney gives a number of illustrations taken from philosophy and classical literature.) Poetry is superior to history, as being more philosophical and studiously serious. The poet's examples of virtue and vice are more perfect than that of the historians. For imaginary examples are more instructive than real examples. And the reward of virtue and vice are more clearly shown in poetry than in history. Poetry is also superior to philosophy as an incentive to virtuous action, because poetry presents moral lessons in attractive forms.

Next, he deals with the various types of poetry separately—pastoral, elegiac, iambic, satiric, of comedy, tragedy, of lyric poetry, and finally, of epic or heroic poetry. The function of comedy is to act as a foil to virtue in life. Lyric poetry is of that kind "most capable and most fit to awake the thoughts from the sleep of idleness to embrace honorable enterprises." And now remains the heroical or the tragical "whose very name (I think) should daunt all back-biters; for by what conceit can a tongue be directed to speak evil of that which draweth with it no less champions than Achilles, Cyrus, Aeneas, Turnus, Tydeus, and Rinaldo? Who doth not only teach and move to a truth, but teacheth and moveth to the most high and excellent truth, who maketh magnanimity and justice shine throughout all misty fearfulness and foggy desires . . . ."

Thus having shown the transcendent excellence of poetry, Sidney considers the objections of its enemies. Many objections against poetry are captious and trivial, and that they are not worth refuting. They are merely poet-haters "*mysomousio*" as he calls the critics of poetry. The preliminary objection to the use of rhyme and verse is answered by saying that: "Verse far exceedeth prose in the knitting up of the memory."

But there are four chief objections to poetry. They are : a man might spend his time in knowledge more profitably than in poetry; that poets are liars and poetry has no concern with truth ; that poetry abuses men's wits, and finally, that Plato had banished poets from his ideal state. Among these charges the one criticised in the detail is the criticism that poets are liars. Opposing this view, Sidney says that of all writers under the sun the poet is the least liar. "Now, for the poet, he nothing affirms, and therefore never lies. For, as I take it, to lie is to affirm that to be true which is false ; so as the other artists, and especially the historian, affirming many things, can, in the cloudy knowledge of mankind, hardly

escape from many lies. But the poet......never affirms." Coming
to Plato, Sidney points out that Plato warned men not against
poetry but against its abuse, just as St. Paul did with respect to
Philosophy. And many great men have honoured poetry.

The rest of the *Defence* deals with a comment on English poetry
of his day. This then is the essence of Sidney's arguments in favour
of poetry and poets.

Let us take his *Defence of Poesie* for analysis. The main points of
critical interest are a complex definition of poetry based both on
Aristotle and Horace, an adaptation of Aristotelian theory, making
poetry a union of philosophy and history thus making poetry the
highest source of wisdom after the *Scriptures*, transforming Plato
into a witness for poetry, and the application of the principles and
literary norms of Scaliger and Horace to English poetry.

Sidney's essential contribution to criticism lies in his redefinition
of poetry in such a manner as to make the moral content of poetry
a part of its essential requirement. Sidney is applying some of the
Renaissance doctrine of ideality to poetry. Thus the *Defence of
Poesie* is more a work of critical synthesis. It combines Plato's
views with Aristotle's poetics. The teachings of Horace are also
included. It is in fact the biggest attempt at critical synthesis.
Sidney never advances a single original point of interest. Even the
new conception of his poetic imitation is the result of combining
Aristotelian concepts with the neo-Platonic doctrine.

He transforms the concept of imitation into one of creation or
ideal imitation according to which the poet imitates not actualities
but the ideal reality behind the actual. Now the ideal word of the
poet is of importance because of its didactic power, and the poet
by presenting an ideal world aims at instructing and delighting
the reader. To quote George Saintsbury :

The importance of this manifesto, both symptomatically and
typically, can hardly be exaggerated. It exhibits the temper of
the generation which actually produced the first fruits of the
greatest Elizabethan poetry, it served as a stimulant and
encouragement to all the successive generations of the great age.
That Sidney makes mistakes both in gross and details......is of
course undeniable. He had a good deal of the merely traditional
mode of Renaissance respect for classical—and for some modern
—authority.

And then he concludes :

> And had his mistakes been thrice what they are, the tone and
> temper of his tractate would make us forgive three times over.[1]

Sidney's achievement is summed up by W. K. Wimsatt and
Cleanth Brooks as follows :

> The sources of Sidney's *'Defence'* were classical but the spirit
> was not sternly classical. Sidney sends up the joyous fireworks of
> the Italianate Renaissance. His colors are enthusiastic, neo-
> Platonic, ideal-purple and gold. The motion is soaring. He is
> essentially a theorist of the exuberant imagination.[2]

A History of Criticism and Literary Taste in Europe (1949), Vol. II, pp. 174-176.
[2] *Literary Criticism : A Short History*, p. 174.

CHAPTER FIVE

DRYDEN AS LITERARY CRITIC AND MAN OF LETTERS

English Criticism before Dryden

In the history of almost every nation the art of criticism is the last to be developed and brought to perfection. Criticism, by its nature, presupposes a substantial literary output that can be criticised, and from which canons of criticism can be extracted in accordance with the genius of that nation. Moreover, as the critical spirit is the offspring of retrospection and reflection, it generally thrives only under a reaction from a time of imaginative effort and artistic achievement. When the poets and singers of a nation are busy giving permanent expression to the creative energy that is in the air, they have hardly the time or the inclination to stop and enquire into the psychological and intellectual processes by which works of imaginative art are produced. It is when the current of inspiration becomes weak, as it invariably does after a time, that men are spurred to this analysis of literary excellence, which is criticism.

What we have said above will explain why in England criticism was not attempted till the beginning of the age of Elizabeth, and did not settle on the lines on which it has since developed, before the Restoration. Before the Elizabethan age, England had produced little imaginative work of value, if Chaucer is excepted. And Chaucer was a man much in advance of his times who founded no school and left no successors. The Elizabethans had no continuous indigenous literary tradition from which they could formulate principles of criticism. But their loving study of the classics inaugurated by Wyatt and Surrey in the previous generation inclined them to pay absolute reverence to the models furnished by the classics and principles of criticism laid down by Aristotle and the ancients and to apply these principles without reservation or modification to the literature of their own times. The influence of the classics on the creative work of the period was on the whole good.

The University Wits and their successors who had turned with disgust from the lifeless fifteenth century verse imitators of Chaucer, and the doggerel of Skelton found ample freedom for the expression of individual genius by taking the classics as their models. And, at a later stage, particularly in Milton, the study of the classics had a salutory chastening effect. It served as an antidote to the violence and exaggeration of the Elizabethans—qualities which were inseparable from their super-abundant energy. But in the field of criticism itself; the slavish adherence to Aristotelian maxims tended to make criticism academic and pedantic, and to divert the theory from the practice of letters considerably. Thus Webb and Puttenham, the pioneers of Elizabethan criticism, devoted their treatise to the classification of writers according to their subjects and the literary forms in which they specialised and to the discussion of metre and other technical questions. They did not concern themselves, as the modern critics do, with the literary worth of individual authors, or with the discussion of the emotional and intellectual basis of their work. These and other Elizabethan critics were for the most part engaged in a heated controversy over the propriety of using rhyme in poetry and the respective merits as an alternative to the old alliterative rhythm and the classical metres. The interminable wrangles did not, fortunately, interfere with the work of the poets who for one or two attempts uniformly favoured rhyme.

Side by side with this controversy over rhyme, there arose a more important one in which the critics engaged with equal zest and which resulted in Sidney's *Apologie for Poetry*, written in reply to the puritan assault on the theatre. But it is in its ultimate scope, a defence of imaginative art against the suspicions with which men of high but narrow purpose have always consciously or unconsciously tended to regard it. The argument of Sidney's book is this briefly. Of all arts poetry is the most true and the most necessary to men. Its outward form, metre and the ornament are of little importance, as verse is nothing more than a means of securing a fitting raiment for poetry. Poetry again, more than any other art, has the power of moulding the character and the actions of men to noble business and issues. For this reason, the poet should not shut his eyes to the ugly side of life but must by means of comedy, hold up vice and wickedness to ridicule, thus fulfilling his role as the teacher of mankind. These are the main ideas of Sidney, who closes his work with an assertion that each form of poetry has its own peculiar import, and a lament over the decay unto which English poetry had fallen in the sixteenth century.

That Sidney was able to take such a lofty and a philosophic view of the function of poetry is all the more to his credit where we consider that his critical contemporaries rarely escaped from the vagueness of far-fetched analogies and generalities and their main interest was in matters of technical skill and detail.

Dryden as Critic

The advance from the critical work of Sidney and of his contemporaries to that of Dryden is a remarkable one. It is with Dryden that criticism in the modern sense of the word begins. This advance was in a measure due to the intellectual movement that affected the country. The creative energy that was so abundant in the Elizabethan writers had gradually spent itself. A reaction had set in against the extravaganzas of the Elizabethan writers, real or fancied. Correctness gradually became the pre-eminent ideal of those who wished to excel in literature. But side by side with this negative aspiration, there was a positive one—the desire to observe minutely and depict faithfully the customs and manners of the age and the world of men and things. The new writers were perhaps not profound observers of life, but their social portraiture and didactic writings exhibit remarkable acuteness and precision. This new intellectual movement was directly responsible in a large measure for the great advance in the literary arts of satire and criticism and for the new departure in philosophy.

The next most important influence that affected English criticism at this period was the work of French critics like Saint Evremond and the practice of the great dramatist Corneille. Saint Evremond, along with Dryden was responsible for popularising in England the contemporary French ctiticism which interested itself chiefly in the discussion of theories of form and formation of aesthetic principles for general application. The impact of French critical thought was on the whole for good, so far as Dryden and other writers of the period immediately following the Restoration were concerned. But the influence of the later French critics headed by Boileau with his cut and dry rules, proved entirely harmful as is evident from the writings of the eighteenth century critics like Dr. Johnson, who deified correctness, treated the form of a literary work as something separable from its matter and indulged in the pernicious habit of awarding marks, as it were, to authors they criticised and classifying them according to their work. Dryden's critical works betrays occasional lapses of this sort but it is on the whole free from them. It was more definitely and beneficently influenced by the *Discourses* of Corneille in which the great dramatist first uttered a mild protest against the tyranny of the Classical Unities—a protest which Dryden voiced more loudly in his *Essay of Dramatic Poesy* (1668).

We have indicated above the principal influence which shaped Dryden's critical views. We must however observe that this orginal contribution to the art of criticism completely overshadows his indebtedness to the contemporaries and earlier writers. He is the first English critic who has a strong hold on his life and reality. He does not, as the critics who came before and after him too often did, consider literature as something apart from life, or as a craft in which excellence could be attained by faithful adherence to certain rules.

The passion for observation which we have noted as a characteristic of his age is strongly present in him and reveals itself in his zeal for the following of Nature. Nature in that age, used to denote three very different things :—(1) An ideal which, it was assumed, all poets and artists should aim at expressing and holding up for emulation of mankind ; (2) the principles of sound reason, which the poet had constantly to keep before him; and (3) the world of reality faithfully to be occupied by the poet. Dryden, while implying by the word 'Nature', all these three conceptions to a certain extent seems to lay special stress on the last. Speaking of Chaucer he says, "Chaucer followed Nature everywhere ; but was never so bold as to go beyond her". He must have been a man of most wonderfully comprehensive nature because, as it has been truly observed of him, he has taken into the compass of his *Canterbury Tales* the various manners and humours (as we call them) of the whole English nation in his age. It is sufficient to say according to the proverb *that here is God's plenty*. We have our forefathers and great grandames all before us, as they were in Chaucer's days ; their general characters are still remaining in mankind and even in England......for mankind is ever the same and nothing lost out of nature though every thing is altered". These words show how clearly he recognised that the artist's business is to depict the abiding reality of life freed from the accidental associations of time, place and nationality.

The next great characteristic of Dryden as a critic is his absolute openness of mind, his desire and ability to pass unbiased judgement on all literary questions that came up before him. He was no revolutionary in taste and it was not his purpose to throw overboard all the accepted critical canons of his day. His burning interest in such academic questions as the true nature and aim of the tragedy and the heroic poem his reverence for the ideal epic which would embody in itself all the great virtues of Homer and Virgil show that he did not think lightly of the standards of the past. He was rather, a reconciler of ancient and modern canons and views of literature, and showed respect to orthodox opinions wherever he could. But he did not make a fetish of such opinions and wherever his sure instinct or sound common sense advised a repudiation of accepted notions he did not hesitate to make it ; see, for instance, his just and reasoned appreciation of Chaucer against the opinion of Cowley (who was accepted as a great authority in his day on such matters) and his preference of Chaucer to Ovid.

He is generally at his best when he sets himself to try the value of dogmatic principles "cautious, respectful, seeming to comply with them till the time comes for the stroke that ends the encounter and leaves the arena cleared for the next antagonist". The importance of his word does not lie so much in his particular judgements which are at times wrong, *e. g.*, his preference of the verse of Waller and Fairfax to that of Spenser and Milton, which proceeds from his admiration for the expert handling of the heroic couplet by the former poets. But what is valuable is his general attitude towards literature as an art and craft. He is "sceptical, tentative, and disengaged", not inevitably pledged to dogmas and principles. It was this openness of mind that enabled him to see the super beauty of Shakespeare's plays and the great qualities of Milton and

Chaucer, though his own gifts were of a different order altogether. The very fact that no literary estimate of these poets had crystallised before him gave him the freedom to speak out, and he did so with generous enthusiasm and true insight.

Another great merit of Dryden's criticism is that it is informal and intimate. He carries his learning lightly and establishes with the minimum of effort that sympathy between reader and writer so essential for the understanding of a true work of art. Of this happy knack of his Mr. Vaughan truly remarks, "This Dryden and not Sainte Beuve who is the true father of the Literary Causerie and he remains its unequalled master. There may be other methods of striking the right note in literary criticism. Lamb showed that there may be ; so did Mr. Pater. But few indeed are the authorities who have known how to attune the mind of a reader to a subject which beyond all others cries out for harmonious treatment so skilfully as Dryden." In his critical writings one is equally struck by the conversational ease of manner so characteristic of the French and the depth of study for which English scholarship has always been distinguished. And like Sainte Beuve after him, Dryden often combines biography and criticism as with great effect, as in his remarks on Chaucer in the "Preface to the Fables".

The merits of Dryden's criticism that we have indicated so far are Dryden's own ; they are not generally to be found in other writers of his time. But in other respects he simply followed the trend of his age, though he achieved more substantial results thereby than other writers. We refer to his handling of the comparative and historical methods of criticism. The comparative method consists in comparing two writers or two forms of art either for the sake of placing the one above the other or for the sake of drawing out the essential differences between the two. The latter method alone is legitimate, it enables the critic to define exactly, by reference to other writers or forms of art, the particular aesthetic value of his subject. The former method which aims at determining the relative worth of writers is for purposes of classification, harmful and misleading as it is impossible to determine the comparative value of men of such diverse and distinctive types of genius as great writers generally are. The Restoration critics generally used the comparative method to classify authors. Dryden is not altogether free from his bias as will be seen from his comparison of Homer and Virgil, but it must be said to his credit that he very often employs comparisons with great effect and vividly brings out the characteristic excellence of his author, *e.g.* the comparison between Chaucer and Boccaccio in the "Preface to the Fables".

Lastly, Dryden was the first English critic to make systematic use of the historical method. In this he was influenced by the French critic Dacier. His knowledge of social and literary history was by no means full or authoritative but such as it was he used it often with success and saved himself from errors into which critics who depend upon impression or authority alone generally fall.

Dryden's Satires

It is sometimes said that Dryden's satires were actuated merely by the motive of profit in writing his satires. The composition of the *Medal* is specially attributed to the fact that he received payment for writing it. But even in the case of the *Medal*, this explanation is by no means the correct one. In undertaking the composition of his first great satire *Absalom and Achitophel* whether or not at the request of Charles II, Dryden found there his first great literary opportunity. And of this he took advantage in a spirit far remote from that of either the hired bravos or the spiteful writers of the lampoons of that age. For this opportunity he had unconsciously been preparing himself as a dramatist, and it was in the nature of things and in accordance with the responsiveness of his genius to the calls made upon it by time and circumstances that in the season of political crisis he should have rapidly perceived his chance of decisively influencing public opinion by exposing the aims and the methods of the revolutionary party.

This he proposed to do not by a poetic summary of the rights of the case or by a sermon in verse on the sins of factiousness, treason and corruption, but by holding up to the times a mirror in which under a happily contrived disguise, the true friends and the real foes of the king and the country should be recognized. This was the form of satire later commented by Dryden himself as the species mixing serious interests with pleasant manners to which among the ancients several of Lucian's dialogues belong. Dryden says "of the same kind is mother Hubbard's Tale in Spenser and if it not to be vain to mention my own—the poem of *Absalom* and *Mac Flecknoe* (1682).

The political question at issue was that of the succession of the Catholic claimant to the throne or of his exclusion in favour of some other claimant, perhaps the king's son Monmouth whom many believed legitimate. For many months Shaftesbury too who after abandoning a succession of Governments had passed into the opposition, and seemed to steer clear of storms. Two parliaments had been called twice in turn—twice the exclusion Bill had been rejected by the Lords. Then as the Whig leader seemed to have thrown all hesitation to the winds and was either driving his party or being driven by it into extremities from which there was no return.

A tremor of reaction ran through the land. The party round the king gathered confidence, and even evidence supposed to be adequate was gathered. Shaftesbury was committed to the tower on a charge of high treason. It was at this time that Dryden's great effort to work upon public opinion was made. *Absalom and Achitophel* was probably taken in hand early in 1681, and published on the 17th November in that year. Shaftesbury, it is known, was then fearing for his life. A week later, in spite of all efforts to the contrary, he was acquitted by the Middlesex grand jury. Great popular rejoicings followed and a medal was struck representing the sun emerging from the clouds. But this momentary rejoicing not withstanding, the game was all up and within a few months. Monmouth in his turn was arrested and Shaftesbury became a fugitive in Holland. *Absalom and Achitophel Part I* is complete in itself being intended to help in producing a direct result at the Government, and it is not to be regarded as a mere instalment of a longer whole. *Absalom and Achitophel* veils its political satire under the transparent disguise of one of the most familiar episodes in Old Testament history, which the existing crisis in English affairs resembled sufficiently to make the allegory and its interpretation easy. The attention of the English public and the citizens of London with whom the affair was familiar was sure to be arrested by a series of characters whose names and distinctive features were borrowed from the Old Testament. Also the analogy between Charles II and David's early exile and final triumphant establishment on the throne was a common piece of Restoration poetry. The actual notion of adapting the story of Absalom and Achitophel to the political situation was not new to literary controversialists of the period.

In 1680, a tract entitled *Absalom's Conspiracy* had dealt with the supposed intentions of Monmouth. Also a satire of 1681 had applied the name of Achitophel to Shaftesbury. For the rest, Dryden was careless about the fitting of the secondary figures of his satires exactly with their scriptural bias and boring the reader by a scrupulous fidelity to minute detail. *Absalom and Achitophel* remains the greatest political satire in English literature, partly because it is frankly political and not intended like *Hudibras* by means of a mass of accumulative detail to convey a general impression of the vices and follies, defects and extravaganzas, as of a particular section or sections of the nation. With Dryden every bit is calculated and every stroke goes home. In each character, brought on the scene these features only are selected for exposure or praise which are of direct significance for the purpose on hand. It is not a satirical narrative complete in itself which is attempted, the poem is intended to lead up to the trial and conversion of its hero. The satirist has his subsequent treatment of the subject well in hand.

Through all the force of the invective and fervour of the praise there runs a consciousness that the political situation may change. This causes a constant self control and weariness on the part of the author. Instead of pouring forth a stream of Aristophanic interpretation or boyish fun, he is adapting himself so nicely to the reactions of the more important of his characters, to the immediate issue of that treatment, both of the temper of his principal supporters and some of the loyal minority. The king is moved to interfere. His protest and his paternal threat allay the tumult. The tone in the main is lofty and dignified, especially in the principal parts, as for instance the scene of the temptation and of the king's pronouncement. The speeches are proper to epic or grave drama such as we should expect in a heroic poem and not a satire. Occasional archaisms foreign to Dryden's own natural style, point directly to the influence of the English epics.

Further the verse, especially in these main parts of the structure is the very purest in style and most musical in sound which only Dryden could compose, that is to say, the best of its kind found in the English language.

Dryden's Absalom and Achitophel

The poem is an announcement and a prophecy of the royal triumph and an appeal to the nation for grateful acquiescence.

Its plan is one of extreme simplicity, a situation rather than a story. A young illegitimate prince is incited to rebellion by the art of a treacherous statesman ; he is taught to cultivate popularity and does so with treacherous success. All this is stated in outline and abstraction only. The prince's position becomes a national danger owing to the caprice of mob. Sketches, again abstract with slight indentifying touches, are given up to this point.

An important question to be determined is, in what sense is *Absalom and Achitophel* a 'satire'. It is not so described by the author, whose title for it is *Absalom and Achitophel A Poem* and it should be compared or rather contrasted with his attack on Shaftesbury and his party in the following year which he calls "*The Medal—A Satire Against Tradition*". *Absalom and Achitophel* is commonly classified as a satire. It does not fit in any other known class such for instance as an "epic", and it does contain important satiric element in the portraits of which the representation of Buckingham as Zimri may be taken as a specimen. The figure of Achitophel is partly satiric, that is to say it is intended as a hostile picture of the man Shaftesbury. And it is these elements of passages in the work, partly because they are detachable and quotable that are perhaps the best known. The work is really unique. There is no parallel in Dryden or elsewhere. It bears no resemblance as a whole to Roman satire, as we know it in Horace, Percius or Juvenal. An analogy has been alleged to Juvenal's IV satire. That satire, it is true, is a story and does comprise satiric portraits of individuals. Domitian summons his council to dicuss the cooking of a remarkable fire turbot and the various councillors are described. But it is more than doubtful if Dryden owed any thing to this work. The former resemblance is slight, and the substance and spirit are totally different. Juvenal's piece is essentially dependent on an undignified theme, Dryden's is on a dignified one. Juvenal could not give nor ever tries to give any thing like the scene of the Temptation.

Satire and Satirists

Dryden's nominal rank is that of a poet ; but the more accurate description of him is a man of letters. He was a teacher of literature of all kinds. A fine prose writer and translator, a dramatic and verse essayist. He spent seven years at Cambridge and was all his life essentially a book man, though any thing but a pedant. He was one of the earliest men who made authorship his profession and faced the world upon that ground. He was in the prime of his life when he published his *Absalom and Achitophel* and his *Mac Flecknoe*, satires which will always be remembered among the highest specimens of the art. He went to work to satirise with the same bluff haughtiness with which every thing else was by him. His warm nature made him scorn and laugh as it made him love, and his bright wit and fine versification were as ready for an enemy as to praise a friend. He makes no disguise of his relish for satire and says plainly that you have a right to attack a particular person when he has become a public nuisance. His ethics of satire is in an unsatisfactory state and I fear that if you apply the moral text simply and make your justice your standard you would have to strike out a vast deal of every good satire. Who is to be the judge when a man has become a public nuisance ? Obviously the satirist himself. But Dryden was sincere and he seized the throne with genuine impulses but there is a difference between a spontaneous effusion of rage and hate and a cold and malignant preparation of bitterness. The satire which indignation makes will always be the most sympathised, and the genial man like Dryden is most admired.

Dryden professes in his essay on satire to prefer Juvenal to Horace for his own reading. There are the marks of personal heat in Dryden's satires and generally a blending of humour and passion, a qualification of scorn by fun which show that it was natural for him to hold that opinion. In him as in Juvenal, the personality and the savageness are accompanied by traces of the satirist's other private qualities—his wisdom, fancy and homeliness. The goodness of his nature shows itself even when he is angry. Consequently, you sympathise with and do not pity so much his victims, though Dryden's great successor Pope, polished and elaborated more, he has not more brilliant strokes than Dryden, nor finer sounding lines. Besides, though Pope had more personal characteristics, he was not a goodhearted man as Dryden was. The faults with which Dryden's memory is betrothed are strictly weakness, deficiencies of moral energy. All his impulses were good. He was not malignant nor artificial, as a satirist he will bear honourable comparison with indeed a superior of Pope if the motive of that satire be contrasted.

Dryden's Prose Style

Dryden is also one of the few great poets who are also masters of prose. And his mastery is all the more remarkable for the fact that before he wrote there was no popular prose style in English. The Elizabethans wrote prose of many kinds ; Lyly's euphuistic prose, the vigorous though often clumsy vernacular of Lodge, Nashe and Dekker, the terse epigrammatic prose of Bacon, etc. can be named. But none of these authors had succeeded in forging a vigorous and light style combining in itself the freedom of the vernacular and the grace and chastity which literature requires—a style that could be used for the general journeyman work of literature. The fact was, the age was on the whole one of poetry and the greatest minds found freer and happier expression in poetry rather than in prose. This explains why even Milton, who wrote prose, which, with all its extravaganzas, rises to great heights of grandeur, did not find himself at home in prose. But Dryden who, though in his younger days a contemporary of Milton, was as much a product of the Restoration as Milton was of the Age of Elizabeth. He was the first great English writer to realise the need for a plain workaday prose. The age of poetry had passed away and even the great poets of the Restoration loved in poetry those qualities which are merits in prose—clearness, precision, close thinking, etc. Prose was then on the whole more congenial to the spirit of the age than poetry and this resulted in the triumph of prose. The four great influences which operated towards the close of the seventeenth century to bring about this result were the pulpit, politics, miscellaneous writing, and criticism.

Dryden left his remarkable impressions on English prose through the last medium ; but it is significant that according to Congreve, he should have acknowledged Archbishop Tilloston as his master in the art of familiar intercourse. Tilloston's religious writings reveal a pleasant combination of simplicity and grace, but it is easy to exaggerate his influence on Dryden ; for the latter's prose has the same combinations in a much higher degree. The truth seems to be, as Prof. Saintsbury says, that Dryden felt the need for a style which could adequately express his opinions of literary matters which strongly interest him to enable him to carry on an argument with an enemy or lavish encomiums on a friend or a patron. He found by practice that he could handle prose easily for these purposes. But as his main interest lay in poetry and not in the other harmony of prose there is no trace in his prose writings of those mannerisms, idiosyncracies, and peculiarities which have kept the greater part of Elizabethan prose from the beaten track of English prose traditions.

The chief characteristics of Dryden's prose is as we have already pointed out, its unique combination of simplicity and grace. Dryden's main aim was not to write prose that would be admired but to express his ideas adequately. There is a remarkable directness in his style. This is to a large extent achieved by the avoidance of the long, balanced sentence which had been popular with writers like Hooker and Clarendon ; also by the sparing use of parenthesis. Dryden steers clear of clumsy classicisms on the one hand and vulgarisms and slangs on the other. Few writers have made occasional use of colloquialisms with greater effect ; he commands an ample vocabulary and a power of strong terse expression—the latter an index of his vigorous common sense. His other qualities as a stylist are his genial humour, his biting satire, his good natured egotism, strongly tinged by a vein of modesty and his keen interest in all things that interested the world of life and letters about him.

The chief defects of his style are his weakness for freer indulgence in conceits or figures of speech and his fondness for quotations. The first two faults are those which he inherited from the practice of the Elizabethans and the latter he shared with many of his contemporaries who expressed by means of copious quotations, the exaggerated respect for authority which was the characteristic of Restoration literature.

We must not close this short exposition of Dryden's prose style without extracting here Dr. Johnson's famous praise of Dryden's

Prefaces ; for the Doctor, however much he differed from Dryden as a critic, goes in this respect to the foot of the master. Johnson says "None of his prefaces were thought tedious. They have not the formality of a settled style in which the first half of the sentence betrays the other. The clauses are never balanced nor the period, every word seems to drop by chance though it falls into the proper place ; nothing is cold or languid, the whole is airy, animated and vigorous : what is little is gay ; what is great is splendid. He may be thought to mention himself too frequently ; but while he forces himself upon our esteem we cannot refuse him to stand high in his own. Every thing is excused by the play of images and the splendidness of expression. Though all is easy, nothing is feeble ; though all seems careless there is nothing harsh ; and though since his earlier works more than a century has passed they have nothing yet uncouth or obsolete."

Dryden's Criticism of Homer, Virgil, and Ovid

The volume of *Fables Ancient and Modern* (1699) includes translations of the first book of the *Iliad* and versions of portions of Ovid's *Metamorphosis*. Dryden's translations of the *Aeneid* have been published earlier. In view of these translations his critical remarks on these writers in the Prefaces to the *Fables* are of great interest. His comparison of the poetic qualities of Homer and Virgil is very striking though it is marred by the suggestions of a desire to classify Homer as the first of epic poets and Virgil as the next. "If invention be the first virtue of an epic poet, then the Latin poems can only be allowed the second place." But we must never overlook the fact that Dryden is pointing out the want of originality in Virgil's plot, lay his finger on a primary drawback of the Latin poet. Shelley too remarks this in his *Defence of Poetry* (1821) : "Virgil with a modesty that will become his genius had affected the fame of an imitator, even whilst he created anew all that he copied." Dryden, again, shows unerring intuition in pointing out that excellence of language cannot cover up deficiency of thought or imperfect fidelity to the deeper realities of life. And in his profoundly true remark that "that which makes them excel in their several ways is, that each of them has followed his own natural inclination as well in forming the design as in the execution of it." He anticipates the Romantic criticism of nineteenth century with its insistence on the doctrine that every great poet is a law unto himself.

Dryden's remarks on Ovid and his preference of Chaucer to that writer against accepted opinion of his day is a remarkable instance of his critical independence and insight. He does justice to the beauty of Ovid's language but revolts against the obtuseness that confused between wit and conceits and jingles, and his historical sense tells him that it would be invidious to compare the language of Ovid written when the Latin language was as its zenith with that of Chaucer who had to forge for himself a new poetic style out of chaos. He acknowledges that Ovid's "turns of word" are unrivalled in their neatness and delicacy but points out with a rare perception that this excellence is a characteristic of highly artificial poetry. And he implies that he prefers the naturalness of Chaucer "but Chaucer writ with more simplicity and followed nature more closely".

Dryden's Treatment of Chaucer

The modernised versions of Chaucer included in the *Fables* are : (1) "Palamon and Arcite". This is based on the "Knight's Tale" of Chaucer, and Dryden has in many places added to or altered it as he thought fit. He had great admiration for this story and he considered it as a good subject for an epic as Homer's and Virgil's plots ; he has divided the work into three books and paraphrased his original with the utmost freedom, but his additions are not so great as is usual with him. The sustained objects of workmanship that characterises "Palamon and Arcite" justifies to a certain extent Dryden's boast, "I will go further and dare to add that what beauty I lost in some places, I give to others that had not there originally". (2) "The Hind and the Fox." This is not a very much extended but considerably altered version of Chaucer's "Nun's Priest's Tale". The version however suffers slightly from a comparison with the original for it has little of the sly satire that runs like an undercurrent in the latter. (3) "The Flower and the Leaf." (4) "Wife of Bath's Tale". (5) "The Character of a Good Parson."

Dryden's appreciations of Chaucer is one of his most enduring claims to fame as a critic. Spenser had indeed spoken of Chaucer as the well of English undefiled and expressed his admirations for him in unequivocal terms in the *Shepherd's Calendar* and the *Faerie Queene*. But Dryden was the first Englishman to attempt a reasoned appreciation of Chaucer, though the latter's literary excellence was of a kind that could not be appreciated by writers of the Restoration and his language was to Dryden, as well as to most of his contemporaries, a stumbling block. Dryden was able to get over these difficulties because as he himself says "I found I had a soul congenial to his, that I had been conversant in the same studies." Dryden had not, indeed, Chaucer's profound knowledge of human nature, his quiet humanity, or his simple unaffected delight in natural beauty. But he had the eye for the follies and foibles of mankind, the same bubbling humour and the same knack of bringing off a character, or a situation in a few strokes ; and in place of this gentle irony that was so powerful a weapon in Chaucer's hands, Dryden possessed the more dreaded and subtle weapon of satire. It is this similarity of temperament that enables Dryden to pierce beneath the accidents of time and language to the innate virtues of his great predecessors. Though a great admirer of the power of invention in Boccaccio, he rightly argues that Chaucer is superior to Boccaccio in refinement in spite of his being hampered by the stricter medium of poetry.

Dryden's Dramatic Criticism

Dryden is essentially a critic of the Restoration age. The themes of his numerous critical writings are the favourite themes of his age. Drama and satire were the two important forms of literature during this age. And it was in the dramatic field that his best critical work was done. The new political and social set-up of England had brought about a revolution in taste, which brought into fashion the French neo-classical drama. The English theatre-going aristocracy regarded this form of tragedy with admiration, and there was not wanting an attitude of disparagement towards the earlier British theatre.

The French drama was especially marked by structural

correctness, respect for decorum, dignity of mode and speech, love of high-flown rhetoric, and strict adherence to the unities of time, place and action. In the romantic drama of pre-Restoration England, these qualities were lacking. Thus various questions relating to the form of French drama came to be actively and acutely discussed. These questions concerned themselves with the value of the Unities, the use of narrative in drama instead of action in some places, the use of rhyme instead of blank verse. Since the French dramatic critics had largely borrowed (with modifications) from the ancient Greek and Roman dramatists, the question of the authority and the superiority of the ancients over the moderns itself became a burning issue for the Restoration man of letters.

The essential critical problems for the Restoration age were :

(1) The relative values of the ancient and modern dramas.

(2) The relative values of the neo-classical French theatre and the romantic dramas of the English stage.

(3) How does the drama of the Restoration compare with the pre-Restoration dramas of England ?

(4) The nature of tragi-comedy, the purely English dramatic form.

(5) The problem of the Unities.

(6) The themes of love and honour in drama.

(7) The use of narrative instead of action.

(8) The use of rhyme instead of blank verse.

The *Essay of Dramatic Poesy* is seminal to Dryden's criticism. It is in the form of a dialogue. The dialogue as a literary form was commonly in use in the post-Renaissance period. The influence of Plato and Cicero accounts for this. It is urged against this form that it never leads to finality of conclusions. But it has conspicuous advantages. It affords an opportunity for the consideration of any subject from different points of view. At the same time, if finality of assertions is wanting, there is also the absence of unwanted dogmatism. When very serious issues become problematical, the dialogue affords a convenient form for focusing attention on the many important aspects of the problems under consideration. The dialogue as a form never forces a judgement on the reader, but it invites him to think and form his own conclusions. Essentially Socratic in origin, it requires considerable skill in handling. Dryden's handling of this form is admirable, and enables him to introduce sobriety and sanity in judgements, a serious regard for contrary opinions, and above all the heated animosity of partisan pamphleteering is avoided.

Summary of the Essay of Dramatic Poesy

This dialogue is among four persons, Crites, Eugenius, Lisideius and Neander (Dryden himself). Crites is for the ancients. Eugenius stands for the last age. Lisideius argues for the literature of France. Neander praises English drama.

In his address "To the Reader" Dryden tells us that the drift of the ensuing discourse was chiefly to vindicate the honour of the English writers, from the censure of those who unjustly prefer the French to them.

The subjects of the essay are judiciously introduced. The naval victory over the Dutch in June 1665 is incidentally made the occasion for a comment on the condition of poetry in England at that time. Crites observes that he should like this victory better if he did not know how many bad verses he should have to read on it. After some inconsequential comments, the literary controversy settles down to a dispute as to the comparative merits of the ancients versus the moderns. All the four interlocuters agree that their discussion should be limited to dramatic poetry. As a preliminary to so serious a discussion, Lisideius defines a play as:

A just and lively image of human nature, representing its passions and humours, and the changes of fortune to which it is subject, for the delight and instruction of mankind.

For the ancients the central points in Crites's arguments are, that the ancients wrote according to rules which have the sanction of antiquity, and they have strictly adhered to the Unities, the unity of time, the unity of place, and the unity of action. Crites's interpretation of the Unities is borrowed from the Italian and French critics of the Renaissance, who, in their turn, obtained the Doctrine of the Unities from Horace. The moderns disregard these rules of composition. In their plays, that which should be the business of a day takes up an age. Instead of one action, we have "epitomes" of a man's life, and instead of one spot of ground, which the stage should represent, there are more countries than can be shown on the map.

If the ancients contrived their plots well, they wrote better. A good part of the best writings of the old is lost to us. If many things appear flat to us it is only because we do not understand the ancients. Above all, Crites concludes by pointing out that Ben Jonson, "the greatest man of the last age," was "a professed imitator of Horace" and "a learned plagiary of all the others".

Eugenius answers Crites by pointing out the defects of the ancients and the comparative merits of those writers of the last age. It is pointed out that though the ancients made the rules, they seldom obeyed them. In this the moderns are superior to the ancients. The ancients did not know how to divide a play into several parts or Acts. The singing of the chorus was the only way of indicating changes in Acts. Sometimes the choruses sang more than five times. This was against the Aristotelian rule which divided a play into four parts, *Protasis*, *Epitasis*, *Catastasis* and *Catastrophe*. Thus the Greeks had only a general undigested notion of a play, and cannot be said to have consummated the dramatic art.

The plots of the tragedies of the ancients are also, like-wise, unoriginal, mostly worn out tales borrowed from myths and epics. Their dramas deal with stock themes. The Roman comedians, too, who imitated the Greeks, hardly ever wrote a play of their own. The plots as well as the characters are transparent.

The most signal defect, according to Eugenius, of the ancients is that they did not preserve poetic justice. Instead of punishing vice and rewarding virtue, they have often shown a preposterous wickedness, and an unhappy piety. Nor do we find excellence of wit in their writings.

Lisideius refers the French drama to the English. He lists nine principal counts against the English stage and demonstrates comparative merits of the French dramatists in these respects :

1. The seventeenth century neo-classical tragedy and comedy of France more successfully and consistently obey the laws of the three unities. The real time in these plays seldom exceed thirty hours. In the unity of place they are more scrupulous. The action is limited to the very place where the play is supposed to have begun. The unity of action is even more conspicuous. There are no burdensome underplots and subplots. The English introduce

many subsidiary plots and themes (especially in tragi-comedies).
The tragi-comedies, according to Lisideius, are the curse of the
English drama.

> There is no theatre in the world that has any thing so absurd
> as the English tragi-comedy. It is a drama of our own inven-
> tion...here a course of mirth, there another of sadness and passion,
> and a third of honour and a duel : thus, in two hours and a half,
> we run through all the fits of Bedlam.

2. This inter-mixture of disparate elements in the same play
destroys the very aesthetic effect it is supposed to produce.

3. The French tragedy is always based on some historical person
or incident. In this respect, the French go further than the ancients ; interweaving truth with fiction, the French dramatists mend
the intrigues of Fate, and dispense with the severity of History.
Even the historical tragedies of Shakespeare cannot stand comparison with the French tragedy. The historical plays of Shakespeare are so many chronicles of kings.

4. There is an economy of plot in the French plays, concentrating on those aspects of the action which produce unity of effect.
They thus gain more time and freedom for the development of the
verse.

5. Besides a severe economy in plot-construction, the number
of heroic characters is also restricted ; in most plays there is one
central and dominating hero, who commands our attention. Corneille's tragedies afford the best illustration.

6. The dramatically unnecessary parts of the plot are explained
to the audience through narration. Battles, deaths, murders, etc. are
reported rather than represented.

7. The introduction of dramatic narration enables the French
writer to introduce those passions which can never be properly
imitated on the stage. For instance, dying cannot be properly
put on the stage, without making the "acting of dying" comi-
cal. But by powerful narration the same effect could be better
produced.

8. The French plays never "end with a conversion" or "simple
change of will". A villainous character must remain consistently
villainous in all the five acts. This principle is not often adhered
to in the English plays.

9. Above all, Lisideius praises French drama, because of the "beauty of their rhyme". Rhyme is preferable to blank verse in tragedies. (This is one of the two most important points at issue).

Through the mouth of Lisideius, Dryden is in fact only presenting the dramatic theory of the French classical dramatists of the seventeenth century, especially that of Corneille.

Neander (who is Dryden himself) presents the brief on behalf of the English theatre. It is through the mouth of Neander that Dryden advances his own critical positions. Neander's defence may be divided into three parts : *(1)* The criticism of French Tragedy and the comparative superiority of English plays. *(2)* A critical evaluation of Shakespeare and Ben Jonson, and a practical criticism of Jonson's the *Silent Woman*. *(3)* Defence of dramatic rhyme as against blank verse.

Neander sees no special merits in the French plays. If they preserve the Unities in their drama, and maintain a strict economy of plot. If they succeed in focusing attention on the hero, if they contrive their plots more regularly, and observe the laws of comedy, and decorum of the stage with more exactness than the English, it must be pointed out that the French plots are barren and they want the variety and copiousness of the English drama. Neander affirms :

> First, that, we (the English) have many plays of ours as regular as any of theirs (of the French) and which, besides, have more variety of plot and characters ; and secondly, that in most of the irregular plays of Shakespeare or Fletcher...there is a more masculine Fancy and greater spirit in the writing..."

Neander's judicial estimation of Shakespeare and Ben Jonson are mere encomiums. Neither the special qualities of their genius nor the merits of their dramatic arts are analyzed. But though encomiums they are true assessments of the authors formulated in inimitable language.

His *Examen* of *The Silent Woman* is not only the first example in English literary criticism, of practical criticism, but it is also the first attempt towards the practical application of theoretical doctrines to a play, and judge the play in accordance with critical doctrines. The critical theory which lends support to the *Examen* is essentially neo-classical. Neander's attempt is to demonstrate that the play obeys the Unities, the laws of comedy and the laws of the decorum of the stage. There is variety in characterization and copiousness in plot construction without sacrificing unity of effect.

Having thus defended the English theatre, Neander passes on to the discussion of rhyme. Accepting the general doctrine that all poetry is imitation, Neander maintains that a mere imitation will not give delight. Poetry must give delight in the first place. Instruction comes only in the second place. The function of the poet is imitation in a particular manner with a view to giving pleasure. Thus a poet should not reproduce reality as it is, and what is merely natural has no place in a work of art. Prose and its nearest poetical equivalent, the blank verse, may be nearer to actual speech. But the essential question "To what extent can they give pleasure?" remains.

A poet who aims at giving pleasure will be compelled to use rhyme instead of blank verse or prose because the latter is too close to the nature of conversation.

> To take every lineament and feature is not to make an excellent piece ; but to take so much only as will make a beautiful resemblance of the whole, and, with an ingenious flattery of nature, to heighten beauties of some part, and hide the deformities of the rest.

This is the function fulfilled by rhymed verse. Art does not aim at mere copying. Dryden (Neander in the *Essay*) is neither a simple realist nor naturalist. The general direction of Dryden's criticism is that art should improve upon life. Art should aim at the creation of beauty out of the raw materials of life. Thus if blank verse is admitted in dramas on the plea that it adds to the delight, then it may further be argued that rhyme enhances this delight. To affect the soul, and excite the passions, and above all, to move admiration (which is the delight of serious plays) a bare imitation will not serve.

In the Dialogue on *Dramatic Poesy*, it is Crites who first introduces the subject of rhyme and condemns its use in serious plays. His arguments are as follows :

1. Rhyme is unnatural in a play because dialogue there is presented as the effect of sudden thought. One may speak noble things *extempore*, but not verse *extempore*.

2. Neither can one give the effect of conversation through rhyme. We cannot call a servant or bid the door be shut in rhyme.

Neander, on the contrary, maintains that rhyme is more natural and more effectual than blank verse in serious plays. (We must note that Dryden is emphatically defending rhyme in tragedies and not in comedies). The argument that dramatic language should be natural is opposed by the contention that :

The plot, the characters, the wit, the passions, the descriptions, are all exalted above the level of common converse...with proportion to verisimility.

Thus heroic rhyme is nearest to nature as being the noblest kind of modern verse. Neander further argues that if rhyme is improper in plays, it is equally improper in epics. For in the epic too, we have dialogues and discursive scenes as in plays. Hence, since Crites has allowed rhyme in epics, if rhyme be proper for one, it must be proper for the other. Though verse is not the effect of sudden thought, nothing prevents the representation in verse of sudden thought.

Crites points out that rhyme is most unnatural in repartees, or short replies. According to Neander, this is not a special objection against rhyme alone. The same could be urged against blank verse. Neither is it valid to assert that a servant cannot be summoned in rhyme. Neander urges that such short passages need not be in rhyme.

It has to be noted that the discussion "rhyme versus blank verse" can only be admitted if it is granted that verse is the proper medium for plays. If verse is completely abandoned, and prose and common speech are advocated, then we are accepting a principle of naive realism. On the contrary, blank verse is acknowledged to be proper for dramatic poetry, then it may be shown that rhyme is equally proper.[1]

In this context we must also take into account the view on rhyme

---

[1] It may be noted that after 1678 Dryden abandoned rhyme. His first play in blank verse is *All for Love*. In adapting blank verse Dryden was not contradicting his own views. But by this time the slowly increasing influence of Shakespeare and the Elizabethans became a decisive factor in his versification. His preference for his own English predecessors prompted him to abandon what is essentially foreign.

given by Dryden in the "prefaces" to his plays. These views are consistent with what Dryden expresses through his own interlocutor Neander. In the *Defence of Dramatic Poesy*, he writes defending rhyme :

> I am satisfied if it (rhyme) causes delight ; for delight is the chief if not the only end of poesy...poesy only instructs as it delights. It is true, that to imitate well is a poet's work ; but to affect the soul, and excite the passions, and above all, to move admiration which is the delight of serious plays, a bare imitation will not serve. The converse, therefore, which a poet is to imit-ate, must be heightened with all the arts and ornaments of poesy, and must be such as, strictly considered, could never be supposed spoken without any premeditation.

In another preface [to *The Rival Ladies*, 1694] Dryden lists the advantages rhyme has over blank verse :

> *1.* It is a help to memory which rhyme so knits up by the affi-nity of sounds.
> *2.* In the quickness of repartees it has a particular grace in that the sudden smartness of the answer, and the sweetness of the rhyme set off the beauty of each other.
> *3.* Rhyme applies an appropriate restraint on the lawlessness of the poetic imagination. The great easiness of blank verse only spurs this wild faculty and the poet might say many things which might be omitted. But when the difficulty of artful rhyming is interposed then the fancy gives leisure to judgement to come in, and the poet is made cautious in his utterances. Rhyme thus regulates fancy, and enables the operation of judgement.

We here arrive at Dryden's fundamental positions. The question is not whether rhyme is natural or not. The central critical assump-tions of Dryden are two : *(1)* That a play is not a realistic imitation of nature. *(2)* That the creative faculty, imagination, should be subordinated to judgement. If freedom of conception and spont-aneity of imagination are stressed in dramatic composition than blank verse (even prose) will be proper to serious plays. If on the other hand, we admit the assumption that in artistic creation the final arbiter is judgement, then rhyme is more helpful. The very fact that it restrains fancy, instead of being a defect, is a positive merit.

Thus the problem of "Rhyme versus Blank Verse" is one which cannot be solved by dramatic or utilitarian considerations. In Dryden's analysis the problem is related to basic aesthetic issues concerning the nature of imitation and the roles of imagination and judgement in the process of imitation. We can only conclude at present by pointing out that Dryden's theories are essentially neo-classical.

A Final Assessment

Dr. Johnson's famous verdict that Dryden is the father of English criticism appears to be, on the face of it, incontrovertible when we take into account the condition of English criticism before Dryden's time, and also both the quality and the quantity of his total critical output. (The principal merits of Dryden's critical and poetic theories have been briefly outlined in the sections above). Dryden's critical independence, the freedom of his enquiries, and the boldness of his conclusions further entitle him to the rank of one of the originators of English literary criticism.

In his works, we have not only criticism, but criticism becoming self-conscious, formulating its own principles. He develops his own critical methods and illustrates the application of principles to dramatic criticism. He frees himself from the contemporary trends both at home and abroad. He accepts freedom of judgement and the freedom of imagination in literary compositions. Rejecting the French playwrights and their critics, he upholds the English tragicomedy. He rejects the servile observation of the Unities. Even the Aristotelian doctrines are criticised and rejected. Thus, in the context of the Restoration age, Dryden shows a remarkable originality of critical thought, and independence of critical judgement.

But in spite of all this originality and independence, Dryden's literary criticism is a product of the trends of the time. Essentially neo-classical in his affinities, his best contributions to criticism lie in the modifications of ancient doctrines rather than in the creation of new theories. His theory of imitation is neo-Aristotelian. His

theory of the function of judgement in literary composition is
Horatian. His doctrine that drama should give delight in the first
place, and instruction only in the second place is not infrequently
found in seventeenth century criticism. He seldom, if never, introduces a critical problem which his age is not interested in.
Consequently the nature of the creative mind, its faculties, its
operations, its psychologies are examined. In sum, in Dryden's
critical theory, literature is viewed as a craft, the craft of giving
delight. It is the various aspects of this craft of literature (and not
the art of literature) which engage his attention. And therefore it
will be erring too much on the side of charity to consider Dryden
as the father of English literary criticism.

CHAPTER SIX

LITERARY CRITICISM OF WORDSWORTH AND COLERIDGE

Romantic Criticism : Introductory

The romantic movement in literature brought into prominence new critical problems. The ideas about the function of criticism changed and the critical emphasis fell on different places. The sphere of literary criticism widened and it began to invade aesthetics and social criticism. With Samuel Taylor Coleridge criticism became philosophical. To say this is not to say that it was criticism which ushered in the new movement. In a very limited sense even this is true. It was long after the Elizabethan Renaissance in England that criticism properly so defined made its appearance in England. As has already been pointed out, Dr. Johnson would consider Dryden as the father of English criticism. English neo-classicism too preceded its criticism. But in the romantic movement, creative writing and critical theories together challenge the old order.

One of the first conceptions to be refuted was the neo-classical conception of the social conditioning of the literary process. In the eighteenth century, the impact of social environment on literature was considered to be of great importance. This accounts for the acute interests in social factors manifested in neo-classical literature. As one of the consequences of this conception of literature, a movement of literary criticism was brought into being which threw emphasis on the organic unity of the national literature with the national culture. This movement took the shape of a debate as to the relative merits of the ancients and the moderns. As against this the romantic writers like Wordsworth and Hugo developed a critical interest in the creative process of the individual writer. This interest developed further on account of the vogue of individualism and the sensibility ushered in by Sterne and Richardson. The interest in the individual psychology of the creative artist became the notion of the "genius". In critical matters the idea of the genius was emphasized to the exclusion of all other considerations.

In fact all the important characteristics of the romantic schools of criticism originate in this conception of the genius. The notion of inspiration, the conceptions of imagination, of spontaneity and originality, and the stress on freedom from the rules in composition, the doctrine of the organic form, all can be finally traced back to the root conception of the "genius". Hence arises the romantic preoccupation with the biography and psychology of the poet. And hence, we have Coleridge defining poetry as that which a poet composes. The romantic critic recognised no laws of composition for judicial criticism except those of "genius" manifested in feeling and imagination. In effect, the changes evident in romantic literature and criticism were the results of changing attitudes to life and value.

To understand the real scope of romantic criticism we must survey briefly the historical development of criticism in England. Literary criticism in England originated with the humanists. These humanists were chiefly preoccupied with the problems of language, style and rhetoric. This was no doubt a salutary trend during the early stages in the growth of English language. But the continuity of this critical tradition well into the age of neo-classicism was far from being beneficial to creative writing. This linguistic and rhetorical bias formed itself towards the end of the eighteenth century into the doctrine of poetic diction. Even during the neo-classical period, literary thought did not emancipate itself from the discussions as to the rules and principles of composition. The fundamental questions concerning the nature of poetic creation, the nature of poetry, the nature of the pleasure derived from poetry, etc. were ignored.

But the signs of a change were evident in the last quarter of the eighteenth century. There was a growing sense of democratic liberalism in thought, and this supported by a philosophic rationalism tended towards individualism in literature. It was this spirit of individualism which was behind the new spirit of critical enquiry which examined the ancient rules and practices with a sceptical frame of mind. Strict adherence to ancient literary forms was not insisted upon. The old Aristotelian conception of imitation was reinterpreted to include the idea of original creation.

Above all, a new interest in human psychology became evident. The psychology of aesthetic appreciation, the psychology of knowledge, of moral action and of poetic creation, engaged the attention of philosophers and poets. In England Edmund Burke propounded a new theory of aesthetic thought. In Germany Lessing and Goethe and Baumgarten laid the foundations of a new science of aesthetic. Later critics and poets of Germany made this aesthetics the basis of their literary programmes. English romantic criticism was influenced by the conclusions arrived at by Schelling, Kant, and the Schlegel brothers. Coleridge's criticism was considerably indebted to these continental influences. Together with this powerful interest in the mental phenomena of man and his consciousness, there appeared a new sociology and new anthropology from France through the writings of Rousseau. In his social theory, all men are born free and with equal original endowments which the artificialities of institutions and civilizations suppress. From these sources romantic criticism obtained its tools of interpretation and criteria of judgement. The result was a revaluation of the ancient masters. Dryden, Pope, and the neo-classicists in general were condemned. Spenser, Shakespeare and Milton were reinterpreted in accordance with the new critical canons.

To Coleridge, Shakespeare is primarily a genius with an intuitive perception of the workings of the human heart. Interest is focused on the study of dramatic characters and psychology. The most important part of Coleridge's Shakespeare-criticism lies in the study of Shakespearean characters. Wordsworth sees in Shakespeare a profound imagination shaping and moulding the raw material of observation. And what interests Keats most in Shakespeare is his "negative capability".

The romantic interest in Milton grows into a kind of Milton cult. Till the beginning of modern criticism, our knowledge of Milton's writings was mostly based on the interpretations given by the romantic critics. Wordsworth and Coleridge imitated Milton. Shelley was influenced by him. And even Keats, who later disliked Milton, was in the early days under the romantic spell of Milton's poetry. Spenser's interest in mediaeval romance was behind much of the mediaevalism of romantic poetry.

Thus both in theory and practical application, romantic criticism widely diverged from both the Renaissance and the neo-classical schools of criticism. The two pioneers of this new critical movement were Wordsworth and Coleridge.

A Note on Wordsworth's Literary Criticism

Wordsworth's literary criticism is mostly contained in the prefaces and essays accompanying the various editions of his poems. Of these the most important are the preface to *Lyrical Ballads*, 1800. "Note to 'The Thorn'," 1800, Appendix to *Lyrical Ballads*, preface to *Poems*, 1815, and the Essay supplementary to the preface, 1815.

The most celebrated piece of literary criticism is the 1800 preface. In it he deals with three important problems. 1. The nature of poetry; 2. the nature of poetic diction; and 3. the function and nature of a poet. These essays constitute a bundle of critical documents of unequalled interest. They deal with enquiries into fundamental problems relating to art and literature. Never before in English literary criticism had there been a genius who asked so many basic questions and sought to answer them.

M. H. Abrams (*The Mirror and the Lamp*) sums up the contents of the 1800 preface as follows :

1. Poetry is an overflow of feeling ; 2. it is opposed to science rather than to history. It deals with truths which are ideal and universal, and not particular and actual ; 3. poetry arises from primitive cries rendered rhythmic by organic causes ; 4. the means of poetry are figures of speech and rhythm, whereby words naturally embody and convey the poet's feelings ; 5. poetic language must not be contrived and artful ; 6. poets are distinguished from other men by their innate intense sensibility and passionateness ; 7. poetry's chief function is to "foster and subtilize the sensibility, emotions, and susceptibilities of the reader. These in brief, consti-

tute the kernal of Wordsworth's literary criticism. The most important doctrines which emerge from Wordsworth's theory are those relating to the nature of poetry, and the nature of poetic language.

The Preface to poems of 1815[1] develops a theory of imagination. Wordsworth's is the first fully developed theory of imagination in the history of romantic criticism. Here, he elaborates the differences between fancy and imagination. This theory will be dealt with in a later section.

The Essay supplementary to the Preface[2], 1815 deals with 1. the nature and function of criticism; 2. a historical criticism of English poetry from Chaucer to the time of Wordsworth; 3. the nature of taste and literary sensibility. Here Wordsworth applies his theories to the task of practical criticism, arriving at a severe condemnation of the theory and practice of the neoclassical school.

Wordsworth's Theory of Poetry : Preface, 1800[3]

By 1800, Wordsworth had rejected the personification and poetic diction of neo-classicism, denounced the morbid and sensational German romanticism, and turned to the simple, sane and healthy life of the common people—the English peasant and farmer. He attempted to restore the native idiom and the tone of spoken voice to poetry.

It may be noted initially that Wordsworth's theory of composition owes much to Locke, Hartley and other eighteenth century empiricists. First, the poet experiences, then he recollects it in tranquillity, and finally, his soul divines the meaning of the experiences before the actual composition takes place. Thus Wordsworth takes up from the eighteenth century a theory of the imitation of nature which he adapts to suit his critical theory. In modifying the eighteenth century view of poetry into a theory of passion and emotion, Wordsworth's criticism is of transitional interest. He faces the old Platonic problem of justifying poetic pleasure. He does this

---

[1] This work is hereafter cited as 1815 Preface.

[2] This work hereafter will be cited as the "1815 supplementary Essay".

[3] Here we are dealing with the 1800 preface mainly.

by uniting the conception of poetic pleasure with that of truth. To know what poetry is, Wordsworth begins by an examination of the nature of poetic truth, of the process of poetic creation.[4]

Poetry is the image of man and nature. The poet writes as a man speaking to man. Poetry's object is not truth individual and local, but general and operative. Poetic truth, for Wordsworth, is operative because it seeks to move the hearts of men. It is general in that it is not to be verified, and is carried alive into the heart by passion, and is its own testimony. Our hearts recognize its truth. The mind of man reflects the workings of the universe. Thus the general representation of human nature pleases us because our psychological structure is parallelled in the workings of the universe as a whole. Thus in poetry, we have an expression, in concrete and sensuous terms, of those principles illustrated alike in the mind of man and the workings of the nature. Thus "poetry is the breath and finer spirit of all knowledge ; it is the impassioned expression which is in the countenance of all science.

Accordingly, the poet who deals with such universal human truths, "is the rock and defence of human nature...". He binds together by passion and knowledge the vast empire of human society, "carrying sensation into the midst of the science itself." The poet relates man to each other and to the world of external nature. The poet can even relate the particular discoveries of the scientist to the world of basic human values in a spirit of love. He possesses a peculiar awareness which redeems him from selfishness and triviality. And he shows the importance of sympathy of human life.

The poet relates isolated and individual experiences to the sum total of man's life. He should, therefore, select for the themes of his poetry those situations which excites our sympathy and increase our emotional sensitivity. Life, at its simplest and at its most unfortunate levels, can afford such illustrative situations. We can discover general truths of man's experiences in the life of a humble half-witted person, a shepherd, a leech-gatherer, or an idiot boy. The poet should kindle our passionate sympathy. The idea of passion is central in Wordsworth's theory. Passion is not acquired by stylistic devices, but arises from the nature of the poet's perception. Thus for Wordsworth, the poet is a man speak-

---

[4] I am, in the following sections, mostly summing up the views of Rene Wellek in *A History of Modern Criticism*.

ing to man. The poet differs only in degree from other man. He has more lively sensibility and more enthusiasm and tenderness. To quote Wordsworth :

> The sum of what was said is, that the poet is chiefly distinguished from other men by a greater promptness to think and feel without immediate external excitement, and a greater power in expressing such thoughts and feelings as are produced in him in that manner.   (1800 Preface)

The poetic process is an attempt to translate into words the power of real passions and experiences. Compared to the original experiences the process of composition is somewhat mechanical, and the poet, however great he may be, can never adequately recapture the originality of those experiences :

> ...his (the poet's) employment is in some degree mechanical compared with the freedom and power of real and substantial action and suffering.

The poet writes under one compulsion only, the necessity of giving pleasure. The poetic pleasure is not utilitarian ; neither is it the pleasure which the satisfaction of particular wants can give. It is the general pleasure resulting from the recognition of the universal significance of human experiences, and which pleasure only poetry can give for "poetry is the image of man and nature." Wordsworth connects poetic pleasure and the process of poetic composition. He says :

> ...poetry is the spontaneous overflow of powerful feelings ; it takes its origin from emotion recollected in tranquillity ; the emotion is contemplated till, by a species of reaction, the tranquillity gradually disappears, and an emotion, kindred to that which was before the subject of contemplation, is gradually produced, as it actually exists in the mind. In this mood successful composition generally begins, and in a mood similar to this it is carried on ; but the various causes, are qualified by various pleasures, so that in describing any passion whatsoever, which are voluntarily described, the mind will, upon the whole, be in a state of enjoyment.

Theory of Poetic Language

Essentially, the Wordsworthian theory of poetic language is a criticism against the theory of poetic diction. The central doctrine is that the language of poetry is identical with the language of everyday communication. Thus figurative language is not poetic. It is artificial. Wordsworth advocates a purely natural idiom of expression. It may be noticed that his poetry is derived from his conception of what poetry is. But his theory of poetic language is contradictory, and we shall see the contradiction later. Because the poet is a man speaking to man, his language should not differ from that of others. The poet thinks and feels in the spirit of human passions. Therefore, his language should be the language of men.

It may be safely affirmed that there neither is, nor can be, any *essential* difference between the language of prose and metrical composition.

(It is important to note that Wordsworth restricts his observations to lyrical poetry). The idea of passion is very important here also. Artificial language can never have passion. But rustic speech in its primal simplicity is passionate. The language used by farmers or rustics is supposed to be highly charged with emotion. Besides the qualities of naturalness and universality, he emphasises that poetic language must be in a state of vivid sensation. Such a language, if selected, judicially, and variegated with metaphors, can give that pleasure peculiar to poetry.

Several arguments can be levelled against Wordsworth's theory. T. S. Eliot, in the *Use of Poetry and the Use of Criticism* (1933) lists some counts against Wordsworth's doctrine. Wordsworth does not take into account the fact the poet is using language as a medium of artistic communication. Secondly, a selection of language used by men "is not the same as the language of ordinary speech. A specially "selected language" has all the qualities of figurative expression. Moreover, figures of speech can really express great passion. Metaphorical communication is especially charged with passion. Thus when Wordsworth attacked the adulterated, distorted, and glossy and unfeeling poetic diction of the eighteenth century, he had forgotten the fact that in his (Wordsworth's) best poetry, these very qualities were present.

In passion we speak figuratively. But passionate and figurative language is the language of primitive men. Wordsworth tells us that "the earliest poets wrote naturally, feeling powerfully in a figurative language." Thus true rhetoric lies in spontaneous expression, whereas the rhetoric of the eighteenth century poets lay in artificiality. He further explains how the language of early poets differed from that of ordinary speech. This difference was a legitimate one, because the early poetry was the poetry of extraordinary occasion. And the language of extraordinary heroic occasions too differed from that of the ordinary men. Such, for example, is the poetic language of Homer. Thus Wordsworth tends towards a theory of poetic primitivism. His theory of language recommends the poetry of strong passion and heroic occasions written in an elevated metaphorical language which the primitive bard was supposed to have used.

It should be pointed out here that both in the theory of poetic diction and of poetic composition, Wordsworth is inspired by psychological considerations. His interest is primarily psychological. The same interest pervades his theory of metre. Wordsworth justifies the use of poetic metre although metrical language is not the same as the speech of rustics. But in his explanation, the end of poetry is to produce excitement in coexistence with an overbalance of pleasure. The presence of metre helps the poets in the production of the just kind of pleasure. The regularity of the metrical rhythm helps the poet further in the control of the excitement caused by poetry. All pleasure, says Wordsworth, originates in the perception of similitude in dissimilitude, and dissimilitude in similitude. In the metrical alternation of sound, the reader discovers these, which enhances the pleasure already present in the poem.

We have to conclude, after carefully examining Wordsworth's theory of poetry and language that his approach is psychological. It is this approach which unites together his various doctrines into one consistent theory, in spite of their apparent contradictions.

The Doctrine of Poetic Sincerity

The next important doctrine that is emphasised in the prose

writings of Wordsworth is the doctrine of sincerity as a principle of poetic excellence. In simple language, the more sincere the experience described in a poem, the greater the poem is. In the very greatest of poems there is (and should be) a correspondence between the subject in the poem, and the poet's convictions. Wordsworth employs this as a constant standard of judgement.

Here again, the critical problem shifts to psychology and the biography of the author. We should be on guard against two errors. We must not impute to Wordsworth the opinion that poetry is the direct reflection of the author's life. If the life of a poet is without blemish, it does not follow that his poetry should as a consequence be without faults. Wordsworth makes a distinction between objective poetry and subjective poetry. To the former group belongs the poetry of Shakespeare and Homer. In this case the life and ideas of the poet is of no concern in the judgement of poetry. But in subjective poetry such as that of Burns, for instance, it is impossible to forget the authors. The second error to be avoided is the conclusion that Wordsworth is against the "art" of poetry. The principle of sincerity does not imply that any direct and spontaneous expression of the poet's own convictions will give us good poetry.

In fact Wordsworth lists a number of faculties essential for the making of good poetry. They are, observation sensibility, reflection, imagination, fancy and judgement. Poetic sincerity is not the same thing as artistic carelessness. Later, Wordsworth recognised rules of art and workmanship and he took infinite pains in revision. The revisions incorporated in the second edition of *The Prelude* (1850) are relevant cases[5]. Revision and technique are consistent with initial inspiration. He appreciated the value of discipline in poetic composition. In fact, the doctrine of sincerity deals with the end and aim of poetry rather than with the initial process of composition.

Poetry is a manipulation of feelings for the purpose, and that purpose is man's edification. The emotional effect of poetry is of crucial importance. Poetry should affect the sensibility of the people, should induce the right kind of feelings and the right kind of awareness. It should humble and humanise men, purify and exalt them. Thus it produces a cathartic effect. Poetry is an element in

---

[5] David Perkins in his work *Wordsworth and the Poetry of Sincerity* examines this problem of sincerity exhaustively.

the effect towards the unification of sensibility. This aim can only be fulfilled by a poetry which is sincere.

Wordsworth's Theory of Imagination

Wordsworth's theory of imagination is fully set forth in the 1815 preface[6]. The central points in his theory of imagination are the distinction that is drawn between fancy and imagination, and the theory that the mind is a creative entity. It is not passive, and does not passively reflect the external world. But it is active, and it half-creates the world it perceives. This faculty of mind which creates is the faculty of imagination. It may be noted that the theory of imagination refutes the early associationist psychology. The psychological theory of perception, as developed in the eighteenth century, especially by David Hartley, was a mechanistic theory. According to this, the mind merely reflects the external world, and perception is similar to the reflection of an image in a mirror. Cognition is the result of accidental association, and hence the word "associationist". Wordsworth opposed this theory. To him, the mind has two faculties, fancy and imagination, the one passive, the other active.

Fancy merely reflects the external world. It is not related to our cognition. Through the power of fancy we never understand what it is that we perceive. It can only give us impressions. But imagination creates the patterns of perceptions. Poetically speaking, the power of imagination creates a poetic image. Imagination has the poetic power of "conferring, abstracting, and modifying" the original impressions in order to load them with new significance. It can thus shape and create.

Florence Marsh *(in Wordsworth's Imagery)* explains the theory of imagination as follows : Imagination, as Wordsworth defined it, becomes the name for the mental power that transforms the literal to the figurative. It has no reference to images that are merely a faithful copy, existing in the mind, of absent external objects ; but it is a word of higher import, denoting operations of the mind upon those objects, and processes, of creation or of compositions,

[6] Coleridge's criticism of Wordsworth's theory of imagination is not given here. It will be dealt with later.

governed by certain fixed laws. It is the power of the mind to do more than associate mechanically. The mind can confer on objects properties not inherent in them, it can abstract from them some of the properties that they actually possess, and it can modify an image by another. In every case the mind alters the object creatively. Wordsworth takes the example of Milton's use of the word "hangs" *(in Paradise Lost, Book II)* to illustrate this modifying power of imagination[7]. Above all, it is through the power of imagination that man recognizes his kinship with the eternal. Thus imagination operates upon the raw-material of sensation to illustrate the evidence of eternal truth. Fancy merely relates to temporal or wordly enjoyments.

Fancy is given to quicken and to beguile the temporal part of our nature; imagination, to incite and to support the eternal. (1815 Preface)

Wordsworth rejects an intellectualist approach to truth. Such an approach is relevant only to science understood in the narrowest sense. Intellect, the chief instrument of science, is rejected by Wordsworth. It is a false secondary power which multiplies distinctions. But true knowledge is knowledge of reality obtained through insight. Poetry (as created by imagination) is the sensuous incarnation of this philosophical insight. Imagination gives us this unified vision of reality. Thus Wordsworth relates truth and poetry through the theory of imagination.

Wordsworth's Criticism and The Lyrical Ballads

Before we apply the theory of poetry in the 1800 Preface to the poems of the *Lyrical Ballads*, we must here restate Wordsworth's doctrines.

In the *Lyrical Ballads*, Wordsworth's aim was to produce poetry "well-adapted to interest mankind permanently and likewise important in the multiplicity and quality of its *moral relations*" (italics

[7] See Chapter xiii of *The Prelude*. Here Wordsworth describes a mystic experience which he had by moonlight on Mount Snowdon. Imagination is compared to this experience.

mine). This stress on the moral relations has apparently obscured Wordsworth's stress on pleasure. He frequently refers to the pleasure, excitement, and enjoyment of the sensations which poetry should arouse, "those grand elementary principles of pleasure, by which man knows and feels, and lives and moves."

> We have no sympathy but what is propagated by pleasure . . . we have no knowledge . . . but what has been built up by pleasure, and exists in us by pleasure alone . . . The end of poetry is to produce excitement in co-existence with an over-balance of pleasure. (1800 Preface)

It was Wordsworth's principal intention to illustrate the principle of pleasure in poetry. The conception of pleasure has been degraded to mean a trivial titillation of the senses. To Wordsworth, pleasure was a channel of experience profitable to man's whole personality. But he does not confine himself to a mere intellectual and spiritual conception of pleasure. Pleasure was neither bodiless nor simply metaphysical. The enjoyment of pleasure depends on the capacity for registering experience.

The special quality of Wordsworth's great poetry lies in its power to give acute pleasure by stimulating imagination to perceive the beauty and newness inherent in the commonplace experiences of our daily life. This fact must be carefully noted. This is the special quality which he sought to give through the poems in the *Lyrical Ballads*.

Hence arises Wordsworth's psychological description of the origin and purpose of poetry.

> The principal object then I proposed to myself in these poems was to make the incidents of common life interesting by tracing in them, truly though not ostentatiously, the primary laws of our nature : chiefly as far as regards the manner in which we associate ideas in a state of excitement.

Wordsworth believed that in moments of crisis men do not behave conventionally, and that therefore, they express themselves more forcibly and with convincing originality. He points out:

> Low and rustic life was generally chosen, because in that situa-

tion the essential passions of the heart find a better soil in which they can attain their maturity, are less under restraint, and speak a plainer and more emphatic language ; because in that situation our elementary feelings exist in a state of greater simplicity, and consequently may be more accurately contemplated.

The effectiveness of this doctrine is fully borne out by the poems in the *Lyrical Ballads*. "Lines composed above the Tintern Abbey" touches the high water mark of English poetic achievement. In this poem, it is the dissociation of his sensibility, and its later fusion through the ministry of nature which constitute the essential theme. Of the poetic quality of the poem there is no controversy. It may be further established that it fully substantiates the essential doctrine of pleasure laid down in the Preface. We have, then, to examine the criticism levelled against the inferior pieces in the *Lyrical Ballads*. Let us take one of the poorest and (a frequently criticised) poem in this volume, "The Thorn".

Critics usually point out the ineptitude of this work, the triteness of its theme, and the prosaic diction of its verse. But such an extreme denunciation is unfair. Its essential theme is taken from ordinary and rustic life. It deals with the emotional distress and the mental frustration under which a helpless woman suffers. The poem gives us the story of Martha Ray who had been most cruelly jilted by her lover and fiancé, the 'unthinking' Stephen Hill. Stephen Hill loved Martha :

> And they had fix'd the wedding-day ;
> The morning that must wed them both ;
> But Stephen to another maid
> Had sworn another oath ;
> And with this other maid to church
> Unthinking Stephen went—Poor Martha ;
> On that woeful day
> A cruel, cruel fire, they say,
> Into her bones was sent.
> It dried her body like a cinder,
> And almost turn'd her brain to tinder.

Martha was big with child at that time. The child was born, and it died, or was probably killed. Whatever the case, she went to the "thorn", on the bleak mountain top every day and remained there for long hours. The child was buried there, or was put in the pond which was nearby. This is the theme of the poem. The theme is balladic. It deals with an unhappy romantic affair. The simplicity of the diction and the rime scheme are similar to that of the popular ballads.

Wordsworth achieved his object, that of presenting a mind in a state of excitement and making it a fit theme for lyrical poetry. There is a vivid picture of the psychological crisis through which this luckless woman is passing. There is considerable pathos expressed in appropriate language in a passage like the following :

> "But what's the thorn ? and what's the pond ?
> "And what's the hill of moss to her ?
> "And what's the creeping breeze that come ?
> "The little pond to stir ?"
> I cannot tell ; but some will say
> She hanged her baby on the tree,
> Some say she drowned it in the pond,
> Which is a little step beyond,
> But all and each agree,
> The little babe was buried there,
> Beneath that hill of moss so fair.

To quote Helen Derbyshire : It is

> a great and remarkable poem : It is easy to see the elements out of which it was made : the "elementary feelings" or "essential passions of the heart" love of maid for man, agony at the lover's desertion, love of mother for child, misery of the distraught mind which seeks relief in the wild or calm companionship of nature.

This indeed is a true judgement. With the exception of a few poems like the "Idiot Boy" and "Michael", it is easily seen that the theory of poetry and poetic pleasure given in the Preface is applicable to the poems of the *Lyrical Ballads* I have taken. "The Thorn" as a case for illustration[8].

[8] "The Thorn" must be read in conjunction with Wordsworth's "Note to 'The Thorn' ".

Many readers have the impression that Wordsworth's views on the poetic diction to be the most important part of the Preface. Too much has been made of Wordsworth's assertions, that he endeavoured to bring (his) language of poetry nearer to the language of men, and that poetry takes its origin recollected in tranquillity. These views can be better understood as indicating a deliberate dissent from Gray's doctrine that poetry has a language peculiar to itself. Wordsworth's stress is on "the selection of the real language of men" and fitting it to metrical arrangement. Wordsworth does not aim at dialectal poetry, or in the indiscriminate use of ordinary expressions. It has certainly to be admitted that a rigorous application of his theory of poetic language is impossible to the task of composing any good poem. The greatest danger in such an application would be the unevenness of style which results from it. In this aspect, the poems of the *Lyrical Ballads* fully illustrate both the weakness and strength of the theory. Within the same poem, we will find lines of great merits and also those of less than mediocre quality. These lines,

> I've measured it from side to side ;
> It is three feet long, and two feet wide.

from "The Thorn" have been condemned by all. But within the same stanza of the poem, occur the lines :

> High on a mountain's highest ridge,
> Whereof the stormy winter gale
> Cuts like a scythe, while through the clouds
> It sweeps from vale to vale :

This description is beautiful and accurate. The central image in the lines becomes truly poetic. And it is not possible to find fault with the poetry here in any manner. It is poetry of the very first order.

Thus among the principal theories in the 1800 Preface, with the exception of the theory of poetic language, all the others are adequately illustrated by the poems of the *Lyrical Ballads*.

But then it is unreasonable to expect a strict correspondence between a theory and a work of art which it generates. No poem can be a mere translation of a pre-conceived theory in the form of a non-logical verbal structure so that it illustrates aesthetically the operation of the theory. Indeed, a poem as poem, must transcend the very theory which initially shaped its conception, in order to be unique and original. And no poem is great unless it is unique and original, even while conforming to a tradition.

Coleridge as Critic

Coleridge's influence on English literary criticism is very great. Twentieth-century criticism has been considerably influenced by Coleridge. Critics like George Saintsbury, Arthur Symons, J. H. Muirhead, I. A. Richards, and Herbert Read all agree in regarding Coleridge as one of the greatest, if not the greatest, of English critics. If the reputation of Coleridge as a literary critic stands today very high, it is particularly on account of the fact that Coleridge was the first English critic to attempt to ground literary criticism in philosophy, psychology, and metaphysics. Thus with Coleridge, literary criticism begins as a serious intellectual discipline of wide scope. Criticism is not merely the art of judgement ; nor is it a set of practical rules for the writer. It is a branch of philosophy dealing with the nature of art, and the psychology of aesthetic appreciation.

The introduction of philosophy into literary criticism begins with Coleridge, and Coleridge's opinions on art and literature show this philosophical bias. It is probable that his literary criticism suffered on account of the influence of contemporary European philosophy. Since Coleridge attempted to base literary criticism in philosophy, it is necessary for us to trace the philosophical development of Coleridge. Coleridge wrote to a friend in 1816 :

I am convinced that a true system of philosophy—the Science of Life—is best taught in poetry.

Coleridge has essentially a philosophy and the main strength of his criticism lies in this philosophical basis. There were two stages in the development of Coleridge's philosophical and critical mind. In the first stage, Coleridge was a follower of Hartley and was an Associationist. He changed his philosophical allegiance to the idealist transcendental philosophy of the German School after his visit to Germany in 1798-99. The main characteristic of Coleridge's literary criticism lies in his repudiation of the typically eighteenth century philosophy of Hartley. In the early period of his career Coleridge was deeply influenced by Hartley and Hume. He thus came under the influence of the philosophy of Associationism. We must understand Associationism before we study Coleridge's theory of imagination and his theory of poetry. The Associationist philosophy is essentially a mechanist philosophy, and it implies Necessitarianism.

Associationism originated with David Hume and David Hartley. Hume was a sceptic as regards the powers of reason as is shown by his book the *Treatise of Human Nature* (1738). Hume and Hartley both repudiated the supremacy of reason. Hartley studied the limitations of human reason. Before Hartley's time reason was supposed to be a supreme faculty through which man understood nature. Hartley disclaimed any special superiority for reason and showed that it is better to trust instinct without being duped by any logical illusion. Following Newton's example he attempted to introduce the experimental method of reasoning into moral subjects. His philosophy was a kind of moral Newtonianism. There was a search for a psychological and moral counterpart of reason, a principle which would unify the moral world as gravitation had unified the physical. Hume had already advanced the principle of association of ideas as this unifying principle in human experience. Hartley (in his *Observations on Man*, 1749) elaborated his theory.

Hume divided human experience into two groups, impressions which include all our sensations, passions, and emotions as they make their first appearance in the soul, and ideas; and the faint images of these in thinking and reasoning. These ideas are held together in the mind by memory, and imagination associates and unites simpler ideas into complex ones. Thus the principle of association functions by means of the relations of resemblance, nearness in time and place, and cause and effect.

These are therefore the principles of union or cohesion among our simple ideas and in the imagination supply the place of that inseparable action by which they are united in memory. Here is a kind of attraction.

(*Treatise of Human Nature*)

From this associative principle are derived the complex ideas comprising "relations, modes and substances". For example, as regards "substance", we have no idea of it apart from a collection of particular qualities. Thus the ideas of a substance (for example the idea of iron) as well as that of a mode of being (for example the idea of duty) are nothing but the collections of simple ideas that are united by the principle of association. This was the fundamental principle underlying the system of philosophy subsequently developed by David Hartley who influenced Coleridge before 1798.

Hartley is chiefly remembered for the development of the moral principle of association of ideas. He carries the application of Hume's theory further. Hume had explained the laws of cohesion on the principle of ideas. Hartley goes further and uses this principle of association not only for explaining the mechanism of mental process but also for the evolution of our moral characters from childhood to manhood. The development of the moral sense is itself out of simple sensations. Hartley's theory explains the formation of human character by circumstances through the univeral principle of association. As a corollary to this, Hartley holds that it is possible to improve man's moral and intellectual conditions by education. The moral sense is not a birth-bond. It is acquired through the principle of association.

We associate the sensations of pleasure with certain objects although pleasure can be associated with the wrong objects. But since there is a providential design in the universe, the human mind instinctively associates pleasure with the right objects. Thus under proper educational discipline our characters are shaped for us partly by unseen powers that impress themselves upon our minds. We need only a wise passiveness in order to proceed from childhood to youth to the final years of moral maturity and wisdom. We begin then with sensation, proceed by associating pleasure with loftier and loftier objects until we reach the stage when the presence of God is felt everywhere.

This doctrine of Association implies Necessitarianism. Necessitarianism maintains the doctrine that the moral order of the world and its perfection necessarily follow from the laws of human nature conceived on the Associative basis and the external world conceived as providentially arranged. If we want to produce better behaviour and if we want moral perfection, then we must allow the operation of the principle of association of ideas. Associationism and Necessitarianism together thus lead to a materialist psychology and a mechanistic conception of the world. After Coleridge's visit to Germany (and also after his acquaintance with Wordsworth) he repudiated all these doctrines. From Hartley's mechanistic Associationism and Necessitarianism, he changed his allegiance to the Kantian Transcendentalism, on the basis of which he developed his later theory of imagination as an active and creative principle as opposed to the Hartleyan notion of the imagination or fancy as a wise passive agent. Coleridge writes to Thomas Poole in 1801 :

If I do not delude myself I have not only completely extricated myself from the opinions of time and place, but have overthrown the doctrine of Association, as taught by Hartley......
especially the doctrine of necessity.

This brief introduction to the pre-romantic psychology and moral philosophy was necessary on account of the fact that romantic criticism in its theoretical aspect implies chiefly the repudiation of these psychological theories.

Foreign Influences on Coleridge's Criticism

Coleridge is the most eclectic of all English critics. Philosophical plagiarism is the most serious charge that can be levelled against Coleridge the critic. René Wellek observes :

Coleridge's lecture on "Poesy or Art" (1818) which has been used by several expositors of his aesthetics as the key to his thought is with the exception of a few insertions of pious sentiments a little more than a paraphrase of Schelling's Academy Oration of 1807.

René Wellek briefly examines this charge of plagiarism. He concludes that "many or most of Coleridge's key terms and distinctions are derived from Germany".
The chief foreign influences on Coleridge are thus those of Kant

and Schelling. The lecture on "Poesy or Art" closely parallels
Schelling's views. The fundamental philosophical distinctions
accepted by Coleridge are Kantian. Coleridge too accepts the distinction between Reason and Understanding. Reason is concerned
with ultimate values or the perception of unity in manyness. But
Understanding operates in a limited sphere. This distinction is the
ground work of Coleridge's speculation on the nature of fancy and
imagination. Coleridge maintains "my opinion is that deep thinking is attainable only by a person of deep feeling and that all truth
is a species of revelation". He writes in one of his letters :

My most serious pre-occupation is the metaphysical investigation of the laws by which our feelings form affinities with each
other and with words.

Coleridge philosophizes on the basis of his experience. He borrows
from German philosophy the conception of the Idea that unites all
experience in not merely general notions, but in any form of mental
image or impression.

Coleridge's theory of beauty too is German in its origin. In the
apprehension of beauty the soul projects itself into the outward
forms of nature. Beauty is not a subjective factor. Coleridge
examines the relations between the natural symbol and the mind
which experiences the symbol. According to him the symbol
and the mind both participate in a common spiritual life and the
experience of the beautiful is a consequence of this participation.

Coleridge's Aesthetic Theory

This essay contains Coleridge's maturest views on the nature of
poetry and art. The main object of the essay is to define the true
nature of the arts. Coleridge's views are essentially similar to those
of Schelling. He maintains that art is not a mere imitation. It is
not a mere copy of nature, but its re-creation. To copy nature is
idle rivalry. Coleridge writes :

...you must master the essence...which presupposes the bond
between nature and the highest sense and the soul of man. There

is an analogy between the process of nature and intelligence which it is the business of the poet to interpret.

He further adds that :

> ...to make the external internal, the internal external, to make nature thought and thought nature—this is the mystery of genius in the fine arts.

In every work of art the conscious is so impressed upon the unconscious as to appear in it. Thus the artist in copying nature does not copy external nature, but he communicates to us through symbols the spirit of nature. This theory of creative imitation is borrowed from Schelling's book *The System of Transcendental Idealism.* For Schelling, poetry gives "what philosophy cannot present"—the unconscious in action and creation. For both philosophers and artists nature is but the idle world appearing in constant limitations. The difference between Schelling and Coleridge is this : Schelling's philosophy is generally pantheistic, Coleridge's is theistic[1].

The peculiar maturity of Coleridge's aesthetic theory lies in the attempt to study the relation between form and content. The neo-classical poetic theory had excluded the importance of theme in the discussions on poetry. To them poetry was essentially metrical composition. But Coleridge addressed himself to the task of elucidation of the form and the content problem. Some of the finest parts of the *Biographia Literaria* 1817 deals, with this problem. Coleridge poses a few basic questions. How does a poem differ from other branches of compositions in which language is used ? What is the basis of this difference ? It is (or is it not) the function of poetry to justify such differences ? In the attempt to answer these questions, he mixes philosophy and criticism.

Coleridge defines poetry in terms of the function of a poet. Poetry is that which is composed by a poet. And the poet is one in whom imagination works. The conception of poetry is wider than the conception of a poem. Poetry is that which brings the whole soul of man into activity. The immediate object of a poem

---

[1] Coleridge's aesthetic theory on the nature of poetry is not fully developed. It remains fragmentary and incomplete.

is pleasure and not truth. But the immediate object of poetry is truth. Thus what distinguishes a poem from poetry is the distinction between the objects of both. The distinguishing criterion of a poem is the degree to which it gives immediate pleasure through proportionate beauty. But the criterion to examine its excellence is derived from its qualities as poetry, because poetry is related to truth. The ideal poet not only produces poems but composes poetry. Thus poetry is an imaginative synthesis or a special insight. Related to this idea is the notion of the aesthetic unity of the form. A poem is an organic unity. We derive pleasure from poems because we are appreciating the element of organic unity in it. This conception of organic unity is advanced by Coleridge as the essential distinction between the poetic verbal structure and the non-poetic verbal structure.

Coleridge's Theory of Imagination

Coleridge's greatest contribution to the history of criticism is the elaboration of the theory of Imagination. In propounding this theory, the greatest influences on him were Wordsworth, Schelling and Kant.

After his acquaintance with Wordsworth, Coleridge discovered that the mechanistic theory of mind, which he had held so far, was defective, for it failed to explain the active function of the mind. Listening to Wordsworth, he found that he was a person and not a "something" that was merely the receptacle of external impressions. It was this peculiar fascination of the creative genius of Wordsworth which made Coleridge examine the old theories. The new theory of the human mind divides all mental activity into fancy, and imagination. This division leads to two distinct types of philosophy and poetry.

After Coleridge's return from Germany there was a growing conviction that insight into truth is essentially dependent upon the soul and the emotions. The mind affects the will and is in turn influenced by the will itself. His philosophy is drawn from his own experience of the emotions and love. His conviction of the vivifying power of imagination is drawn from his craving for love. He wrote to Thomas Wedgewood :

Love is limitless sensation. I....think ideas never recall ideas no more than leaves in a forest created each other's motion —the breeze it is that runs through them—it is the soul, the state of feeling....

There is an inherent relationship, according to Coleridge between nature and the human soul. All things represent the infinite, and this "infinite" which is the ground and source of all nature, is arrived at through a special insight. This insight which is the gift of a few only is essentially the gift of imagination. The Coleridgean theory of imagination as a creative faculty analyses the special nature of the insight which reveals the infinite in all finite things. But it must be noted that Coleridge was never a pantheist. Instead of a pantheistic faith Coleridge affirms faith in a personal Being. He subordinates nature to the human soul. Thus when man appreciates natural beauty, man is not yielding to an external function. On the contrary, he is only appreciating the mystery and beauty of the inner life, which mysteries manifest themselves in the sensual world, and the sensual world mirrors our spiritual experiences.

Coleridge maintains that there are ideal and symbolic meanings in nature. But the average man has no special faculty to understand them. Oppressed by the cares of the world, physical illbeing, and the tyranny of the senses, he lives in the world of actuality. To break through this world of actuality, one needs the faculty of imagination[2]. Imagination presupposes a sense of harmony and spirit. This harmony is manifested through the outward forms of nature. Thus in the imaginative approach to nature is hidden a form of consciousness.

This theory of imagination is similar to that of the German Idealist philosopher Schelling. Coleridge develops his theory in the *Biographia Literaria* according to the philosophy of Schelling. Schelling (in his *System of Transcendental Idealism*) accords to the faculty of imagination a high function as the organ of artistic and philosophical truth. The quality of imagination which makes it common to philosophy and art is its power of reconciling opposites and discovering the ground of harmony between the contradictories. The transcendental philosophy of Schelling explains the principle

---

[2] These views find poetic expression in the "Ode to Dejection."

of unity of life through the nature of imagination. In the ordinary consciousness imagination makes a distinction between the self and the world. In the philosopher, imagination is the power of mediating on this ground of distinction. In the artist, imagination plays the function of reconciling opposites and giving them an outward and objective expression. Schelling thus concluded that art and poetry are therefore superior to all forms of knowledge. He further maintained the inherent interdependence of subject and object through the power of imagination. And this power which unifies all contraries was denoted by Coleridge as the "Esemplastic Power". This power unifies and creates experience and it constitutes the essential principle of unification in human consciousness. Separation between thought and feeling, reason and emotion is bridged on account of its activity. Coleridge accepted this theory of Schelling. The whole self of man is involved in the apprehension of reality. Coleridge thus fully formulated his philosophical conception of imagination.

Although it was Wordsworth who initially prompted Coleridge to the study of the faculty of imagination, it was the theory as developed by Coleridge which Wordsworth accepted with some minor modifications. In the *Excursion* Wordsworth wanted to give a poetic exposition of this philosophic theory of imagination.

Coleridge's analysis of mental activity makes a distinction between fancy, primary imagination, and the secondary imagination[3]. Fancy is arbitrary and lawless. It is not controlled by any higher power of judgment and selection. And it has no serious purpose. Then there is the primary imagination which belongs to all men, as the essential basis of all human perception, both to the scientist and the poet. It is merely the repetition in the finite mind of the eternal act of creation in the infinite *I AM*. Coleridge's primary imagination corresponds to what Kant calls simply the "imagination."

According to Kant, imagination is a universal human faculty which reconstructs experience. The data of the senses is arranged into various forms and designs in the process of perception through the power of imagination. Thus Kant makes imagination a cognitive faculty, and gives it no special poetic status. Here Coleridge disagreed. To Coleridge imagination is a poetic faculty in its most

---

[3] About the nature of the fancy Wordsworth and Coleridge differed.

highly developed form. It is a "dim analogue of creation." The Kantian imagination is not the faculty of poetic invention. It is only a synthesising power with little of creative freedom.

Above the primary imagination is the activity of the secondary imagination. It is this which *is the* poetic faculty. The secondary imagination dissolves the work of the primary in recreating it and thus transforming the sense impression already modified by the primary. To quote a long and relevant passage from the *Biographia Literaria* :

> The imagination then I consider either as primary, or secondary. The primary imagination I hold to be the living power and prime agent of all human perception, and as a repetition in the finite mind of the eternal act of creation in the infinite *I AM.* The secondary I consider as an echo of the former, co-existing with the conscious will, yet still as identical with the primary in the kind of its agency, and differing only in degree, and in the mode of its operation. It dissolves, diffuses dissipates, in order to re-create ; or where this process is rendered impossible, yet still, at all events, it struggles to idealize and to unify. It is essentially *vital* even as all objects (as objects) are essentially fixed and dead.
>
> Fancy, on the contrary, has no other counters to play with but fixities and definites. The fancy is indeed no other than a mode of memory emancipated from the order of time and space; and blended with, and modified by that empirical phenomenon of the will which we express by the word *choice.* But equally with the ordinary memory it must receive all its materials ready-made from the law of association."

Wordsworth and Coleridge on Imagination

In creative as well as critical writing, Wordsworth and Coleridge so closely co-operated with each other that it is not possible to discuss the achievements of one without referring to those of the other. In criticism as well as in poetry this mutual influence was beneficial to both. Although we discuss separately the respective theories of imagination held by Wordsworth and Coleridge, they together constitute one complete phase of the romantic movement. There are superficial differences between the Wordsworth's theory of imagination and Coleridge's. But Coleridge did not differ vitally from Wordsworth about 'imagination'. (See *Literary Criticism : A Short History*, by William K. Wimsatt, Jr., and Cleanth Brooks)

The superficial difference relates to the conception of fancy. In the 1815 Preface, Wordsworth wrote :

> To the mode in which Fancy has already been characterized as the power of evoking and combining, or as my friend Mr. Coleridge has styled it, "the aggregative and associative power" my objection is only that the definition is too general. To aggregate and to associate, to evoke and to combine, belong as well to the imagination as to the fancy; but either the materials evoked and combined are different; or they are brought together under a different law, and for a different purpose. Fancy does not require that the materials which she makes use of should be susceptible of change in their constitution, from her touch ; and, where they admit of modification, it is enough, for her purpose under which the processes of fancy are carried on is as capricious as the accidents of things, and the effects are surprising, playful, ludicrous, amusing, tender, or pathetic, as the objects happen to be appositely produced or fortunately combined. Fancy depends upon the rapidity and profusion with which she scatters her thoughts and images, trusting that their number, and the felicity with which they are linked together, will make amends for the want of individual value ; or she prides herself upon the curious subtlety and the successful elaboration with which she can detect their lurking affinities.

And further Wordsworth separates fancy from the knowledge of spiritual truth :

> Fancy is given to quicken and beguile the temporal part of our nature, imagination to incite and to support the eternal...

Coleridge objected to this in the twelfth chapter of the *Biographia Literaria* :

> If by the power of evoking and combining, Mr. Wordsworth

means the same as, and no more than, I meant by the aggregative and associative, I continue to deny that it belongs to all to the imagination ; and I am disposed to conjecture, that he has mistaken the co-presence of fancy and imagination for the operation of the latter singly.

Wordsworth merely distinguished between fancy and imagination as an inferior and as a superior mode of imaging, while both are inventive, fancy was an inferior and arbitrary way of imaging, and imagination was a superior faculty.

Coleridge, on the other hand, made a distinction between three types of mental faculties, the fancy, the primary imagination, and the secondary imagination. But fancy, as Coleridge explains it, is only a mode of memory, and receives its material ready-made from the law of association. The primary imagination is a universal faculty, and it is at the source of all human perception. The secondary imagination is the poetical faculty, the special gift of the creative imagination. It is essentially vital and it struggles to idealize and unify. It reveals the underlying unity inherent in life and relates man to nature and to reality. But it may be pointed out that Wordsworth uses precisely this conception of the nature and function of imagination in *The Prelude*. It is thus futile to attempt to separate the two theories of imagination.

Wordsworth and Coleridge as Critics—A Summary View

Wordsworth and Coleridge are the two of the greatest minds produced by the romantic movement. It will be useful therefore to compare briefly their critical achievements.

Wordsworth was not a critic in the usual sense of the term, in spite of the fact that his prefaces and essays constitute the manifesto of the new age of romanticism. His main work in criticism was destructive. He rejected the eighteenth century personification and "the poetic diction" and the morbid and sensational German romanticism. He brought poetic interest to bear upon the simple, sane and healthy life of the common people—the English farmer and the peasant. He revived the native idioms and tone of the spoken voice to poetry. In one sense, this was a move in the direction of romanticism and democracy ; in another sense, it tends towards realism. On the positive and creative side, his interest in the psychological state of experience as fit themes for poetry, his stress on passion, his formulation of the principle of poetic pleasure all continue to be influential even in our own day.

Coleridge, on the other hand, considered criticism to be an important part of literary study. In his opinion it is the function of criticism to formulate the rules of literary composition. He writes in the *Biographia Literaria* :

> The ultimate end of criticism is much more to establish the principles of writing than to furnish rules how to pass judgment on what has been written by others ; if indeed it were possible that the two could be separated (Chapter XVIII).

The most important thing which distinguishes Coleridge's criticism from Wordsworth's (and indeed from those of most others) is his philosophical interest. His eminence as a critic is, to a great extent, due to his philosophy.

In his youth he was influenced by the materialist philosophies current in the later half of the eighteenth century. Among these we may note Godwin's mechanistic philosophy and Hartley's associationist psychology. But later his thought developed in the direction of idealism. Apart from Kant, and Schelling, his writings show the influence of Plato and seventeenth century English Platonists. Coleridge's views on literature are briefly as follows :

> Literature should give a vision of life. This vision is apprehended by imaginative intuition. Poetry should be *ideal, representative* and *generic,* characters should be clothed with *generic* attributes, with the common attributes of the class, and not with such qualities as one remarkable individual might possess. He thus disagreed with Wordsworth's theory of the theme and diction of poetry. Rustic life and diction had no place in his theory of poetry. To him language was the product of the *inner* as well as the *outer* life. Language was the product of thought, of the philosophers and not of clowns and shepherds.

In his criticism we have no excessive subjectivism characteristic of the typically romantic thinkers. He was both subjective and objective as Ernest Bernbaum points out (in *A Guide through the Romantic Movement*). It is this quality of his thought which has made a special appeal to twentieth century critics like Herbert Read and I. A. Richards. Herbert Read says :

He [Coleridge] made criticism into a science, and using his own experiences and those of his fellow poets as material for his research, revealed for the first time some part of the mystery of genius and of the universal and eternal significance of art (p. 33).

And I. A. Richards maintains (in *Coleridge on Imagination*) :

Coleridge's criticism is of a kind that requires us—to reconsider our most fundamental conceptions, our conceptions of man's being—the nature of his mind and its knowledge.

CHAPTER SEVEN

MATTHEW ARNOLD : CRITIC OF SOCIETY AND LITERATURE

The Background of Victorian Thought and Criticism

The prophetic indignation evident in the critical writings of Matthew Arnold can be better understood when we take into account the forces in art and thought which he attacked. The four decades between 1850–1888 during which Arnold wrote, his various books dealing with poetry, criticism, culture, and religion were important so far as the social developments in Britain were concerned.

The year 1851 saw the opening of a new era in English history. The Great Exhibition (in London) of this year symbolized the main characteristics of the social and industrial structure of England in the Victorian Age. Briefly, it was an age of technological advancements, growing industrial productivity, superficial material prosperity, rapid developments in theoretical science endorsing a universal belief in the inevitability of human progress, and the hey-day of unfettered capitalistic and imperialist expansion on every side. But the other side of affairs presented a gloomy picture. Along with the growth of material prosperity there accompanied the materialistic spirit in its worst sense. Emphasis on science and technology obscured not only the humanistic studies, but also the human spirit. An aggressive competitiveness and a profit-motive replaced the more positive forces of social cohesion. Apart from the superficial prosperity, there was wide-spread poverty as a consequence of the unplanned economic growth, and crime; violence, brutality, and social insecurity were among the common features of Victorian life. Arnold saw beneath the outward appearances of life, the forces of hatred and disintegration which were rampant. While scientific theories were demolishing the foundations of religious thought there were no alternative philosophy of life. Nor had the various forms of Christianity in England the necessary hold on popular minds.

It is with such a confluence of forces that Arnold was pre-occupied in socio-ethical criticism. His advocacy of poetry and culture must be considered in relation to the contemporary forces. In this situation, it was a synthesis which was needed and Arnold sought to provide it. The most influential school of thought which the England of the Victorian days had was the French Positivism of Saint Simon and Auguste Comte. Their philosophy laid stress on material reality and social forces. This philosophy opposed religion and metaphysics. Positivism influenced thinkers, and literary men alike. This was further supported by the Darwinian discoveries. On the whole, science reinforced positivistic and scientific materialism. Thus was the romantic influence on literature under-mined, and realistic tendencies encouraged. But at the same time, the idealist and romantic forces were not completely eradicated.

Thus we see in the Victorian period two contradictory forces were at work, the idealist-romantic, and the positivistic-materialis-tic. We have a tradition of writers who stressed the scientific advancement, material progress, and industrial prosperity. For instance, Macaulay, John Stuart Mill, Darwin, Huxley, Frederick Harrison, John Morley, and (the father of Sociology) Herbert Spencer. But Carlyle, Newman, Ruskin, Arnold, Pater and Swinburne were writers who rebelled against this materialistic tradition.

Arnold, more than any one else, felt bitterly the disappearance of values in life. To him, such a state of affairs was the outcome of an alienation of man from his main sources of moral and spiritual inspiration, namely poetry and literature. According to Matthew Arnold, literature has an edifying role to play both in individual and social life. When society and literature are separated, the sequel will be Philistinism. Literature moulds life through the powerful and profound application of ideas to life. The best tradition of European poetry has been one continuous tradition of an attempt to grasp the inner significance of life through the application of ideas.

Arnold's interest in society as an educationist has also to be taken into account. The need for a sound policy of general education was great. The need was especially felt because in Arnold's time democracy had taken root firmly in England. It was the masses who were going to shape the destiny of the future. Already signs of social insecurity were being acutely felt. The tempo of life was increasing. In the words of Trevelyan, it was an age of "parliamentary confusion, of weak governments, of rapid combinations and dissolutions of political partnership". (Quoted in *The Educational Thought and Influence of Matthew* by W. F. Connell).

Arnold's Socio-Ethical Criticism

It is more convenient to consider Arnold's views on society and life separately from his literary criticism. As we have pointed out earlier, he was interested in both types of criticism, the socio-ethical and literary. The remarkable thing about Arnold's criticism is the consistency of his views, "the consistent consistency" in the opinion of Saintsbury (in *The History of Criticism*).

Arnold starts with a milieu whose main features have been outlined above. His interest in social criticism is only too apparent in all his literary essays. In *The Function of Criticism* social criticism parallels his literary criticism, and the conclusions of both reinforce each other.

Arnold took a serious view of the cultural situation in England in the Victorian Age. He had always been concerned with the possible danger of vulgarization and the fragmentation of society. Thus he devoted himself to the analysis of, and prescription for, the current culture crisis. In the collection of essays *Culture and Anarchy*, he outlines the pressing defect of current life. Accordingly, he developed a theory of culture as a necessary force for social regeneration. About the role of culture in society Arnold writes in the Preface to *Culture and Anarchy* that :

The whole scope of this essay is to recommend culture as the great help of our present difficulties, culture being a pursuit of our total perfection by means of getting to know, on all the matter which most concern us, the best that has been thought and said in this world ; and through this knowledge, turning a stream of fresh and free thought upon our stock notions and habits...

From this statement we notice three points regarding Arnold's conception of culture. The aim of culture is total perfection ; culture is essentially a way of life and not mere intellectual acquisitions ; and thirdly, culture is an instrument of social amelioration. Culture as a way of life (and as different from mere knowledge) is a special conception of Arnold. It is this kind of culture which is a remedy from anarchy. "Through culture seems to lie our way, not only to perfection but even to safety." Culture is always opposed by Arnold to anarchy. Indeed, Arnold equates anarchy with the aimlessness which unguided liberalism is bringing about.

The usual conception of culture is "a smattering of the two dead languages of Greek and Latin". But there is another view in which :

all the love of our neighbour, the impulses toward action, help, and beneficence, the desire for removing human error, clearing human confusion ; and diminishing human misery, the noble aspiration to leave the world as better and happier than we found it...motives eminently such as are called social—come in as part of the grounds of culture, and the main and pre-eminent end......It moves by the force....of the moral and social passion for doing good.

Thus culture is the systematic "pursuit of a harmonious expansion of all the powers with the beauty and the worth of all human nature." Although Arnold himself was a great scholar and student of classical literature, yet he does not merely equate culture with learning. It is not mere learning which is the essential feature of a cultured individual. There is also the "sheer desire to see things as they are" or to "render an intelligent being more intelligent".

Culture, according to Matthew Arnold, is an internal condition which relates to the growth and predominance of our "humanity proper, as distinguished from our animality." In this sense culture even goes beyond religion. In *Culture and Anarchy*, Arnold further explains the nature of perfection attained through culture. It is a trinity of:

harmonious perfection, general perfection, and perfection which consists in becoming something rather than in having something, in an inward condition of the mind and the spirit.

In Arnold's opinion, religion fulfilled this function of making the individual inwardly perfect in the past. But he regarded the nineteenth century forms of Christianity as having failed in their specific tasks. Arnold disliked the dogmas, the ritual, and the practices of Christianity. To him religion itself was morality touched with emotion. And ''God was the eternal, not ourselves, which makes for righteousness''. And instead of the traditionally Christian conception of the sinful character of human nature, Arnold advanced a dualistic conception of the individual as having a lower (animal) existence and a higher (human) order of nature. The truly integrated and cultured individual conquers the lower through the power of the higher. Thus in social thought Arnold begins with a humanistic conception of the nature of man. In his humanism lay his initial antipathy to all institutionalized and even mystified forms of religious worship and practices.[1]

Of all the eclectic writers, Arnold was the most eclectic. His theory of the individual and his doctrine of ethical idealism are composite ideas borrowed from such varied sources as the Stoics, Carlyle, Emerson, Thomas Arnold, Goethe and the Bible, to mention only the most important sources. The essential system of thought which he distilled out of all these various sources may be called ''ethical idealism''.

Arnold's view of man and his ethical responsibilities marked him out distinctly (not only from the religious tradition of thought, but also) from the liberal-romantic line of thought on the one hand, and from the naturalistic scientific tradition, on the other. As opposed to romanticism, Arnold advocated a kind of ''cultural classicism''. In maintaining that man has both an animal and a human nature, Arnold reflects the romantic stress on feeling and impulses. At the same time, in this very conception is implied at once the rejection of the purely biological conception of man as part (the highest

---

[1] See his books dealing with religious criticism : *Literature and Dogma ; God and the Bible; Last Essays on Church and Religion.*

part on account of the evolutionary process) of nature. Arnold thus rejects not only the old religion, but also the new religion of science.

Arnold's pre-occupation with the impact of science on society is evident in *Literature and Science*. At that time the controversy between the advocates of the new science and those of the classical studies had become very acute in educational matters. The questions posed were outwardly simple. There are two kinds of knowledge— of nature (science) and knowledge of man (humanities). Which should receive greater encouragement ? Arnold supported a humanistic programme of education based on the humanities and classical literature. The study of literature is the study of the operation of the human forces in society. Arnold's best plea on behalf of the classical education is contained in his lecture "On the Modern Element in Literature"[2] (Published in 1869). The modern age stands in need of an intellectual deliverance. Modern life has become immensely complex and rapidly changing. Our grasp of the main problems of life is only partial. Consequently there is despair, confusion, and depression. How to understand the complexities of our age ? The best method is that of comparing our age with other ages who had similar problems. The Athenian civilization and culture of the fifth century B. C. had similar problems. And we find in its literature an adequate interpretation of the age. In the ancient poets and dramatists we find an adequate interpretation of the problems of life. Thus Arnold showed that classical literature possessed a relevance to the situation of nineteenth century England. He advocates the spirit of Hellenism, "an unclouded clearness of mind, an unimpeded play of thought" which sees things as they really are (*Culture and Anarchy*). Arnold thus opposed mere scientific education which denies man a knowledge of himself.

Here we have outlined the salient points in Arnold's social criticism. These arguments of Arnold have had a considerable influence on the neo-humanists of America, Irving Babbitt, and Paul Elmer More. It was essentially the ethical theory of Arnold which appealed to them. Also the rejection of both the romantic and the positivistic attitudes at the same time by humanism has its origin in Arnold's criticism of life.

At the same time Arnold has been very severely attacked by those modern critics whose affiliations are not chiefly humanistic.

[2] See Arnold's *Schools and Universities* and "On the Modern Element in Literature".

For example F. R. Leavis attacks Arnold. T. S. Eliot's attack on Arnold is well-known.

Eliot's criticism of Arnold is not merely from the standpoint of a literary critic. Eliot opposes the whole set of theoretical conclusions which emerges from Arnold's essays and lectures. Arnold's humanistic conception of culture is rejected by Eliot. Instead, in his *Notes towards the Definition of Culture*, Eliot examines the possibility of a religiously oriented culture. In the *Idea of a Christian Society*, Eliot provides an alternative conception for Arnold's culture. It is not unnatural that a critic and thinker of Arnold's stature provoked considerable controversy.

Poetry and Morality

Arnold has been frequently criticised for his view of the relation between poetry and morality. In his poetry and criticism, Arnold assumes as axiomatic that religion is dead, and the only function of religion was to emotionalize the moral code. Poetry is itself a religious act. In a sense poetry is superior to religion. He wants poetry to teach and inculcate a moral code. In this opinion regarding the high function of poetry Arnold is truly in the romantic tradition. He quotes one his earlier passages about the future of poetry at the beginning of his "The Study of Poetry":

The future of poetry is immense, because in poetry, where it is worthy of its high destinies, our race, as time goes on, will find an ever surer and surer stay. There is not a creed which is not shaken, not an accredited dogma which is not shown to be questionable, not received tradition which does not threaten to dissolve. Our religion has materialised itself in the fact, in the supposed fact; and now the fact is failing it. But for poetry the idea is every thing; the rest is a world of illusion of divine illusion. Poetry attaches its emotion to the idea ; the idea *is* the fact. The strongest part of our religion is its unconscious poetry.[3]

[3] This passage contains many of those inaccuracies of definition, and vagueness of expression for which Arnold has been in recent times severely attacked.

Thus the poetry of the future will replace religion. It is in poetry that the essential religious sentiments coalesce into one thing. Poetry, and religion should all be united. Spiritual discipline will come from the ennobling effects of poetry.

Further, it is the function of poetry to interpret life for us. In "The Study of Poetry", he writes:

> More and more mankind will discover that we have to turn to poetry to *interpret life for us, to console us, to sustain us.* (Italics mine).

This is precisely what he means by a criticism of life. In his essay on Maurice de Guerin, he writes :

> The grand power of poetry is its interpretative power....

One of the worst defects of Arnold's critical procedure is that he does not keep up the distinction between morality and life, and between life and religion in discussions. All the didactic arguments of Arnold's theory lead upto his famous comment that "poetry is a criticism of life". (This statement is found in many of his essays in different contexts). It is clear that "life" does not mean the social mode of existence. Arnold's definition of poetry as a criticism of life is not the same thing as using poetry for socio-economic propaganda. By "life", Arnold implies the moral and emotional elements in human existence. "Life" is thus moral and spiritual. "Criticism", in this sense, means an "interpretation and healing representation". In the Preface to the First Edition of Poems, 1853, he points out :

> The greatest poetry appeals to the great primary human affections....

Thus great poetry affects man through primary human affections, and has a transforming power. By a "criticism of life", Arnold means this transforming power of life. Life is not defined in socio-economic terms, but in terms of moral law, truth, and feelings. These are the general conceptions in Arnold's critical theory which are concerned. And it is precisely these larger and indefinite connotations which Arnold gives to conceptions like "morality" and "life" which are severely criticised by modern writers. F. R. Leavis writes ("Matthew Arnold as Critic" in *Scrutiny*, Vol. VII, No. 3) that : in

> Arnold as a theological or philosophical thinker had better be abandoned explicitly at once.

Poetry and the Contemporary Age

While Arnold is preoccupied with the larger conception of life, he does not neglect the practical problems of contemporary life. In his theory of poetry and of criticism, we also find an analysis of the intellectual and historical forces which shaped life in the Victorian Age. About this aspect of Arnold's criticism, Vincent Buckley writes (in *Poetry and Morality*, 1959) :

> This modernity [of Arnold] consists largely in what we may call his representative self-consciousness, in his sense of the age in which he lives as an age both special and historically important. Arnold has it in a high degree, and is anxious to estimate and represent the spirit of his age, the *Zeitgeist*.

This sense of his age further finds expression in the doctrine of the role of ideas in poetry. In "The Function of Criticism" he lays it down as axiomatic that poetry is always an application of ideas to life. In great poetry there is a profound and powerful application of ideas to life. In judicial criticism Arnold uses this conception frequently. His criticism of the romantic poets, especially of Shelley, springs from the fact that they had an insufficient grasp of the complexities of life. They lacked a set of mature ideas. The same criticism is applied to the neo-classicals. They had no serious concern with life in their own age. They, according to Arnold, made no effort to apply the ethical ideas of the age in their poerty. He praises Goethe because he is "the clearest, the largest, the most helpful thinker of modern times".

Poetry, according to Arnold, must influence the mental atmosphere of its age, by dealing with the ideas with which men of that age live. We have seen that he praises (in *Culture and Anarchy*) the Athenian writers of the fifth century B. C. because they dealt with the analysis of the social forces and fully reflected the age in their works. Arnold sees the poet as the true representative of his age, and of his particular society.

Arnold on the Function of Criticism

(In making this analytical summary, several sections dealing with social and political criticism have been omitted, and attention has been focused on "What criticism is").

There are seven central ideas which are elaborated by Matthew Arnold in his "The Function of Criticism".

First, Arnold defends the critical activity. He points to the superiority of European literary criticism. In it we have sustaining ideas of life. In English literary criticism, on the other hand, there is a comparative intellectual barrenness. While Arnold admits that the critical power is lower than the creative ability, criticism, at its best, fulfils a valuable function. He rightly points out that Wordsworth's Prefaces are more valuable than the "Ecclesiastical Sonnets, and Johnson's *Lives of the Poets* is better than his tragedy, *Irene*. Then we can not generalize and say that criticism is always inferior to creation.

Second, there is a great difference between creation and criticism. Creation is not possible always, while criticism can be written at any age. (Here Arnold advances his conception of what poetry is).

The creative power works with materials and elements. It cannot operate without these elements. By "elements" Arnold means the raw-material of experience or "ideas", "the best ideas on every matter which literature touches". Literature touches the best ideas current in any time. Poetry may not discover new ideas, but it uses those ideas which already exist for "the ground work of literary genius is a work of synthesis and exposition, not of analysis and discovery." Arnold further explains that the poetic process lies in :

the faculty of being inspired by a certain intellectual and spiritual atmosphere, by a certain order of ideas . . of dealing divinely with these ideas, presenting them in the most attractive combinations. . . .

Arnold thus concludes that great epochs in literature are rare, because all ages are not ages of great and divinely inspired ideas. For poetry to flourish, we need not only poetic genius, but also an age of great ideas. To quote Arnold again :

> ...for the creation of a master-work in literature two powers must concur, the power of the man and the power of the moment, and the man is not enough without the moment; the creative power has, for its happy exercise, appointed elements, and those elements are not in its own control.

This is a questionable thesis. The defect of this "theory of the moment" lies in the fact that we have no means of discovering which events or ideas are great in the sense in which Arnold uses it. For the greatness of an "idea" or "element" used in poetry is available to us only through the poet's own interpretation of it.

Third, from this position, Arnold attempts a definition of the critical task. He maintains that as contrasted with the creative activity the critical task has its elements under its own control. It is the business of the critical power :

> in all branches of knowledge, theology, philosophy, history, art and science to see the object as in itself it really is. Thus it tends, at last, to make an intellectual situation of which the creative power can profitably avail itself. It tends to establish an order of ideas, if not absolutely true, yet true by comparison with that it displaces ; to make the best ideas prevail. Presently these new ideas reach society, the touch of truth is the touch of life, and there is a stir and growth everywhere ; out of this stir and growth, come the creative epochs of literature.

Fourth, having described the nature of the critical task Arnold applies his criterion of criticism to the romantic poets. The romantic revolution at the beginning of the nineteenth century promised much, but fulfilled little. The truth is that the romantics were separated from the current ideas in their time. They had insufficient data to work with. In other words :

> English poetry of the first quarter of this century, with plenty of energy, plenty of creative force, did not know enough.

Fifth, Arnold examines the impact of the French Revolution as a source of ideas on the creative art of the times. He maintains that this revolution did not produce much creative writings. Compare it with Renaissance. Here again, Arnold's arguments, while consistent, are one-sided. He says that movements like the Reformation and the Renaissance were disinterestedly intellectual and spiritual movements. But the French Revolution took a political and practical character. And, therefore, it did not become the source of a great literary and creative activity. Arnold misses no opportunity of attacking whatever is English. He points out that compared to the English Revolution of the seventeenth century even the French Revolution was more intellectual.

Sixth, Arnold has a deep-rooted dislike of the utilitarian, the pragmatic, and the practical. Whenever an idea is rendered practical, it ceases to have any creative or ennobling effect. The greatest defect of the English character lies in its practical turn. Arnold praises Burke, the only great Englishman of that age because :

> His [Burke's] greatness is that he lived in a world which neither English Liberalism nor English Toryism is apt to enter— the world of ideas, not the world of catchwords and party habits.

Arnold repudiates the self-complacent notion of progress. The average Englishman is too conceited with the apparent prosperity around him and he congratulates himself. Arnold quotes the instance of a most heinous crime of murder committed by a mother on her new-born infant to prick this bubble of self-satisfaction. With ironic contempt, Arnold quotes the newspaper headline, "Wragg is in custody".

The fundamental requirement of criticism is that it should be *disinterested*. It must "keep aloof from practice". How to attain this critical disinterestedness ? We had better quote his own words :

> By keeping aloof from practice ; by resolutely following the law of its own nature, which is to be a free play of the mind on all subjects which it touches ; by steadily refusing to lend itself to any of those ulterior, political, considerations about ideas, which plenty of people will be sure to attach to them, which

perhaps ought often to be attached to them, which in this country at any rate are certain to be attached to them quite sufficiently, but which criticism has really nothing to do with. Its business is, as I have said, simply to know the best that is known and thought in the world, and by in its turn making this known, to create a current of true and fresh ideas. Its business is to do this with inflexible honesty, with due ability ; but its business is to do no more, and to leave alone all questions of practical consequences and applications, questions which will never fail to have due prominence given to them. Else criticism, beside being really false of its own nature, merely continues in the old rut which it has hitherto followed in this country, and will certainly miss the chance now given to it. For what is at present the bane of criticism in this country? It is that practical considerations cling to it and stifle it, and subserve interests not its own ; our organs of criticism are organs of men and parties having practical ends to serve, and with them those practical ends are the first thing and second ; so much play of mind as is compatible with prosecution of those practical ends is all that is wanted.

(Arnold analyses the function played by one literary journal after another in his day and rejects each as not having a disinterested critical role to play).

The "disinterested course" which criticism must take is determined by the law of its own being, Arnold tells us. For criticism is :

the idea of a disinterested endeavour to learn and propagate the best that is known and thought in the world, and thus to establish a current of fresh and true ideas.

For Arnold judgment is only a subsidiary function of criticism. Judgment must always be supported by fresh knowledge. Hence the critic must seek knowledge zealously. The English critic must learn more and more from Europe. Judicial criticism, which seeks to place an author in a tradition may not be much dependent on new knowledge. Here what is necessary is an intimate and lively consciousness of the truth of what one is saying. But this according to Arnold, is not the most satisfactory part of a critic's work. That part is the search for new knowledge which makes criticism "sincere, simple, flexible, ardent and ever-widening its knowledge''. In this search for new ideas criticism is very similar to creation.

These are the fundamental ideas in Arnold's essay ''The Function of Criticism''. What we notice is the remarkable consistency of his theory. Poetry as well as criticism is concerned with ideas, and in the preoccupation with ideas lies the justification both for the creative and critical activities.

On Poetry and Poets

In *The Study of Poetry*, Arnold gives us his serious reflections on the nature of poetry.[4] This essay has two parts. In the first part he examines the nature of poetry. In the second, he applies his doctrine of poetry to the history of English poetry for judicial criticism.[5]

Dealing with the nature of poetry, Arnold begins with the conception of the high function of poetry which has an immense future, and a great destiny. We must be able to distinguish a true classic of poetry from an inferior one. In the field of poetry the good is the enemy of the best. We must therefore discover the best poetry. In poetry the distinction between the excellent and the inferior is of paramount importance because of poetry's high destiny. Arnold says :

> In poetry, as a criticism of life under the conditions fixed for such a criticism by the laws of poetic truth and poetic beauty, the spirit of our race will find, we have said, as time goes on and as other helps fail, its consolation and stay. But the consolation and stay will be of power in proportion to the power of the criticism of life. And the criticism of life will be of power in proportion as the poetry conveying it is excellent rather than inferior, sound rather than unsound or half-sound, true rather than untrue or half-true.

How can we discover the best poetry? Arnold's answer lies in the theory of ''poetic touchstones''. These touchstones are ''lines and

---

[4] This essay was written in 1880.

[5] In this respect, ''The Study of Poetry'' may be compared to Wordsworth's 1815 Preface.

expressions of the great masters", which are of undisputed and undisputable excellence. Such touchstones are found, for example, in Shakespeare and Milton :

> If thou didst ever hold me in thy heart,
> Absent thee from felicity awhile,
> And in this harsh world draw thy brath in pain
> To tell my story....
>
> *(Hamlet)*

> *Or*

> And courage never to submit or yield
> And what is else not to be overcome ?
>
> *(Paradise Lost)*

Familiarity with such lines as these quoted above can be used as a criterion for judgment and comparison. In these lines are expressed characters of a high quality of poetry. What is this high quality ?

To Arnold, this lies in the seriousness of both thought and style. They are inseparable. Thought reflects style. "The best poetry acquire their special character from possessing, in an eminent degree, truth and seriousness". Truth and seriousness are, Arnold further argues, one and the same in great poetry. The two qualities are closely related. He says :

> The two superiorities are closely related, and are in steadfast proportion one to the other. So far as high poetic truth and seriousness are wanting to a poet's matter and substance, so far also, we may be sure, will a high poetic stamp of diction and movement be wanting to his style and manner. In proportion as this high stamp of diction and movement, again, is absent from a poet's style and manner, we shall find, also, that high poetic truth and seriousness are absent from his substance and matter.

Sublimity of style is the reflection of the sublime seriousness of the truth of the content. This view of the poetical style, Arnold held consistently throughout his critical career. In *The Study of Celtic Literature,* Arnold writes :

Style, in my sense of the word, is a peculiar recasting and heightening, under a certain condition of spiritual excitement, of what a man has to say, in such a manner as to add dignity and distinction to it.

In the Preface to 1853 edition of *Poems* occurs for the first time the term "grand style". In his essay on *Translating Homer,* he develops the basic idea. In his own words :

I think it will be found that the grand style arises in poetry when a noble nature, poetically gifted treats with simplicity or with severity a serious subject.

The second part of *The Study of Poetry* gives us Arnold's views on the great English poets. According to him, Chaucer "lacks the high seriousness of the great classics." Coming to the neoclassical age he remarks :

We are to regard Dryden as the puissant and glorious founder, and Pope as the splendid high priest, of our age of prose and reason, of our excellent and indispensable eighteenth century. . . Dryden and Pope are not the classics of our poetry, they are classics of our prose.

Nor is Arnold able to appreciate Burns. His poetry perpetually deals with "Scotch drink, Scotch religion and Scotch manners." Burns is compared to Dante. We cannot but remark that this comparison is more than unfair. In this context he clarifies what is meant by the powerful application of ideas to life in poetry :

But for supreme poetical success more is required than the powerful application of ideas to life ; it must be an application under the conditions fixed by the laws of poetic truth and poetic beauty. Those laws fix as an essential condition, in the poet's treatment of such matters as are here in question, high seriousness ...the high seriousness which comes from absolute sincerity.

Arnold concludes this essay by prophesying about the prospect of survival for poetry. He rejects that democratic charlatanism which foretells the decline of classics. Great poetry will always have currency and supremacy by the very *"instinct of self-preservation of humanity"* (Italics mine).

Concluding Remarks on Arnold's Criticism

One is astonished by the severe strictures made by some modern critics on Arnold, F. R. Leavis and T. S. Eliot both have been relentlessly demolishing the critical system built by Arnold. One may ignore F. R. Leavis. But Eliot's remarks on Arnold's criticism are vitiated by his own theological preoccupations. Eliot dislikes Arnold's rationalized form of Christianity. He also opposes the Arnoldian theory of poetic high seriousness, and the grand style. But, Eliot is himself very similar to Arnold, when he [Eliot] says that literary criticism must be completed from a religious and theological point of view. J. M. Robertson points out that Arnold had no "gift for consistency or for definition," (in *Modern Humanists Re-considered*). Now, in the field of critical discourse "consistency of definition" can never be an unmixed blessing.

Neither is the charge levelled against Arnold that he is a propagandist or an advocate of criticism well-founded. As a theoretical critic he has advanced the most comprehensive theory of the sublime element in poetry. As a practical critic, he strictly and with a remarkable consistency applies his doctrine to poets and poetry.

He has widened the field of critical enquiries. His fundamental aim was to diagnose the social and cultural ills of the nineteenth century, and to formulate a synthesis of man's knowledge, his poetry, and religion leading towards perfection. There is a lucidity and clarity in Arnold's generalisations. As Saintsbury points out :

Systematic without being hide-bound, well-read...without pedantry, delicate and subtle, without weakness or dilettantism ; Catholic without eccleticism ; enthusiastic without indiscriminateness;...Mr. Arnold is one of the best and most precious of teachers on his own side.

We may consider Arnold not only as a critic but as a Critics' Critic.

CHAPTER EIGHT

T. S. ELIOT ON CRITICISM AND DRAMA

Introduction

Eliot is not only the most famous poet of his time, but also its most famous critic. Eliot's criticism is especially important because his is the criticism of a great poet and dramatist. Eliot's own theory is that the only criticism that is worth reading is the criticism of practising poets. Whether this statement can be raised to the status of a general theory or not is immaterial. It is not merely a matter of accident that the great critics in English literature are also its great poets—Philip Sidney, Ben Jonson, Dryden, Samuel Johnson, Coleridge, and Matthew Arnold.

Like Matthew Arnold, Eliot too has a comperehensive critical mind. His numerous essays and lectures deal with almost every important aspect of literature and criticism. Besides, Eliot is seriously concerned with the major issues which vex the minds of modern thinkers. He is concerned with the survival of culture and civilization. He is concerned with the problem of values. He is concerned with religion and its impact on the creative mind. Thus as a critic of life and letters Eliot surveys the whole of human experience. As a literary critic Eliot maintains that the literariness of a work of art can be ascertained by literary standards. But as a critic of life Eliot maintains that the greatness of literature cannot be ascertained by purely literary considerations. Such statements of Eliot show the complexity of critical presuppositions which enter into his pronouncements.

The Historical Situation

It is with Eliot that many new trends in modern criticism begin. What is called the New Criticism has considerably been influenced by his writings. Historically speaking, one of his important contributions is the reaction against romanticism in general which he strengthened. The anti-romantic and anti-humanistic reaction had its origin at the beginning of the twentieth century. Romanticism was the most powerful influence for nearly two hundred years. But a reaction against romanticism entered modern literature through two sources, the American and the English.

In America, at the beginning of this century, two influential critics, Irving Babbitt and Paul Elmer More had begun to question the fundamental assumptions of romanticism. Irving Babbitt, in his book *Rousseau and Romanticism* repudiated the philosophy of Rousseau. Eliot was influenced by this repudiation of Rousseau.

In England, T. H. Hulme had already inaugurated an era of literary classicism. He, too, opposing romanticism and humanism, attempted to revive classicism in art and criticism. Such efforts at a repudiation of romanticism and humanism finally culminate in Eliot. Thus Eliot is the modern representative of literary classicism. As a critic he belongs to the tradition of Ben Jonson, Dryden and Samuel Johnson. But the great classical and neo-classical critics before Eliot concerned themselves chiefly with the analysis of literary works, and we do not find in them any elaborate theory of poetic composition or the process of literary creation. But Eliot has his own theories of literature which are advanced in his famous essays "Tradition and the Individual Talent" and "The Function of Criticism".

The most important schools of literary criticism were those of impressionism and "abstract criticism" when Eliot began his literary criticism in the second decade of our century. Impressionistic criticism assumes that the essence of literary criticism lies in the individual's response to a work of art. Criticism is the record of the adventures of a soul among masterpieces. The impressionistic critic considers a high degree of aesthetic sensibility as the only requirement in the appreciation and judgment of a work of art. All other equipments, either in scholarship or in the discipline of a literary tradition, are considered extraneous.

Eliot's Attack on Modern Schools of Criticism

The volume of critical essays entitled *The Sacred Wood* (first publish-ed in 1920) has started many modern trends in criticism. The two first essays, "The Perfect Critic" and "The Imperfect Critic" con-stitute an attack on impressionism and the school of "abstract criti-cism".[1]

The essay "The Perfect Critic" begins by attacking two move-ments in contemporary criticism, the movement initiated, by Matthew Arnold, and that which is called "aesthetic criticism" or "impressionistic criticism". Arnold is dismissed briefly as a propagan-dist for criticism rather than a true critic. And then Eliot examines impressionistic criticism.

Eliot takes Arthur Symons as a typical impressionistic critic. This kind of criticism ends by becoming a common type of popular lite-rary lecture, in which the stories, the characters, and the general qualities of a literary work are set forth. This is one of the worst defects of a criticism depending on mere "impressions" for the analysis of a poem or a play.

Further it is almost impossible to build a criticism upon pure im-pressions. The moment we try to translate the impressions into words, we begin to analyse and construct. Consequently the verbal formula-tions of aesthetic impressions are not the same as impressions. Finally what we have is not criticism, but a few opinions based on the critic's aesthetic sensibility. In the sentimental person, a work of art arouses all sorts of emotions which are the accidents of per-sonal associations. Such a critic is an "imperfect critic".

At the other extreme, we have the "abstract and intellectual" type of criticism which derives from Matthew Arnold. This criti-cism falls into the opposite error ; the error of mistaking criticism for the history of ideas. Such critics seek in a work of art for philo-sophical and historical material. They confuse social criticism with literary criticism. The "abstract" or "intellectual" (or the "scienti-fic") critic seeks to remove the emotional element from criticism, and proceeds on the assumption that poetry is the most highly organised form of intellectual activity. Such a definition of poetry separates intelligence and feeling.

Representatives of these two types of criticism are Coleridge and

[1] I am giving here a summary of Eliot's views as expressed in the volume of essays entitled *The Sacred Wood*.

Matthew Arnold. Their criticism is vitiated by the presence of irrelevant material. But Aristotle (and in the present time, the French critic Remy de Gourmont) provides the best examples of the perfect critic. A true literary critic should have no emotions except those which are provoked by the book. Aristotle's criticism is an instance of this. Everything Aristotle says throws light on the literature which he discusses.

The true criticism is a verbal expression of the structure of perceptions formed in a really appreciative mind. Criticism is part of the development of sensibility. The bad criticism is that which gives the simple expression of the emotions provoked by a work of art. Criticism is not mere feeling ; nor is it mere thought. The defect of modern impressionistic criticism is that it is all feeling, and the defect of abstract criticism is that it is all thought.

Introduction to Eliot's Criticism

The Sacred Wood, is Eliot's first important volume of critical essays and is to be considered as an introductory volume. It anticipates serious critical problems, the relation of poetry to the social and spiritual life of man. In the "Introduction" to this book, Eliot further indicates his critical position. He derives many of his ideas from Remy de Gourmont (1858-1915), and he disagrees with Middleton Murry. Murry is a romanticist; Eliot is a classicist.

Eliot maintains that a critic of poetry must have a general idea as to the nature of poetry. In *The Sacred Wood* he tentatively assumes that "poetry is a superior amusement". It is neither "emotion recollected in tranquillity", nor "criticism of life". In criticism we had better begin by assuming that poetry is "excellent words in excellent arrangement and excellent metre." A poem is an organic unit with a life of its own. It is not a mere biographical data. The emotional content of the poem is different from the real emotion in the mind of the poem. At the same time, poetry has something to do with the life, the ideas, and the philosophy of a poet. The relationship between ideas, and poetry is too complex to admit a simple solution. This view is called the impersonal theory of poetry.

Eliot's impersonal theory of poetry is antithetical to that of Wordsworth and Coleridge. According to the latter, poetry is an expression of emotions. The impersonal theory is also against the generalized romantic notion that poetry is the expression of personality. Eliot's impersonal theory of poetry is the most significant theory on the nature of poetic process after Wordsworth's romantic conception of poetry.

The romantic critic tries to discover the nature of poetry by analysing the psychology of the poetic process and by studying the mental operations of the poet. Thus it was that the conception of imagination received great emphasis in romantic criticism. The romantic poetical and critical theories support each other.

Eliot also takes up the critical problem along with the larger issues involved. His theory of criticism is preceded by a doctrine as to the nature of poetry, and enquiries into the nature of related concepts. His ideas find expression in two celebrated essays, "Tradition and the Individual Talent", and the "Function of Criticism".

Tradition and the Individual Talent

This essay attacks the principal conception of the romantic theory of literature. In the romantic theory, poetry is the product of the inspiration of the poet. The poet is essentially a "genius", a highly individualized mind creating poetry through the power of imagination. Thus the personality of the poet is of great importance in poetic creation. And there is a direct correlation between the biography of the poet and his literary career. The more individualistic the life of a poet, the greater his poetry. The "personalist theory of poetry" further postulates freedom from all traditional influences as a necessary pre-condition of artistic creation.

Eliot's essay attacks these very notions. Instead of the notion of "genius", he advances the concept of tradition. Instead of the theory of mind as a shaping agency, he presents a conception in which the mind is a passive receptacle of impressions. Instead of direct expression of the personality of the poet in poetry, he advocates a suppression of the merely personal.

The "Tradition and the Individual Talent" begins by referring to the absence of the traditional element in contemporary writing. Eliot deplores this fact. As a matter of fact, the best part of a poet's work are those in which the traditional elements assert themselves.

Eliot's concept of tradition is not a passive transference of the poetic practices of a previous generation or generations. In this sense "tradition" is to be discouraged. But true tradition is not passive. It cannot be inherited. It can be obtained by much conscious labour. The most important element in tradition is the "historical sense". Eliot defines the historical sense as a "sense of the timeless as well as the temporal and of the timeless and of the temporal together." It further involves the simultaneity of the past. The historical sense makes a writer aware that the whole of European literature from the time of Homer to his own day constitutes a simultaneous order.

No artist has any importance when considered alone. His significance is that of belonging to a tradition. To understand and judge the work of a new poet or artist, we must compare and contrast him with the other poets and artists in the tradition. Eliot maintains that just as the new poet is influenced by " tradition", so the traditional order itself will be affected by the new. What he means is that just as the past writers help us in judging the new so the poet or artist will in turn help us in judging the previous writers and artists. Thus the past is altered by the present, and the present is directed by the past: this, in essence, is Eliot's conception of tradition. Here, as it is clear, tradition becomes a dynamic concept. How does this dynamic tradition influence the writer? Of course, no writer can accept the past completely, nor can he choose one or two special periods. But to be traditional means to be aware of the main currents of art and poetry. The artist must be conscious of the fact that while art never improves, the material of art is never the same. The artist should recognize the fact that, while the mind of Europe changes, improves and develops, such a process of development is of no consequence so far as his art is concerned. Thus the element of dynamic traditionalism makes the artist aware of the tradition of European thought and art in such a way that the artist's awareness of the present is an awareness of the past. Eliot points to the fact that this theory of poetry demands considerable learning and that it is usually held that learning kills sensibility. But one must not mistake essential knowledge for superficial pedantry. And Eliot remarks that Shakespeare acquired more essential history from Plutarch than most men from a whole library.

According to this theory of dynamic traditionalism the artistic process is a process of continual surrender of the artist to something which is geater than himself, namely, the sense of tradition. "The progress of an artist is a continual self-sacrifice, a continual extinction of personality". The artistic process is thus a continual depersonalization, rather an expression and assertion of personality.

This is the central doctrine in the first part of the essay entitled "Tradition and the Individual Talent". In the second, Eliot presents the psychology of the poetic process. The process of composition is compared by Eliot to the process of a chemical reaction.

When a catalytic agent like platinum wire is introduced into a mixture of oxygen and sulphur dioxide, sulphuric acid is formed. This formation takes place only when the platinum is present. But it itself does not undergo any change although without its presence no chemical reaction will take place. The platinum remains inert, neutral, and unchanged. The mind of the poet is the shred of the platinum. It does not undergo any change in the process of composition. It may use biographical material or material from outside. Thus the poem has no relation to the poet. In the writings of young and immature poets, the mind will find expression. But the more perfect the poet, the greater will be the separation between his own artistic creations and his creative mind. The poet has no personality to express. The poet has only a perfected medium— the mind—in which "feelings are at liberty to enter into new combinations".

Thus in the impersonal theory of poetry, criticism and appreciation are directed not upon the poet but upon the poetry. This theory suggests the conception of poetry as a living whole of all the poetry that has ever been written.

Eliot illustrates this theory by applying it to some examples of great poetry.[2] The quality of a poem does not depend on the greatness of emotion which it expresses. It is not the greatness or the

---

[2] Eliot remarks in this essay that poetry is composed out of "emotions" and feelings. Great poetry may be composed of emotions or of feelings only. He gives the example of the Canto XV of the *Inferno* as poetry composed out of feelings only.

Now this distinction which Eliot makes between emotion and feeling seems to be confusing and irrelevant. Nowhere else in his writings is this distinction maintained; neither does he adequately distinguish between the meanings of the two words. This present writer would suggest that this distinction be ignored, for it is no way directly relevant to the impersonal theory of poetry.

intensity of the emotion "but the intensity of the artistic process, the pressure, so to speak, under which the fusion takes place, that counts". Eliot points to Dante's treatment of the episode of Paolo and Francesca. The artistic emotion evoked is different from the actual emotion. The intensity of poetry is different from the intensity of emotion in the situation. The actual emotion and the artistic emotion may be approximate to each other, as in the case of *Othello* where the poetic emotion is the emotion of the protagonist himself. But in any case, "the difference between the art and the event is always absolute". Take, for example, a typically romantic lyric, Keats's "Ode to the Nightingale". It contains a number of feelings which have no direct relevance to the nightingale.

Eliot supports his impersonal theory with reference to philosophy and metaphysics. His philosophical theory repudiates the notion of the substantial unity of the human soul. Thus the poet has no personality to express, but is only a medium. This medium is the mind of the poet in which various impressions and experiences combine to become poetry. These experiences and impressions need not be those which are important to the poet himself. The appeal of a poem does not depend on the event in the life of the poet or the emotions experienced by him.

According to Eliot, the search for new emotions to express causes eccentricity in poetry. It is not the business of the poet to find new emotions. On the other hand, he must use the ordinary ones and transform them into poetry. And even an emotion which the poet has not experienced will serve his purpose. With this premise Eliot attacks Wordsworth's definition of poetry as emotion recollected in tranquillity. For in the composition of poetry, there is neither emotion, nor tranquillity. The poetic process is a process of concentration rather than of recollection, and poetry is the result of a concentration which is neither conscious nor deliberate. The mind of the poet is not deliberately attempting to compress his material. The concentration of poetic process is a passive process. In fact the bad poet attempts to be conscious where he should be unconscious, and unconscious where he should be conscious. His poetry thus becomes too "personal". To quote Eliot :

Poetry is not a turning loose of emotion, but an escape from emotion; it is not the expression of personality, but an escape from personality.

This is Eliot's impersonal theory of poetry. This theory is made the basis for a new criticism. He examines the nature and function of criticism in the essay entitled "The Function of Criticism".

The Function of Criticism[2]

This essay is in four parts. The first part refers back to "The Tradition and the Individual Talent". On the basis of that essay, Eliot tentatively defines criticism to be the commentation and exposition of works of art by means of written words. He rejects the opinions held by Arnold. Criticism, unlike art, *can never be autotelic*. It has a definite function or set of functions. The function of criticism is the "elucidation of a work of art and the correction of taste".

In the second part of "The Function of Criticism" Eliot refers to the views of Middleton Murry. Murry's views are briefly as follow. There is a relation between criticism and social and religious values. Literary Classicism and religious Catholicism are related. The Classicist will trust authority and tradition rather than individual inspiration. Romanticism, Protestantism, social liberalism are related, and they stand in opposition to the Classical Catholic-Conservative tradition. The Romantic Protestant-Liberal obeys no external authority. The only authority he owes allegiance to is the authority of his own conscience, what is called "the inner voice". This is the same thing as the notion of individual inspiration. The true English tradition is this Romantic tradition. The Classical-Catholic tradition is alien to the English people.

In the third part of "The Function of Criticism", Eliot briefly dismisses these views (given above) of Murry.

In the fourth part, Eliot takes up the critical problem in all its aspects. He begins by referring to the distinction usually (and especially made by Matthew Arnold) made between critical ages

[2] This essay is in the nature of a controversy. The views of Eliot in "The Tradition and the Individual Talent" were challenged by Middleton Murry in an article "Romanticism and the Tradition". "The Function of Criticism" is a counter-attack.

The irrelevant portions of this essay are omitted here. This summary only traces Eliot's theory of criticism without referring to Murry's views, when absolutely necessary.

and creative ages. This is a mistake. Criticism and creation cannot
be so neatly separated. Criticism is of great importance to the
poet. Great ages of criticism had also been great ages of creation.
Criticism is of fundamental importance to the creator. A large part
of creation is critical labour. There is a usual tendency to decry
the critical part of the creative activity. But the best part of
the creative labour is the critical labour of analysing, selecting, and
rejecting.

But to say this does not mean the affirmation of the opposite,
namely creation and criticism cannot be separated. While creation
and criticism should not be separated, criticism and creation should
be separated. This is not mere paradox. Creative activity can be
usefully combined with criticism, but critical activity cannot be
combined with creation. In other words *there can never be creative
criticism*. Creative criticism is neither criticism nor creation. Thus
one of the larger functions of criticism is to aid the poet in the
process of composition.

What is the most important equipment for an ideal critic ? Eliot
answers that it is "the sense of fact". Instead of sentimental
emotionalism, what a critic requires is the sense of fact. A knowledge of fact can never mislead anyone. Those who mislead are
those who supply opinion or fancy instead of facts. Eliot cites the
example of Coleridge and Goethe who read their own personal
opinions into Shakespeare's characters. Even the function of
interpretation itself is not so important. Genuine interpretation
consists in presenting the facts about a work of art. This is also why
the criticism of the practising poet of his own poetry is in a sense
superior to the interpretative criticism of others. How can we
confirm "interpretation" by external evidence ? This is not possible.
Therefore "interpretation" can degenerate into mere verbal
jugglery. The chief tools of criticism are comparison and analysis.
A good critic uses facts concerning a work of art for its analysis.
He compares works of art.

Eliot adds a note of caution. We are, he says, not the servants
of facts but its masters. Mere fact-hunting is not criticism. For
example, the discovery of Shakespeare's laundry bills may not
be very useful. But then scholarship in any form, however humble,
can be of some use to a critic who has mastered the art of criticism.

Further Notes on Eliot's Theory of Criticism

Eliot's reflections on the nature and function of criticism lie scattered in several of his works. In *The Use of Poetry and the Use of Criticism*, Eliot still further elaborates on the nature of criticism.

According to Eliot, there are two kinds of criticism. One type of criticism seeks to find out what poetry is, the other type attempts to answer the question: Is this a good poem? These two types may be called the theoretical and the practical types of criticism. These two types of criticism are in fact inseparable from each other. Any important critic who has produced some influence (like Aristotle, for example) has also attempted to answer both questions. Wordsworth, while explaining the nature of his poetry has answered the general question : What is poetry?

Eliot points out that the "rudiment of criticism lies in the ability to select a good poem and reject a bad poem." It is an important conviction of Eliot that criticism is as inevitable as poetry itself. In "The Tradition and the Individual Talent", he briefly alluded to this. It had been (and it still is) a fashion to decry criticism. And also, students of poetry make a distinction between critical ages and creative ages. Eliot rejects all such gross assumptions. He points out that to ask 'what poetry is?' is to pose the critical question. This is a unique feature in a great poet to stress the need of criticism for creation. Eliot affirms that there is a significant relation between the best poetry and the best criticism of the same age. "The age of criticism is also the age of poetry."

There is an essay entitled "The Frontiers of Criticism" in his latest volume of essays *On Poetry and Poets*. In this essay, Eliot examines the limits of criticism from several angles. It was one of his earliest assumptions that criticism can never be an autotelic activity, and that it has functions beyond the mere interpretations of literary works. In this essay, these special functions are briefly considered.

In Eliot's "The Function of Criticism", the theory of criticism presented was purely literary. He explained the nature of criticism in relation to the nature of poetry. But Eliot was also aware that there could never be "pure literary criticism". A critic interested only in pure literature will become too abstract to be of any general interest. Certainly the literary critic must help his readers to understand and enjoy the poem. But the critic has other functions as well. "The critic must be a whole man, a man with convictions and principles, and of knowledge and experience of life." But at the same time there are "frontiers for criticism beyond which the critic must not go."

Criticism must certainly make use of related fields of study, like psychology, sociology, anthropology, philosophy, and theology. Coleridge has set an example of the use of philosophy in criticism. But then the critic must not make his criticism a mere commentary on other subjects. In this case he ceases to be a literary critic. The other limit to criticism lies in the method of explanation. The recent school of impressionistic criticism has stressed subjective appreciation as the function of criticism. In reaction against this the new criticism stresses the process of explanation. Here again, it is necessary to apply a limit.

The modern interpretative critic uses several methods of explanation. There is the biographical method. There is the psychological method. There is the method of explanation with reference to the source or origins of a work of art. All these types of criticism, when carried too far, cease to be criticism. Eliot cites several relevant examples of these. There is the criticism of his own poems by critics using the knowledge of the origin of the poem as a tool for interpretation. These explanations have been misleading. Then there is the famous example of John Livingstone Lowes's book on Coleridge (*The Road to Xanadu*), which again seeks to explain *The Rime of the Ancient Mariner* through the origin of the images and phrases of the poem in the wide and varied readings of Coleridge. But such an investigation, Eliot maintains, is beyond the strict scope of criticism. Herbert Read's book on Wordsworth is another relevant example of criticism trespassing beyond its proper domain.

Eliot concludes by remarking that just as thirty years ago, the great emphasis placed on appreciation vitiated much of impressionistic criticism, so today, the exaggerated importance placed on scholarship tends to vitiate criticism in the other direction. What is important to note here is that the only true type of criticism which Eliot wholly approves of is what is called "workshop criticism", the criticism of a poet upon his own poetry and that of others. This is no doubt a very restricted view. But the truth is that there is no finality of explanation on the nature of criticism. Just as different ages inspire different types of poetry, so also different generations bring different criteria of judgement and methods of interpretation.

Concluding Notes on Eliot's Criticism

Eliot is the most influential critic of the twentieth century. He is likely to become one of the greatest of English critics. Like Coleridge before his time, he widened the scope of critical enquiry, and attempted to re-examine some of the fundamental issues relating to the criticism of arts. Thus he is important as a theoretical critic. His method of criticism has influenced the contemporary generation considerably. His notion that a work of literature is an "objective correlative" has been the principal critical conception employed by many critics of the modern schools.

The notion of the "objective correlative", (which Eliot defines in "Hamlet and His Problem" in *The Sacred Wood*) implies the conception that poetry is a verbal structure which embodies a set of emotions or an emotion which the poet wants to communicate. Note especially that these are not the emotions experienced by the poet. They are only artistic emotions. This theory refutes the notion that there is a relation between the poem and its author. Having thus separated the poem from the poet, this theory further gives to a poem an independent status of existence. The poem does not communicate any meaning or experience, but is its own meaning and experience. Modern criticism seeks to find out to what extent has a given poem succeeded in being an integral unit.

Another conception which has been influential in modern criticism is the notion of the dissociation of sensibility. Dealing with the metaphysical poets, Eliot points out that between the time of Milton and the modern period, a separation between thought and feeling took place in human consciousness. The importance of intellect was exaggerated. To Eliot, this separation was disastrous as far as art and poetry are concerned. It may be mentioned that this notion of the dissociation of sensibility is untenable. Eliot uses it as a convenient stick to beat those whom he dislikes. He attacks Milton on this score. He praises Donne and the Metaphysicals because they have a unified sensibility.

Eliot's judicial criticism has resulted in some important revaluations. He has enhanced the prestige of the metaphysical poets.

He has reinterpreted the Augustans, and did them some justice, while in the revaluation (if not devaluation) of Shakespeare and Milton he did considerable injustice.

We have to bear in mind that Eliot's criticism is primarily workshop criticism, the criticism resulting from his own experience of writing poetry. Thus the merits and defects of his criticism are those of the practitioner of verse, and his criticism is therefore more useful to the aspiring poet than to the lay men. To say, this is not to condemn Eliot's criticism, but to point out its extreme technical usefulness. At the same time, to the general reader he has been useful in correcting the prejudices which the previous critics had erected in the evaluation of the previous ages. This is especially true in the field of his dramatic criticism. His critical pronouncements on the nature of the poetic drama, and the relation between poetry and drama have some of the most illuminating comments on these problems.

Eliot's Dramatic Criticism

Eliot's growing interest in the poetry of drama has culminated in his interest in the poetic drama. His poetical development shows a steadily developing dramatic art. Towards the close of his literary career, he concentrated his attention exclusively on the drama. Whether we have gained a minor dramatist and lost a major poet in this progress of Eliot from poetry to drama is not our immediate concern. Whether Eliot is a great dramatist or not may even be disputable. But his dramatic criticism is of the highest quality.

In the essay entitled "Four Elizabethan Dramatists" (1924) we find the main tendency of his dramatic criticism. He indicates a point of departure from the usual criticism of the Elizabethans made popular in the nineteenth century by Charles Lamb and Swinburne. In Lamb's dramatic criticism, we have the origin of the deplorable separation between drama and poetry or drama and literature. Lamb paid attention to the poetic qualities of Elizabethan drama, and neglected the function of the plays on the stage. Thus arises the modern opinion (which Eliot rejects) that drama and poetry are two separate things.

Later, William Archer, and also Swinburne held two other extreme views about drama. To Swinburne, the play always exists only as literature. To Archer, the play need not be literature at all. Their views though superficially antithetical, proceed from the same separation of drama and literature.

Eliot opposes this distinction. He maintains that the dramatic element and the literary element in a play are integral to it and therefore inseparable from each other. Mr. Archer condemns all Elizabethan drama except that of Shakespeare. According to Archer, the Elizabethan drama is devoid of realism.

Here lies, (Archer explains *In The Old Drama and The New*) the decisive superiority of the modern drama, especially that of Bernard Shaw, over the Elizabethans. But according to Eliot, the principal defect of the Elizabethans is the same as that of the moderns, that there is too much realism in it. And this is a defect from which even Shakespeare is not wholly free. This effort at realism itself springs from the absence of a dramatic convention. What is essential for the playwright is that he should work within the framework of a dramatic convention.

Eliot points out that the great advantage of the Greek dramatists was that they had a convention. Aeschylus, for instance, did not aim at too much realism. In his play, we do not find that some parts are poetry, and the rest drama. Every part bears an integral relation to the rest. "The imitation of life" is circumscribed. Even the imitation of ordinary speech is carefully employed. Here Eliot lays down a general aesthetic principle which is of fundamental importance.

Life is the material of art. At the same time the dramatist should abstract from life as a precondition of his art.

Thus there is no mirroring of the problem of life in a play. A play is a self-consistent work of art. This theory has to be borne in mind in the study of Eliot's criticism of drama. Eliot explains his doctrine of dramatic convention. It is not a particular convention that is advocated. It (the convention) may be a new selection or structure or distortion in subject matter or technique, any form or rhythm imposed upon the world of action. Eliot then examines the problem of dramatic speech.

The essay "Rhetoric and Poetic Drama" is a defence of the use of rhetoric in drama. Thus it deals with the problem of dramatic medium. In the modern usage rhetoric has a bad connotation. It covers all kinds of bad writing. It is writing used to produce an impression through pomposities in style. A standard criticism levelled against the drama of the seventeenth century is that its style is too rhetorical and therefore artificial. Modern drama, on the other hand, in seeking to improve upon this defect, used the conversational style. This trend is in keeping with the tendency towards realism. The oratorical and the rhetorical styles of writing are avoided.

Against this tendency Eliot advances some arguments. It is impossible to use the "conversational style" in drama. Because conversation as such has no style. The moment the dramatist attempts at any form of style, even the colloquial, it ceases to be natural and realistic. Moreover, the conversational style can become monotonous. It can never provide that variety of style necessary to represent various situations and emotions. Thus both in theme and language, Eliot opposes realism.

A Dialogue on Dramatic Poetry

Eliot discusses some important problems relating to modern drama in the form of a dialogue. The form of, this dialogue is much indebted to Dryden's *Essay on Dramatic Poesy*. Indeed, even in theme, it resembles Dryden's work. The dialogue is among seven persons who are referred to merely as A. B. C., etc. It is clear that the interlocutor E is Eliot himself, for through E Eliot is only expressing some views in a more concise form which he has expressed elsewhere.

The fundamental problems discussed are the problems of the relationship between drama and religion and ethical values, the problems of the form of drama, the relation of poetry to drama, Archer's criticism of the old and the new drama, and the nature of the unities. But the most important problem under discussion is the possibility of poetic drama in the modern age. Let us sum up here the views of Eliot.

The problems connected with the drama have become many and complex. The ancient critics of drama did not bother very much about the contemporary ethics or religious values. They had only one type of drama to consider. And the social ethos was more or less fixed. But the modern critic has too many problems to discuss. Drama is not mere amusement.

Among these problems the most important is the form of the drama. If there is to be a future for drama, then a suitable form has to be evolved. Take the form of the Russian ballet. The ballet revives the more formal element in drama which the modern age needs. And the question of verse drama versus prose drama is essentially a question of the degree of form. The usual opinion that verse is an artificial element in drama is wrong.

People usually think that the emotional range and the realistic representation of truth are both circumscribed by verse. They argue that only prose can give the entire range of actuality of emotions and represent reality. But this is wrong. The human mind in intense emotion tends to express itself in verse. Thus prose drama merely emphasises the ephemeral and the superficial. If we want the permanent and the universal we must express ourselves in verse.

How does Eliot combine the form of the ballet with verse? It is in the sense that the ballet has a permanent form. As has been pointed out, the form is essential for drama. Take the case of the religious ritual. Drama cannot afford to divert from the ritual and liturgy of the church, as it had its origin in religious liturgy. Religious liturgy provides drama with a suitable form. Eliot maintains that the perfect form of the drama is to be found in the ceremony of the Mass. But to say this is not to equate drama and the Mass. The Mass cannot replace drama, any more than drama can replace the Mass. A devout person attending a Mass is not similar to the one attending a drama.

After this initial discussion, the dialogue examines the problem of poetry and drama. What is the relation between the two? Here Archer's theory is examined. Archer made a separation between poetry and drama. He condemned the Elizabethan and Jacobean dramatists for mixing up poetry and drama. According to the same principle, Shakespeare himself ought to be condemned. But "there is no relation between poetry and drama. All poetry tends towards drama and all drama towards poetry."

According to Eliot, a critic like Archer really confuses the issue. The real defects of the Elizabethan and Jacobean drama are not its poetry and its lack of ethical and religious conventions. The real defect is the absence of a *dramatic convention*. This is true even today. It is the lack of artistic conventions which stands in the way of poetic drama today. Eliot sees a definite future for the poetic drama. None of the modern fatalistic philosophies of life can suppress man's permanent craving for poetic drama.

It may be mentioned here that some recent philosophies like Bergsonism and dialectical materialism have considerably tended to suppress the idea of the individual. Bergson's emergent evolution subordinates the individual to a cosmic process of evolution. Every phase of human development, and every action of the individual is accounted for in terms of the evolutionary hypothesis, and the biological motivation. Thus the ineffable mystery and poetry inherent in life are too easily explained away. Bernard Shaw is the worst offender in this. In placing stress on the economic and social problems Shaw removed the poetic element from life. Besides the evolutionary hypothesis, the prevalence of a dialectical philosophy of history has also strengthened the move towards realism in literature. For a genuine revival of drama, especially poetic drama, we have to reject these fatalistic philosophies of life, widen the scope of the drama, and evolve a new dramatic convention.

Eliot's insistence on the need for dramatic convention leads him to a defence of Dryden's theory of dramatic Unities given in the *Essay of Dramatic Poetry*. In Eliot's "Dialogue on Dramatic Poetry", E (Eliot's spokesman in the Dialogue) upholds Dryden's explanation of the Unities. Dryden's view is the soundest and the most commonsense view possible for his time and his place. Eliot maintains that he personally prefers for the future drama the Unities because they help to create more concentration. "The Unities make for intensity, as does verse rhythm".

The central doctrine which emerges from Eliot's theory of poetic drama is the doctrine of dramatic convention. He rejects the contemporary trends towards realism in theme and style. He lays down as axiomatic that, while actuality is the raw material of art, art should always abstract from actuality.

The Themes of Poetic Drama

The dramatic quality of Eliot's poetry has already been referred to. Eliot's interest in drama is shown by the large number of essays dealing with the old dramatists and the new. It is not only the form of the drama which engages his attention, but also the media of dramatic communication. This brings him to the question of the use of poetry in drama. Poetic drama is not merely drama with poetry superadded for embellishment. Eliot holds that poetry which does not justify itself dramatically should not be used in a play. Thus no play should be written in verse for which prose is adequate.

Eliot examines the nature of dramatic prose. The assumption that prose brings the dialogue of drama nearer to actual speech is wrong. The prose style of dramatic dialogue is as remote from the language of normal communication. Thus Eliot makes a triple distinction between speech, prose and verse. He further points out that a mixture of prose and verse should be avoided, because the transition from one medium to the other jolts the audience.

But then the Elizabethan dramatist mixed prose and verse successfully. The reason is that to the Elizabethan audience a mixture of prose and verse was more familiar. Language was then at its earliest stage of development. But today, however, we should strictly avoid such a practice. All parts of the drama should be in verse. For this, a verse form of wide range must be developed in which everything that has to be described and said can be described. Such form when used with skill can develop itself into poetry in the most dramatic situation. This is especially true when the poetic drama has to deal with contemporary themes. Eliot advocates that even the most conventional part of a play should be written in verse with a rhythm very similar to that of normal speech. This point is illustrated by Eliot with reference to the opening scenes of *Hamlet*. We hardly notice that the scene is in verse. Even the ordinary questions and answers are in verse. But the rhythm is so modulated to avoid any discontinuity.

Eliot admits the fact that a poetic drama can be written in prose, *e.g.*, the plays of John Millington Synge. But the language of Synge is based on the Celtic idiom which is naturally poetic in rhythm and speech. But the prose-poetic dramatist is comparatively at a disadvantage in the selection of themes. He must select themes which too are poetic. But a verse-poetic dramatist has a wider range of selection. For instance, Shakespeare has managed to say the most humdrum things in verse.

The use of poetry in drama thus finally leads to the problem of poetic communication. This is examined in the eassy "The Three Voices of Poetry". This indeed is a confusing title. The first voice refers to lyrical poetry, the second to narrative poetry, the third to dramatic poetry. Communication through the third voice presents the problem of dramatic communication. In making a character speak in a drama, the dramatist must achieve simultaneously, communication on two levels. The character must be understood by the other characters and by the audience. This is the complex difficulty of the third voice.

In a play, there are several characters differing in education, intelligence and social habits. Therefore, the use of one poetical style becomes unnatural. Nor can one character, however, important, be given all the poetry. Poetic speech must be found for all the characters, and poetry must be widely distributed. The author is limited by this requirement. Further, even if a suitable form of poetry is given to each character, the poet writing for theatre must see to it that the poetry helps to extract the utmost emotional intensity from that situation. In other words, poetry must forward the action. The author must extract poetry from the character, as it were, and not impose his poetry on the character.

In "The Three Voices of Poetry" Eliot advances the hypothesis that dramatic monologue cannot create character. For character is made in action and in communication between imaginary people. Thus a poet speaking in the first voice (in his own voice as Browning does) will not succeed in bringing a character to life. The first voice can only mimic a character already known to us.

The peculiar advantage of the poetic drama is that here all the three voices are audible (see "The Three Voices of Poetry). First, we have the individual utterances of each character as belonging to that character. Then there are places where the author and the character seem to speak in unison. Eliot points out the great fascination of the line.

"To-morrow and to-morrow and to-morrew..." lies in the fact that here the character and the author together express the same idea. Finally, in the poetic drama, there are the more impersonal utterances like "Ripeness is all".

Eliot here has examined all the serious issues involved in the use of poetry in drama and the advantages of the manner of communication (the third voice) peculiar to the poetic drama.

In "Poetry and Drama" he deals with the subject matter of poetic drama.

Poetic drama should not compete with prose drama and realistic drama in using contemporary material from actual life. Of course, even this can be used by a competent verse dramatist. But properly speaking, the verse dramatist should deal with those fringes and outermost reaches of human consciousness (which are unattainable to the prose dramatist) beyond the range of our ordinary actions and emotions in life. There is an area of interest which becomes known to us only during moment of meditation and reflection. Poetic drama should deal with those areas of consciousness, without at the same time losing contact with the external world.

As against the prose dramatist (Shaw, for example) whose interest is in the analyses of socio-economic problems, Eliot believes that it is the function of all art (especially of poetic drama) to bring us to a condition of serenity, stillness, and reconciliation, by "imposing a credible order upon ordinary reality", and thereby eliciting some perception of an order in reality.

Eliot's Theories Applied to His Own Dramas

It is instructive to see whether Eliot's own dramas conform to the general theory he lays down. Eliot is careful to tell us that his dramatic criticism is the by-product of his own dramatic career just as his poetic criticism is a product of his poetry workshop. (See "Poetry and Drama" and "The Three Voices of Poetry".)

Eliot's earliest attempt at dramatic composition is the fragment *Sweeney Agonistes—Fragments of an Aristophanic Melodrama*. In this fragment Eliot builds up the character of Sweeney through dialogue. The fragment reveals the growth of lust and carnal love in Sweeney in a contemporary setting. The verse style is colloquial. His next play is *The Rock*. This was a spectacle, and he had only to write the choral passages in it. The action and themes were already fixed uopn. Thus as he tells us, it is not a play of the "third voice", but only of the second. It is with *Murder in the Cathedral* that we come to a major tragedy, if it can be called a tragedy. This is one of the greatest plays of the modern age. The test of Eliot's dramatic theory lies in this.

Murder in the Cathedral is a poetic tragedy. It has a historical theme, the murder of Thomas A' Becket for its plot. But the plot has been modified to suit a modern audience. In "Poetry and Drama", Eliot tells us that in this play he wanted to concentrate on death, and martyrdom. Thus the theme is sufficiently poetic, being one of universal interest and relevance to any age. These are subjects which we become aware of in a momentary detachment from action.

In the search for a dramatic convention Eliot has arrived at the use of the traditional Greek device of the Chorus. It is on account of the use of Chorus that Eliot is able to dramatize themes like death and martyrdom. In Eliot's use of the Chorus, the Chorus becomes not only a commentator on the action, but also a partici-pator. In *Murder in the Cathedral*, the chorus consists of the women of Canterbury who thus represent the realistic contemporary environment.

The verse of the drama is not archaic. It is "netural" as Eliot calls it. He imitates the versification of *Everyman*. He varies the rhythm suitably. There are only two prose-passages. The *Murder in the Cathedral* is a remarkable achievement, and to a great extent vindicates Eliot's theory.

His next play *The Family Reunion* has a contemporary theme. It is the home-coming of a son Harry, to celebrate the birthday of the mother. All the family and relations are assembled to receive the son. But he arrives as a split personality, haunted by a guilty conscience. The essential theme of the play is the origin of moral guilt and sin—themes again unsuitable for realistic plays. As in the previous play the use of the Chorus helps Eliot dramatically to objectify the split consciousness of the hero. In this play Eliot's major attempt is to find a versification closer to contemporary speech. His lines of varying length and varying number of syllables, with a caesura and three stresses achieves this object. What he says in "Poetry and Drama" that poetic drama should enter into overt competition with prose drama becomes true in *The Family Reunion*.

It becomes truer in the case of his next play *The Cocktail Party* whose title resembles a realistic comedy. Yet it is no comedy, indeed, it is intensely tragic. It is a complex play with such concen-tration which a poetic play alone could extract out of a set of given incidents and situations constituting plot. The theme of the plot varies from domestic dispute, conjugal disharmony, to martyrdom and death. This play has no chorus and no ghosts. The source of his story lies in the *Alcestis* of Euripides. The versification of the play comes very near to prose. Indeed the rhythms are so distributed that if the lines had not been printed as poetry, they could be easily mistaken for normal speech.

The success of these plays on the stage confirms Eliot's theory that the craving for poetic drama is permanent in human nature. Of course there can never be any final theory about the poetic drama. Each age, each historical situation with its own special complexities, must interpret the reality of experience in its own way.

CHAPTER NINE

CRITICISM : RECENT AND MODERN

1. Twentieth-Century English (British) Criticism. 2. T. E. Hulme : The Father of Modern Classicism. 3. The Bloomsbury Philosophy and Aesthetics. 4. I. A. Richards : Science and Poetry. 5. F. R. Leavis and the Scrutiny Tradition. 6. New Criticism. 7. Yvor Winters.

Twentieth-Century English (British) Criticism

The progress of English literary criticism from the tradition of Arnold and Pater to "New criticism" is astonishingly rapid. Twentieth-century English criticism shows an extraordinary vigour both in the search for new critical standards and in the task of re-interpretation and reassessment. At the turn of the century, the influences of Arnold and Pater were still dominant. In one sense they are still influential. Both Arnold and Pater as critics had definite points of view as regards literature and criticism. Arnold's point of view is opposed to that of Pater. Arnold was both a critic of society and literature. He sought to combine the achievements of the human spirit in a synthesis which he called "culture". Pater on the other hand, was a pure aesthetist. He sought to separate life and literature, and in his criticism, we have the fullest theoretical support for a movement like "Art for Art's sake".

In the critics who immediately succeeded Arnold and Pater, we do not find any precise points of view or definite commitments. To quote from the *Dictionary of World Literature* :

The clear-cut statement of a point of view regarding the nature of literary value, as in many eighteenth-century critics, is rare at the beginning of the twentieth century. In a critic like George Saintsbury (1845-1933), indeed, tolerance is almost indistinguishable from lack of principle ....Their methods were partly impressionistic, partly scholarly, i. e., an "appreciation" of a work or an author would consist of a fairly subjective account of the critic's reaction to the subject, some attempt to demonstrate the organisation of the work and some facts about the author's life, habits, and points of view.

The most important names in criticism at the beginning of the twentieth century were, apart from Saintsbury, Edmund Gosse, Edward Dowden, Sidney Colvin, W. J. Courthope, A. C. Bradley, C. H. Herford, W. P. Ker, J. W. Mackail, and Andrew Lang. It is impossible to assign them under appropriate classifications for the simple reason that none of them had a very clearly defined critical theory or procedure. Their critical habits varied between the idealist Coleridgean methods of A. C. Bradley at one end, and the biographical, scholarly procedure of Sidney Colvin or Edmund Gosse.

The two important critics of the Edwardian age are G. K. Chesterton and Mr. Belloc. One hesitates, by the modern standards of criticism, to call either of them great. As T. S. Eliot points out, Chesterton has an equipment of ideas, without the analytical ability. Accordingly, his criticism seldom touches on art or poetry. His criticism, remains on the level of detached discussions concerning the "ideas" in a book. Chesterton's criticism is at its best in the volume of essays *The Heretics* dealing with some modern authors. He has a brilliant style, full of paradoxes.

In the reaction against the Edwardian critics lies the origin of some powerful trends in modern criticism. This reaction was started chiefly through the influence of a group of writers which included among others T. E. Hulme and Ezra Pound who called their new literary movement "Imagism". Of this group T. E. Hulme was the central figure. His thoughts continued to influence critical ideas till the middle of the twentieth century. Through him we have the new current of critical classicism.

T. E. Hulme : The Father of Modern Classicism

Hulme's contribution to modern thought is great. His life, as well as his work, ended prematurely on the battlefield—a fitting, though tragic, end to the militant career of a relentless crusade against contemporary ideas. Hulme's posthumous influence emanates from a few short poems and a comparatively thin volume of essays entitled *Speculations* (edited by Herbert Read, 1924). In spite of the slender bulk of his literary output, his ideas dominated the critical scene for at least two decades. Many great poets, including T. S. Eliot, are indebted to him. His thought is likely to survive for a long time to come. It might be argued that Hulme's categories cannot be accepted. His premises might not be above criticism. His conclusions might appear untenable and far-fetched. He was also not the first to deliver a broadside against Victorian ideals. But then, Hulme's claim to fame does not lie in these things. He has introduced a peculiar and original point of view in literary thought. It is this originality that makes him an important figure.

The Hulmean point of view is often designated by various names. It may be called the religious, or the classical, or the tragic point of view. If a compound epithet is permitted, the word "religious-classical-tragic" would be more appropriate. Hulme's position not merely includes all these but synthesises the essential factors of each. It may be contrasted with the "liberal-humanistic romantic" tradition. So far as Hulme is concerned, there is a definite antithesis between these two traditions. It is not a question of difference. The latter is completely wrong. Romanticism is allied to humanism and both are related to liberalism. The classical attitude cannot be separated from a world-view comprising the religious and the tragic perception of the ultimate finitude of man.

Thomas Earnest Hulme was an Englishman. He was born in 1883. After a high-school education he entered Cambridge University which he left without taking a degree. He toured Canada and Europe studying philosophy. He got enlisted in the army in 1914 and was killed in action in September 1917.

Only three works appeared while he was alive. The first was his translation of Bergson's *Introduction to Metaphysics*, and the second was his translation with a critical introduction, of George Sorel's *Reflections on Violence*. The only other work of Hulme published during his life time consisted of a few articles and a group of five poems, printed with the title *Complete Poetical Works of T.E. Hulme*. The main tendencies of Hulme's thought were contained in his notes which were published by H. Read with the title *Speculations*, the sub-title of which is *Essays on Humanism and Philosophy of Art.* It is an indictment against humanism and the conclusions that emerge from a consistently humanistic position.

At the dawn of the twentieth century, religions—of all varieties—stood discredited. Science was responsible for this. After the Renaissance, the religious attitude had seldom been considered intellectually respectable. John Donne's lines :

> The new philosophy calls all in doubt
> The element of fire is put out....

inaugurate an era of doubt and scepticism. The seventeenth century had not achieved any religious synthesis. The eighteenth century had enthroned "Reason" and dethroned "Faith". The Pantheism of the romantic period too began to take shape towards the latter half of the eighteenth century. When Wordsworth said that "an impulse from the vernal wood...can teach me more than all the sages can", he was only affirming an article of the Pantheistic creed. Keats meant much the same thing when he wrote : Beauty is truth, truth beauty.

The Idealism and the poetic Pantheism of the romantic period yielded to the mid-Victorian faith in progress. The evolutionary philosophies had a common assumption about the ultimate perfectibility of human nature. The distinction between the different species of beings and that between the organic and the inorganic worlds had vanished. Thus there was a general principle of continuity in the nineteenth century. Hulme calls formulation of this principle, the crowning achievement of the nineteenth century. Hulme opposes this principle of continuity with his principle of discontinuity. Continuity is implied in the popular conception of evolution. It has finally come to assume the "status of a category". The contradictions and antinomies inherent in the Renaissance doctrines were caused by the ignoring of the presence of discontinuity. The reinstatement as a basal doctrine of the principle of discontinuity is Hulme's distinctive achievement. His anti-romanticism, anti-humanism, and anti-liberalism emerge from this doctrine.

By discontinuity or "gap", Hulme means the absolutely unbridgeable, qualitative differences between certain regions of being. There is, for example, a discontinuity between the inorganic world (the world of mathematical and physical sciences) and the organic world (of biology, physiology, and history). Both these worlds are again absolutely different from the world of ethical and religious values. Hulme graphically presents the distinction as follows. Consider the three areas marked off on a flat surface by two concentric circles. The outermost region corresponds to the world of matter, the innermost to that of the religious categories, and the intermediate corresponds to the organic life. Each is self-enclosed, and there is no passage from one to the other by a slow continuous progress. In other words, matter can never produce organic life, and organic life cannot by any means form the basis of explanation for the ethical and religious values. Hulme proceeds to expound a consistent religious aesthetic and literary theory based on the doctrine of "gaps" or "chasms".

One direct corollary to the above doctrine is the belief in the imperfectibility and radical insufficiency of man. Man is a finite being of limited capabilities. He can only strive towards perfection. But perfection is beyond him and will always remain so. Christian theology has the correct conception of human nature, as it makes a rigid distinction between the purely human and the purely divine. We know, on grounds of historical evidence, that man's moral condition has not appreciably improved since the beginning of recorded times. Theology explains it by the dogma of original sin. It affirms the radical sinfulness of man. An attitude embracing the dogma of original sin and the tragic sense of human finitude, Hulme calls the religious attitude, in contradistinction to the humanistic attitude built on an exaggerated notion of human perfectibility and human goodness. For Hulme, the antithesis is between Religion and Humanism on the one hand, and between Classicism and Romanticism, on the other, which leads to "spineless liberalism" and false Utopianism in politics. The doctrine of progress, too, becomes an exploded fallacy. Hulme advocates a return to religion. A civilisation built on humanistic foundations, as ours is, is in total annihilation. If culture and civilisation are to be redirected from the road to ruin, discipline and order, both ethical and political, are essential. Hence the need for a religious revival. Order is not negative and destructive but creative and liberating. When order and discipline are imposed on the realm of letters we have classicism. Thus religion and classicism are related.

Humanism is a word which is rather loosely applied to a number of distinct schools of thought, all of which have one factor in common. They have the welfare of man as their fundamental consideration. And man is the measure of the universe. In letters as in religion, the humanistic movement recognises nothing greater than man. If belief in God is dispensed with, then Religion becomes a mere quest after the "good life".

Hulme cannot tolerate humanism. According to him, it seeks to appropriate "the perfection that belongs to the non-human". "It thus creates the bastard conception of personality. In literature it leads to romanticism." Historically, the mediaeval period is characterised by the dominance of the religious outlook. Humanism dominates the period since Renaissance.

Hulme's definition of classicism, while interesting, is peculiar. Classical art is that which expresses belief in objective ethical values. It must have as its material, the specific human predicament, involving human limitedness, man's frustration, his imperfectibility. Nature and natural forms cannot afford any delight. Natural forms must be subjected to the rigidity, the hard precision of geometric patterns. Hulme instances Indian, Byzantine and Egyptian art as examples of classicism. In poetry, Pope and Horace represent it. The essence of poetry for Hulme is that it must suit certain fixed forms. The romantic emphasis on spontaneity, on the expression of emotion, and on originality is all nonsense.

Nor is the romantic theory of imagination quite tenable. Imagination is only an act of apprehension. And "fancy" is the instrument through which this act of apprehension takes place. Fancy, thus, has a new role to play, supplementing the function of imagination.

Hulme is not describing the classical art of the past with a nostalgic longing for days of bygone glory. He is only stating the feelings of dissatisfaction and disillusion current in his own day. The romantic tradition had become devitalised with its "heroics of romantic poetry, its melodramatic attitudes, cosmic posturings, and wild pursuits of the impossible." In the decay of romanticism was also implied the disappearance of hedonism, utopian liberalism, pragmatism and modernism in religion. Hulme's great and laudable endeavour had been to find a synthetic world-view. His religious categories were formulated for this definite purpose.

In his own day, as in ours, there was so much specialisation that

knowledge had been compartmentalised. Such compartmentalisa-
tion occasions the dichotomy between life and thought, between
subject and object that we see now. Nowhere was this dichotomy
more visible than in philosophy. He criticises the conception of
philosophy itself as a discipline which, while dealing with the human
and personal problems, tries to attain the precision and imper-
sonality of scientific investigation. The consequent fallacy can be
removed only by looking upon philosophy as a mixed subject.
Otherwise philosophers become "something human with quite
inhumanly sharp weapons".

Philosophy and its "canons" must be subjected to a severe
examination. Most philosophies since the Renaissance have a
"family resemblance". They present certain conclusions concerning the ultimate destiny of man. The words of Croce, "the legitimate mystery of the infinite progress and infinite perfectibility of
man" strike the optimistic key-note of the philosophical conclusions
since the Renaissance.

Do we have sufficient historical evidence for this belief ? The
progress of events since the beginning of the twentieth century
tends to shatter philosophical self-complacency. That human
society itself behaves like an insane person has been recognised
by even Erich Fromm, whose diagnosis and remedy for social
ills betray a markedly humanistic approach. There are symp-
toms of dissatisfaction everywhere, in philosophy, in politics,
in art and in literature. Scepticism and confusion are the order
of the day. In the poems of Hardy, A. E. Houseman, Hopkins
and W. H. Auden, in the novels of Kafka, Huxley, James Joyce,
Virginia Wolfe and Rex Warner, there is a prevailing sense of
anxiety and fear.

It is against this background that one must assess the significance
of Hulme's advocacy of the religious categories. The function of
religion is the "conservation of values". While Ethics deals with
certain absolute values it is not concerned with their preservation
in society. The function of the philosophy, of religion and of ethics
must be kept separate. The region of religious knowledge is a "special
region of knowledge, marked out from all other spheres". In this
sphere, the starting point is the understanding of man's true
nature, purified from the mystic halo of glory with which romanticism and uncritical humanism have invested it. Self-knowledge
is the alpha and the omega of the religious attitude. Self-knowledge

reveals a tragic predicament, a gulf between the infinite and the finite, the temporal and the eternal. Art and literature must reveal this "gap" and its awareness is for Hulme, the beginning of wisdom.

The Bloomsbury Philosophy and Aesthetics

Modern criticism and aesthetic theory have both been considerably influenced by what is called "The Bloomsbury Tradition". The most important writers belonging to this tradition are E. M. Forster, Virginia Woolf, Lytton Strachey, Clive Bell and Roger Fry. To this group also belong the economist Maynard Keynes, and the philosopher G. E. Moore.

The philosopher whose doctrines had inspired this group of writers was G. E. Moore. His book *Principia Ethica* defined the Bloomsbury attitude to life and governed its actions. *Principia Ethica* was its Bible. The central doctrine which emerges from this book is the religion of the good life. In this book, Moore, after critically examining the various notions of the ethical good, advances his theory of the moral 'good'. According to him, the conception of the good is a simple, indefinable and unanalysable object of thought. Further, he maintains, that many ideas concerning values in ethics are complex "wholes". And these "wholes" themselves cannot be analysed further into its constituent elements. In a "value", the whole is more than the sum of its parts. This is called the principle of organic unity. For example, "the consciousness of a beautiful object" is the sum of two elements, "consciousness" and "beauty". Neither "consciousness by itself", nor "beauty by itself" has any great value. But the "consciousness of the beautiful object as a whole" possesses a greater value than the sum of its parts. Moore further concludes from this principle of organic unity that all things of intrinsic value are complex wholes. Thus the two essential principles of this thought are the postulates that the good is indefinable, and that in every notion of good there is the principle of organic unity. All the great values of life are complex organic unities.

Among these, "personal affections and aesthetic enjoyments include all the greatest, and by far the greatest goods we can imagine." Here we have the germ of the philosophy of aesthetics and criticism held by the Bloomsbury writers. Appreciation of beauty is the most essential constituent of the good.

Of the two ultimate values "personal relationships" or "love" and "aesthetic enjoyments", aesthetic enjoyment is more permanent. Love can change, or disappear. But art and beauty endure. Therefore the writers of this group turned more and more to art. The creation and appreciation of art became a religion for these writers. Clive Bell (in *Art*) says that "religion is art ; for art is a religion." He continues :

> It is an expression of and a means to states of mind as wholly as any men are capable of experiencing ; and it is towards art that modern minds turn, not only for the most perfect expression of transcendent emotion, but for an inspiration by which to love.

This attitude to art is more developed in Roger Fry, and Virginia Woolf. They maintain that a vision of the universe was the most important thing of all for an artist.

The modern conception of the autonomy of a work of art is chiefly derived from the Bloomsbury aesthetics to some extent. Even Eliot himself has been influenced by this philosophy. G. E. Moore frees art from the restrictions of morality, but at the same time makes art play the function of morality and religion. According to Roger Fry, art has its own specific function. The artistic experience is different from all other experiences, and therefore reference to any other experience, social, ethical, and religious is extraneous to artistic considerations.

The artist's problem is to relate his state of mind, his intuitions about things, to his vision in a coherent, and self-contained work of art. It is such a philosophy of art which a novelist-critic like E. M. Forster or Virginia Woolf inherited.

In the criticism of the novel, Forster employs a fundamental conception. He maintains that the story is the essential element in a novel. The story relates the life of the characters in a novel ; it is narrative of events arranged strictly according to their time-sequence. He expresses (in *Aspects of the Novel*) the desire that the novelist should be able to express values of life without the time-sequence. But this is not possible, for without the time-sequence, the story would become unintelligible. This search for values, and a conversational case of tone characterize Forster's occasional critical essays and his book on the novel, *Aspects of the Novel*.

The best part of the literary criticism of Virginia Woolf is also concerned with the novel. Her comments on the novel begin with a protest against materialism. In her famous essays "Modern Fiction" (1919) and "Mr. Bennet and Mrs. Brown", she criticizes Wells, Bennet, and Galsworthy. All three of them stressed the material side of life. Their vision of life is superficial. Human nature was mistaken for external details. A Russian novelist would do better. He would pierce through the flesh to reveal the soul. Like the Russians she wants to reveal every nuance of the inner life. Reality is spiritual. And in moments of intense illumination, we become conscious of the depths of human feelings. The novelist thus should reproduce his vision of reality. The unity of a novel is emotional. Thus in the various essays on the novel she uses these aesthetic conceptions for critical evaluations. She praises those novelists (the Russians for example) and those dramatists (the Elizabethans) who interpreted reality through literature. She condemns those who were either mere "realists" or "artists".

Mention need not be made here of the development of biography by Lytton Strachey. To quote G. S. Fraser (*The Modern Writer and His World*) :

> Mrs. Woolf and Lytton Strachey, the two most prominent literary critics of the group, had neither the taste for close examination of literary texts, nor the aptitude for every profound general theorising. . . . And they used their narrative gifts, within the critical essay, to recreate a personality, a scene, an atmosphere. We remember portraits from their essays rather than judgment.

To conclude : the Bloomsbury tradition, though influential in formulating some aesthetic theories did not give us genuine literary criticism, but "pleasant, vivid and cultivated conversation about literature". The only significant critical doctrine, which derives from their aesthetics is the principle of the autonomy of art.

I. A. Richards—Science And Poetry (1926)

Ivor Armstrong Richards is, along with Eliot, one of the two most influential critics in twentieth century Anglo-American criticism. Richards's criticism, like Eliot's, also encouraged the close study of the text and the rigorous analysis of a poem. It is on account of the influence that the serious study of semantics has become increasingly important in the literary criticism of the modern age. With Richards, scientific psychology enters into the field of literary criticism. The urge towards scientific explanation of the arts culminates in the critical theory of I. A. Richards. Here neurology supersedes metaphysics as the milieu of critical activity. Richards does not depend on ethics or on any philosophy of truth or beauty in his explanation of the nature and function of poetry. Poetry has a duty to perform, and this duty is essentially psychological. The effect of poetry on a reader lies in the psychological adjustments of impulses. Basic to Richards's critical theory is the neuro-physiological conception of the mind as the product of the nervous system.

In his *Principles of Literary Criticism*, he maintains that the mind is the nervous system. The impact produced in the mind by a poem revolves itself into two streams, the intellectual and the emotional. In the reading of a poem, the emotional stream is, according to Richards, more important, and is made up of the interplay of our interests. This is the active branch of influence. But the intellectual stream (or the thinking) caused by the reading of the poem has no importance.[1]

In Richards's own words (in *Science and Poetry*) :

The active branch is what really matters ; far from it all the energy of the whole agitation comes .... Every experience has essentially some interest or group of interests swimming back to rest.

Richards explains the mental process resulting from the experience of reading a poem by comparing the mind to a system of magnetic needles. Imagine a system of magnetic needles which are free to

---

[1] This is the essence of Richards's theory of belief in poetry. It is a doctrine of Richards's criticism that the quality of belief in a poem in no way influences its poetical quality.

move in any direction. Every disturbance affects the magnetic system and after a number of vibrations they come to rest in a particular direction. For every disturbance "there will be a final position to rest for all the needles into which they will in the end settle down, a general poise for the whole system but even a slight displacement may set the whole assemblage of needles busily re-adjusting themselves" (*Science and Poetry*).

The needles are our interests and the whole of man's mind is thus a delicately arranged system of interests. Every disturbance entering the neuro-physiological system upsets the delicate placing and poising of interests. These disturbances tend to effect the structure of personality permanently. But for a healthy and full life the mind must regain its own equilibrium. It is the function of poetry to help the individual regain his mental equilibrium. In Richards's own words :

> We must picture then the stream of poetic experience as setting back to equilibrium those disturbed experiences.
>
> *Science and Poetry*

Thus by one psychological theory Richards explains both the nature and the value of poetic experience.

Man, is not in any sense, primarily an intelligence ; he is a system of interests. Intelligence helps man, but does not ruin him. In this lies the genuineness of distinction which Richards makes between science and poetry. Science relates to intelligence ; poetry to a system of interests. In a scientific verbal structure what is important is the thought in it. In a poetic verbal structure what is important is the system of interests which it evokes. Thus the poet is not important for his ideas but for his efforts at communication. "It is never what a poem *says* which matters, but what it *is*".

On the distinction between the different uses of words in science and poetry Richards's comments are as follows :

> He uses these words because the interests which the situation calls into play combine to bring them, just in this form, into his consciousness as a *means of ordering controlling and consolidating the whole experience.*

From the above conception of the nature of human consciousness

Richards advances the psychological theory of value. He views the mind as a hierarchy of interests. What will be the difference between the good and the evil according to this system? The good is a free and balanced organisation of the interests of the mind. The evil is a wasteful organisation of the mind. The good life is "the fullest, most active, keenest and completest kind of life". Such a life is one which brings into play as many as possible of the positive interests ; but "conflicts between different impulses are the greatest evils which afflict mankind". Poetry becomes valuable because it helps us in the organisation of our impulses. In ancient times, moral functions and authorities helped the individual to some extent in controlling his inner disturbances. Now under the impact of scientific ideas these functions and authorities are disappearing. Poetry replaces the power of moral authority and conventions. Poetry helps in the ordering and the reconciliation of the impulses and the process of poetic compensation is itself the result of a poet's experience of an inner equilibrium.

This is Richards's explanation of the nature of the poetic psychology. He drives from this conception the chief characteristics of the poem. In this theory it is not the extensive vocabulary at the poet's command but the amazing command of words which is the true characteristic of the poet. The poet has a special ability in disposing and arranging the words. The poet is one who uses words in such a manner that they modify one another, where their separate effects are combined in the mind, and they become part of the whole poetic response. The words in the process of poetic composition fall into their place without his conscious control. Similar is the choice of the rhythm. Rhythm is not governed either by metrical skill or by intellectual considerations. Rhythm paints the instinctive impulses seeking to control itself.

"The motives which shape a poem spring from the roots of the mind. The poet's style is direct, depending on the way in which his interests are organised. That amazing capacity of his for ordering speech is only a part of a more amazing capacity for ordering experience" (*Science and Poetry*).

Thus poetry cannot be written by cunning and study or by craft and contrivance, because the ordering of the words springs not from the knowledge of the technique of poetry but from the actual

supreme ordering of an experience. Rhythm reflects personality.
It is not a matter of trick with words and sounds. Thus I. A.
Richards relates poetry and life. The poet is one who has a
supreme command of life. It is this command of life which is
reflected in his command of words and rhythm.

One significant conclusion which emerges from Richards's pre-
occupation with the study of language and the nature of meaning
is the distinction which he draws between a "scientific statement"
and a "pseudo-statement". In arriving at this distinction Richards
traces the development of different world-views. At the beginning
of history man had a magical view of the world. He inhabited the
the world with spirits, demons and invisible agents who accounted
for all the causations of natural phenomenon. This magical world-
view had helped in pre-historical time in the organisation of human
attitude, but the growth of the scientific attitude has neutralised
nature, deprived it of all magical and spiritual association. There
is a transition from a magical to a scientific view.

By science Richards means a systematic explanation of nature in
terms of causes and effects. In one sense this has an advantage. In
another sense this has a disadvantage. Science can tell us how the
natural process goes on or the natural process is gone. It deals
with the how of things. But the mind of man wants to know the
origin, the reason, and the ultimate purpose of all things ; in other
words, the "why" and the "what" and the "wherefor". Without
these explanations man is not emotionally satisfied. The scientific
statement is one which relates to a natural phenomenon and which
can be verified. It is, therefore, true or false. But a statement
concerning the origin of life or the final cause of existence is a
statement which cannot be verified although such statements give
us emotional assurances. Such a statement is neither true or false
and a statement which is neither true or false is designated by
Richards as a "pseudo-statement". Poetry is thus a series of
pseudo-statements which give us emotional assurance. Here lies the
difference between poetry and science. Scientific statements are
verified to be true or false. The poetic pseudo-statement makes us
emotionally reassured or disturbs us. Thus, rejecting as irrelevant
all other approaches to poetic considerations, Richards maintains
that the poetic experience operates through our emotional organisation. It produces effects upon our feelings and attitudes. In this
sense, poetic truth is the very opposite of the scientific truth.

Scientific truth is verifiable truth. A poetic truth is one which satisfies you. To quote Richards :

A pseudo-statement is a form of words which justifies entirely by its effects in resolving or organising of impulses and attitudes ...; a statement, on the other hand, is justified by its truth, *i.e.*, its correspondence in a highly technical sense with the fact to which it points.

Man needs scientific truth and poetic truth. As Richards points out :

The disappearance of the magical view of the world has brought about a sense of desolation, of uncertainty, of futility, of the groundlessness of aspirations and vanity of endeavour. This situation can be remedied only through a system of statement which is as powerful as that of the magical world-view. Poetry fulfils this function.

This is, in essence, Richards's formulation of his poetic theory. The principal features of this theory are a psychological explanation not only of human consciousness but of human personality, a psychological explanation of the nature of language, and the theory that the progress of knowledge lies in a transition from the magical to the scientific view of the world. We have not referred to the more technical explanation of Richards's psychology as given in *The Principles of Criticism* or in *The Practical Criticism*. Nor have we entered into detailed consideration of Richards's theory of meaning as given in the *Meaning of Meaning*. We have based our analysis on Richards's small book *Science and Poetry*. The reason is that in his small book *Science and Poetry*, Richards collects together the various views and formulates an aesthetic of poetic mind and poetry suitable for literary criticism. *Science and Poetry* closes with a chapter on practical criticism on some contemporary poets.

We have already referred to Richards's formative influence on the New Criticism ; but Richards's views are essentially different from the views of the most of the modern critics. Except in the rigorous study of a poem as a poem and the close textual scrutiny of the lines which Richards's criticism shares with New Criticism, there is nothing in common between them. Richards's is a relativist in ethics and he recognises no universal poetic criterion. John Crowe Ransom in his book *The New Criticism* rejects the psychology of I. A. Richards. According to Ransom, the emotive and the conative phases of poetic experience are not sufficient for the valid world view or realistic ontology which poetry should give us. Mr. Eliot himself dismisses Richards's criticism. To quote from a long passage from Eliot's "Use of Poetry and Criticism" :

> His (Richards's) ethics, or theory of value is one which I cannot accept ; or rather I cannot accept any such theory which is argued upon purely individual psychological foundations.

In spite of Richards's considerable psychology and linguistic equipment, one is sometimes tempted to conclude that his theory of criticism derives directly from contemporary psychology and that it will vanish with the changes and development in our knowledge of human consciousness. Psychology, as it is at present, is not adequately developed to give us a final explanation of that permanent and timeless experience of man which is called the poetic experience.

F.R. Leavis and the Scrutiny Tradition

Leavis is especially remembered as a critic through his editorship of the literary magazine *Scrutiny*. With this journal were associated a number of critics. Apart from Leavis, this group consists of L. C. Knights, Traversi, Martin Turnell, Q. D. Leavis, Denys Thompson and D. W. Harding. The critical point of view of the *Scrutiny* is unique. It rebels against both academicism and against extreme modernism. Leavis himself is a strange case as a critic. He has not advanced any general aesthetic or literary theory. In his several critical works, one seeks in vain for the formulation of any definite doctrine or the clear indication of a point of view.

Generally speaking, his critical method is similar to that of Eliot (from whom he learned much) and of I. A. Richards. It is the method of close textual analysis. But Eliot's textual studies always illustrate his general theories. So do Richards's. But Leavis uses textual scrutiny simply for praising or condemning. This is especially illustrated in his Milton-criticism. However, Leavis remains one of the most influential critics of the day. Although he has never claimed to teach, or practise a generally applicable 'technique' or method of "criticism", he has a large number of disciples.

The basis of his criticism lies in his interest in culture and the problem of maintaining a tradition. One of his early books, *Mass Civilization and Minority Culture*, examines this problem of maintaining a right tradition of moral and aesthetic taste. In his criticism of the authors, past and present, what he seeks is the "quality of life" presented. He is not interested in the "form" of a work of literature apart from its contents. As a moralist, it is the quality of life which interests him. He looks for life-enhancing values in literature. His final criteria for evaluation are those of the "moral taste". In his opinions, the aesthetic taste is too superficial to merit detailed attention. The aesthetic qualities merely reflect the moral aspects inherent in his work.

His criticism of Milton illustrates the virtues and defects of his critical procedure. To Leavis, Milton has no sure grasp of life. His ways of thinking about life is not sufficiently serious. Milton had a "grand obtuseness". For nearly similar reasons, he condemns Shelley. But because of the "moral grasp" he can praise George Eliot and Conrad, and D. H. Lawrence.

Leavis's first important book of literary criticism, *New Bearings in English Poetry* shows his debt to T.S. Eliot. It was from Eliot's *The Sacred Wood* that he obtained many important ideas which are employed in his criticism. In the Preface to his *Common Pursuit*, he approves of Eliot's statement that "The critic...should endeavour to discipline his personal prejudices and cranks...with as many of his fellows as possible in the common pursuit of common judgment". But Leavis has provoked more controversies on minor matters than any other critic, alive today[2]. His next book *Revaluation* (1936) applies the criteria of "moral taste" and "grasp of life" to the great poets. These were the standards according to which modern poets were examined in *New Bearings in English Poetry*. These two books together seek to discover "a great tradition" in poetry. He writes in the Preface to *Revaluation* :

In dealing with individual poets the critic, whether explicitly or not, is dealing with tradition, for they live in it. And it is in them that tradition lives.

[2] See *Revaluation* (1936) and *The Great Tradition* (1948).

In the same preface, he outlines his method of criticism :

> In dealing with individual poets the role of the critic is, or should (I think) be, to work as much as possible in terms of particular analysis—analysis of poems or passages, and to say nothing that cannot be related immediately to judgments about producible texts.

The *Revaluation* is chiefly devoted to fault-finding, except in the case of the Metaphysicals and Pope.

His next book *The Great Tradition* (1948) a collection of essays on George Eliot, Henry James, Joseph Conrad seeks to establish the "great tradition" in the history of the novel. The great tradition in fiction has been a tradition of serious moral concern. "The great novelists are significant in terms of the human awareness they promote, awareness of the possibilities of life."

Leavis's development as a critic after the 1950's is not along the lines of literary criticism. He has become an acute controversialist attacking every thing (and every one, in life or literature) which he does not like[3]. Concerning his defects, George Watson observes in *The Literary Critics* :

> The most serious charge to be made against his criticism is two-fold. He has hurried towards value-judgments, especially in his later work, without respect for the essential delicacy and complexity of literary values ; and he has not known enough about any thing—or cared much about finding out.

As a critic, "he remains a British provincial."

The New Criticism

The New Criticism is the most important among the schools of criticism which have emerged after the First World War. Although the origin of the New Criticism lies in the writings of T. E. Hulme

---

[3] His recent quarrel with C. P. Snow on the "Two Cultures" is a relevant case.

and Pound, it is now principally an American movement. There are several important figures in this movement. But they have no common programme or theory uniting them. They are not unanimous in their beliefs and there are often sharp cleavages of opinion among them. It may further be noted that what is new in the "New Criticism" is not so much any new theory of art and criticism, as much as a new emphasis. What, then, unites the New Critics is a set of basic attitudes. These attitudes originate chiefly in their reaction against certain contemporary schools of criticism which for want of a more suitable name may be called the "extrinsic" schools of criticism.

By the "extrinsic" school of criticism, I mean those schools in which stress is laid on the ideas and the intellectual contents in a work of art. Thus, for instance, the Marxist School of Criticism, and the Humanistic Schools are two examples of extrinsic critical schools. These two do not fully exhaust all the extrinsic schools. There are the psycho-analytical, the biographical, and the sociological, and the relativistic criticism.

The extrinsic critic (be he biographical, sociological, dialectical or humanistic) considers a work of art according to a pre-conceived theory of society, life, or history. A poem or a novel is not considered as such, but only in relation to the set of ideas which it embodies. Thus the Marxist critic judges a poem in accordance with the theory of class-struggle and according to the degree to which the poem reflects this particular datum of the theory. A humanist critic searches in a poem for moral values, and a sociological critic for those components of social dynamics which make up the "social product", namely, a poem or a play. It is clear in any case that art is not interpreted as art, and literature not as literature. The New Critics opposed their critical methods.

Thus the growth of the New Criticism was a vital necessity in the literary situation of the early twentieth century in Britain and America. The reaction against the Edwardian critics which began with Hulme became a major force with Eliot's *The Sacred Wood*. In this volume, Eliot had advocated purely aesthetic considerations in artistic discussions. In America criticism had been dominated by the humanist and Marxist schools. Although they differ ideologically, they are similar in their approach to literature. The humanists derived their ideas from Paul Elmer More and Irving Babbit. Both were social thinkers and they were interested in the impact of literature on the development of human culture and civilization. The Marxists, on the other hand, were concerned with the effective use of literature for purposes of social propaganda. Further, the academic critics transformed literary criticism into the study of biography, psychology, sociology or ethics. In fact, none of these critical schools concerned themselves with the work of art as such.

The school of New Criticism came into being as a revolt against this situation. And the name "New Criticism" gained currency after John Crowe Ransom's use of that title under which were published studies of four leading critics. Among the New Critics the most important names to be considered are those of Robert Penn Warren, Cleanth Brooks, Allen Tate, R. P. Blackmuar, and Yvor Winters.

Another name for this school of criticism is the "Ontological Criticism". By ontological criticism we mean that school of criticism which treats a poem as a definite entity, separate from both the poet and the socio-cultural *milieu* in which it is produced. Thus the "Ontological Critic" or the "New Critic" looks upon the poem as poem, and they oppose all extrinsic studies on the poem. Cleanth Brooks, for instance, in his *The Well-Wrought Urn*, analyses poems belonging to various historical periods in order to arrive at the central conception of what essentially a poem is. Thus the ontological critic resorts to close textual analysis of a poem for its explication and judgment.

One implication of the New Criticism is that criticism has absolute standards and principles. Thus they reject critical relativism. The principle of critical relativism maintains that there are no absolute standards and principles in criticism, and that both the poetry and the criticism of an age are its expressions and are determined by the age. Frederick A. Pottle (in his *The Idiom of Poetry*) is the best exponent of this theory. He maintains that :

Poetry always expressed the basis of feeling (or sensibility) of the age in which it was written.

and that

Poetry is whatever has been called poetry by respectable judges at any time and in any place.

and,

The poetry of an age never goes wrong.

Pottle's arguments make it impossible for us to arrive at any permanent criteria and literary values. Cleanth Brooks (in *The Well-Wrought Urn*) refutes strongly these arguments. It may be noted here that Pottle's criticism is closely patterned after scientific thought. According to him literary criticism needs a Michaelson-Morley experiment. As scientific knowledge develops, so do ideas about literature and criticism. It is easy to see that the parallel established between physics and criticism is obviously wrong, for criticism is not a science in that sense. Criticism is a kind of normative science. Further, while critics of different ages may disagree on interpretations, there is near unanimity among critics of all ages as to which works of art are enduring and which are ephemeral. Pottle overlooks this simple fact.[4]

The most important problem of discussion among the New Critics is the nature of the poem. They always deal with an individual work rather than a writer's achievement as a whole. They seek to illuminate the "centre of the work" itself. With T. S. Eliot, they maintain that a poet has a particular medium to express, and this is language. How does the poetic use of language differ from others ? The distinguishing characteristic of a poem is the peculiar way of handling language. And this peculiarity consists in the irony and paradox of the poem. This view is not only concerned with lyrical poetry. It includes all imaginative literature. Cleanth Brooks maintains (in *The Well-Wrought Urn*) that :

few of us are prepared to accept the statement that the language of poetry is hard, bright, witty ; it is hardly the language of the soul.

We usually consider paradox as intellectual rather than emotional, clever rather than profound, rational rather than divi-

---

[4] Similar, outwardly to critical relativism, is the procedure of "academic criticism". The method of academic criticism, that of insisting on scholarship in the interpretation and appreciation of a poem, has been severely attacked by F. R. Leavis in England. See his *Common Pursuit*. But the present writer cannot agree with F. R. Leavis. Nor is academic criticism simply relativistic.

nely irrational. Brooks argues that "paradox" is the language appropriate and inevitable to poetry. It is the scientific language which is purged of every paradox. To quote Brooks again :

> Paradoxes spring from the very nature of the poet's language : it is a language in which connotations play as great a part as the denotation....The poet, within limits, has to make up his language as he goes.

The New Critics thus seek for the total meaning of a poem. In terms of the total meaning, imagery, dramatic situation, and metre become mechanisms of organization—not ornaments, but a part of complexity out of which the knowledge of a poem grows. The New Criticism regards these things as functional. Thus the emphasis on paradox is part of the search for the total meaning of a poem. The interest in the total meaning of a poem finds expression in such statements as MacLeish's "A poem should not mean/But be".

It is too early to make a definitive assessment of the works of the New Critics. One thing is certain. They are at grips with the central problems concerning literature, and they have raised the level of discussions on poetry.

Yvor Winters as Critic[5]

Yvor Winters is one among the New Critics. In spite of belonging to the school of New Criticism, he does not share many common beliefs with the New Critics in general. His criticism goes against the accepted doctrines of today. His affinity with New Criticism lies in rejecting critical relativism and also in his close analysis of the texts.

[5] Yvor Winters was born in Chicago in 1900. He was educated at the Universities of Colorado and Stanford. His major critical works are : *Primitivism and Decadence* (1937), *Maul's Curse* (1938) and *The Anatomy of Nonsense* (1943). Of these, three works have been collected in one volume entitled *In Defence of Reason.* He has published eight books of poems. The most important among these are : *The Journey* (1921), *Before Disaster* (1934), *Poems* (1941) and *The Giant Weapon* (1943).

He insists that analysis of literary works must rest on a belief on the acceptance of truths and values and that it is the duty of the writer to approximate these truths in so far as human fallibility permits. Of course there is a similarity between his critical stand-point and that of the Neo-Humanists. The similarity lies in that Winters insists, like the humanists, that the moral evaluation of that literature is the fundamental problem in criticism. Further, Winters as well as the humanist warns us against the modern effects of the Romantic Movement. Often, Winters is compared in these respects to Irving Babitt. But there are differences. Babitt is primarily a moralist. Winters is primarily a critic. Babitt considers the aesthetic qualities of a poem as merely incidental, and he concentrates on the moral content of a poem. Winters, on the other hand, concentrates on the art. To him, a poem has two major aspects—"the rational structure" or paraphrasable contents, and the feeling which is largely paraphrasable. This may be examined separately for purposes of critical analysis, but, according to Winters, the two features are simultaneously present in a work of art.

Winters builds his critical standard on these two qualities of a poem. A poem is successful if it displays a proper adjustment of feeling and content to a definable rational frame.

This view, in fact, appears to be a re-statement of an old doctrine that a poem has a didactic element. Winters's dichotomy between the rational content and the moral aspect of the poem is parallelled in the old dichotomy between form and theme. But the originality of his theory lies in defining a poem as a record of the artist's ethical evaluation, his understanding, and his emotional response. Winters maintains that the moral quality of a poem is exactly equivalent to its excellence as a work of art. This principle is illustrated, for instance, in his view about poetic metre. In *Primitivism and Decadence,* Winters argues that poetry should have a regular metrical pattern. His theory is that, since the metre of a work "renders possible a refinement and adjustment of feeling to Motive", the quality of the metrical pattern in a poem has a "moral significance".

Winters compares the creative act to our moral adjustments in daily life. We are called upon to adjust ourselves to the realities of experience by control of emotions. The creative act is precisely of the same nature and it is a moment of delicate moral decision. The difference between the creative act and our ethical adjustment is only a difference in degree. Winters's doctrine of ethical adjustment advocates a balance between our understanding and our emotions. He maintains that if our rational perception weakens, then our feelings are motivated by dreams rather than realities. Such a context is defined by Winters as "madness". The moral person is one who is able to adjust his understanding to reality. With the aid of well-established habits of observation and self-control he can apprehend the true nature of a scene and is able to evaluate experience, correctly. Thus, there is a correlation between the power of the artist and the sum of experience he is able to interpret. The greater and the wider the range of experience the greater the artist. Thus, according to Winters, Shakespeare had a profound understanding of the experience he presented and of the medium (language). This is how he was able to express in language "the feeling detailed and totalled, appropriating the actions portrayed".

His criticism takes us directly to the art. In his view, if the rational structure of the poem is obscure, then there can be no appropriate emotion. Obscurity is an important element in poetry. For him poetry must clearly state its subjects.

In his recent book *Function of Criticism*, Yvor Winters examines the various theories of criticism and literature. His point of view in the book is that any development of literary methods in our century must explain the potentialities of different kinds of subject matter and the potentialities of various literary forms and these in turn are related to a theory of a final cause. Winters examines some of the modern critics in accordance with his point of view. He considers Eliot, therefore, as a critic without any theory or "a contradictory theorist". Ransom is, in his view, an eighteenth century associationist. Blackmur is a relativist because he does not respect any of the principles of new criticism. Similarly, he examines each of the modern critics. He rejects Cleanth Brook's theory of ironical opposition or paradoxical structure. He attacks the Chicago critics because their poetic values are purely formal values.

In the *Function of Criticism*, Winters gives his theory in a summary form :

I believe that a poem (or other literary works) is a statement in words about human experience....In each work there is a content which is rationally apprehensible and each work endeavours to communicate the emotion which is appropriate to the

rational apprehension of the subject. The work is thus a judgment, rational and emotional of the experience, i.e., a complete
moral judgment in so far as the work is successful.

CHAPTER TEN

MOVEMENTS IN LITERATURE
AND CRITICISM

1. Naturalism. 2. Marxism and Literary Theory. 3. Impressionism. 4. Symbolism.

Naturalism : Philosophical and Literary

Literary naturalism is a combined product of philosophical naturalism and the scientific evolutionary doctrine advanced by Charles Darwin. In order to avoid confusion in the use of the word 'naturalism', we had better approach the concept of naturalism systematically. In a paradoxical sense the Romantic poets who were chiefly idealists of some variety or other also dealt with nature. Consequently, there is sometimes a tendency to confuse Romantic naturalism with what is called "the naturalist movement" in literature and criticism.

There are two broadly contrasted sets of the theories about the world. They are the supernatural or the religious theories which postulate the concept of a Spirit or God either immanent in or transcendent to nature. The other theories include realism, naturalism, and materialism which consider the process of nature as autonomous and self-explained. The supernaturalist points out the inadequacy of purely naturalistic or materialistic categories for an explanation of the world and of human nature. Thus in this view the human and the natural are distinct and separate, but the naturalists (like the realists or the materialists) explain nature by purely natural categories. Thus naturalism challenges the various arguments of the super-naturalist and the idealist and holds that the universe requires no supernaturalist cause and government but is self-existent, self-explanatory, self-operating and self-directing. Naturalism views the world process as purposeless and deterministic. According to this theory, man's ethical values, compulsions, and cultural activities can all be justified on natural grounds without recourse to super-natural explanation. Thus, the general argument of the naturalist is that there is no reality beyond nature. In aesthetics, the doctrine of naturalism brought into prominence the systematic study of nature from a realistic point of view. In this sense, artistic naturalism is simply the theory that the artist's only function should be to observe closely and report clearly the character and behaviour of man's physical environment. The artist should not seek any hidden reality or essence. He should not attempt to correct or complete nature by idealising and generalising. He should not impose value-judgment on nature. He should simply describe what he finds around him. Naturalism is a special literary movement. It refers to the practice and doctrines of the nineteenth-century School of Realism. In fact, realism in literature—rather "neo-realism" in literature—has come to be called naturalism. This naturalism is a branch of realism. The essential distinction between realism and naturalism is that realism in literature is briefly a repudiation of the sentimental, romantic and the idealistic, whereas naturalism not only repudiates these but goes further and postulates a philosophy of life based on purely materialistic and mechanistic conceptions. Thus literary naturalism springs from a theoretical manifesto advancing a new conception of reality in terms of the new Physics of Newton, the Biology of Darwin and the Sociology of Herbert Spencer.

The novel was the form most commonly chosen by the naturalists. For, the form of the novel, vast and complex as it is, had provided the scientific fiction writer ample scope for his ideas. It was the French writers of the last half of the nineteenth century who developed the naturalistic technique of fiction. Thus naturalism presents an optimistic and unified theory of man and nature. The great naturalist novelists were Flaubert, Zola and Guy de Maupessant. The fundamental dogma of the movement is expressed by Zola in the title of the book *The Experimental Novel*. Zola explains naturalism as a scientific method applied to nature.

According to Zola, the main task of the artist is to represent and explain what happens in nature, and art must aim at literary transcription of reality that the artist obtains by making an analytical study of character, motives, and behaviour. The naturalist novelists argue that all moral judgments are merely conventional and has no real basis in nature. So the artist should seek to understand and not to approve or condemn. Human behaviour is regarded as largely a function of environment and circumstances. The novelist should exhibit taste in detail with no false idealism of character, no glossing over the ugly and no appeal to support hidden forces.

R. G. Collingwood in *Idea of Nature* says :

In its narrowest sense, evolution means the doctrine especially associated with the name of Charles Darwin...that the species of living organisms are not a fixed repertory of permanent types, but begins to exist and cease to exist in time.

About materialism, he says :

The idea of the world of nature as self-creative, and self-regulating, combined with the idea of nature as a machine, gave rise to a materialistic theory of nature. The leader of this movement was the neo-Epicurean Pierre Gassendi (1592-1655) who held that the quantitative and mechanical nature described by Galileo was the only reality, and that mind was merely a peculiar kind of pattern or structure of material events.

Regarding the new theory of evolution advanced by Spencer and others, Collingwood says :

The history of life was thus conceived as the history of an endless succession of experiments on the part of nature to produce organisms more and more intensely and effectively alive.

George Saintsbury, (in *The History of the French Novel*) dealing with the origin of naturalist-novels, writes :

For they claimed—and the justice, if not the values of the claims must be allowed—to have rested their fashion of novel-writing upon two bases. The substance was to be provided by an elaborate observation and reproduction of the facts of actual life, not in the least transcendentally inspired, or in any other way brought near Romance, but considered largely from the points of view of which their friend Taine, writing earlier, used for his philosophical and historical work—that of "milieu" or "environment" and that of heredity....The treatment, on the other hand, was to be effected by an intensely personal style....

The Naturalist-novel, as practiced by Zola, rests on three principal supports, or rather draws its material from and guides its treatment by three of several processes or doctrines.

Dealing with its defects he writes :

But as concerns the definitely human part of their matter, immense stress is laid on the Darwinian or Spencerian doctrines of heredity, environment evolution and the like. While, last of all in order, if the influence be taken as converging towards the reason of the failure comes the "medico-legal" notion of a "lesion" of some flaw or vicious and cancerous element which develops itself variously in individuals...it must surely be obvious that insistence on the "lesion" even if the other points of the theory were unassailable, is grossly excessive, if not wholly illegitimate... it must be evident that Heredity, Natural Selection, Evolution, Environment etc., are things which, at the very best can be allowed an exceedingly small part in artistic re-creation....

Yet the master error lies, farther back still, in the strictly "Naturalist" idea itself—the theory of Experiment, the observation—document—"note" all for their own sake.

George More Says (in *Confessions*) on the new art of Zola :

The idea of a new art based on science in opposition to the art of the old world that was based on the imagination, an art that should explain all things and embrace modern life in its entirety, in its endless ramifications be, as it were, a new creed in a new civilization, filled me with wonder and I stood dumb before the vastness of the conception and the towering height of the ambition.

Emile Zola holds (*The Experimental Novel*) :

We see that the novelist is made up of an observer and an experimenter. The observer gives the facts just as much as he has observed them, establishes the solid ground on which the characters and events move ; then the experimenter appears and institutes experiments, that is, makes his characters move in a particular story, in order to show the succession of facts, would be such as is required by the determinism of the things studied.

In other words, the influence of social environment, of heredity, of the time or environment of heredity, of the time or social condition, as a materialistic novel must play a perfectly inevitable part in determining the causes of events.

Dealing with Zola and Naturalism, Turnell writes :

> His (Zola's) theme like that of any other considerable novelist was nature and destiny of man, but the nature and destiny of man interpreted in terms of a naturalist philosophy. He shows us humanity imprisoned in a rigorously determinist world from which every vestige of genuine spirituality has been banished, and which impinges on man's consciousness at every moment of the day.
>
> Zola did not claim any originality for his philosophical views. He maintained with some show of reason, that what he called Naturalism had always been an element in French thought and that Montaigue had actually used the word in the same sense as himself. He was also at pains to bring out his debt to the philosopher. In spite of his contradictions, he wrote in *Une Campaigne* that the positivist Diderot is the true master of the Naturalists : he was the first to insist on exact truth in the theatre and the novel.

Again he says :

> The first principle of Realism was no more than a demand for a greater degree of verisimilitude. Zola never claimed that the representation of reality should be "photographic" or that the novel should be a mere "slice of life".

Marxism and Literary Theory

Between 1850 and 1950, so many revolutionary theories of far-reaching implications have been advanced in the different sciences each of which is so ambitious in its scope that it attempts to provide a satisfactory explanation for every aspect of the reality of experience. Darwin's evolutionary hypothesis, Marxism, and the psychological systems developed by Freud, Jung, and Adler are theories which provide, in terms of their own concepts, explanations of life and consciousness. Theories about man's life and consciousness affect creative literature and criticism. Darwinism, for instance, has shaped very much the attitudes of the literary realists, and naturalists. Far more influential on literary theories and criticism have been Marxism and the Depth Psychologies of Freud, Jung, and Adler.

Karl Marx has advanced a theory of historical progress which is generally called Dialectical Materialism. The word "Dialectical" derives especially from Hegel, in whose history of philosophy, historical developments are explained on the basis of a conflict between a thesis, and an anti-thesis, and which conflict is reconciled in a synthesis. "Dialectical" in this context refers to this process of movement through conflict. In Hegel's philosophy the cause of the conflict was the evolution and manifestation of the Idea. Marx borrowed the conception of the historical process substituting matter in the place of Hegel's Idea. Hence Dialectical Materialism.

Marx's theory essentially holds that life is evolution (according to natural selection). In human history all developments and progress have been caused in the process of economic evolution. Human society is moving towards (in the final end) a classless egalitarian society, with no 'state' or government, with neither wants nor scarcity. The movement towards this goal is through conflicts of one economic class with another endlessly till the classless and wantless structure is established. Thus Feudalism, and Capitalism, for example, are various economic structures of society in two different periods of evolution. Each economic structure leads to a social organisation which in turn produces its own culture, religion, and literature. This in a nutshell is the Marxian interpretation of literature.

It is easily seen that, according to this theory, literature is determined by socio-economic factors. Thus socio-economic realism becomes the most important criterion of excellence accepted by the Marxist literary theory. In fact, Marx maintains that the mode of production or material life determines the social, political, and intellectual processes of life. Social existence determines consciousness. He notes that :

> It is not the consciousness of men that determines their being, but, on the contrary, their social being that determines their consciouness.

(quoted from *Literature and Art* by Marx and Engels, selections from their writings, New York : International Publishers, 1947.) Correlating literature and economic developments, Marx asks :

> Is Achilles possible side by side with power and lead ? Or is the Iliad at all compatible with the printing press and steam press ?

These, then, are the basic conceptions in the Marxian theory of literature[1]. One need not point out the tremendous impact this theory produced during the decades 1920-1940 on English and American literature and criticism.

One immediate consequence of this theory is the conclusion that art has a socio-economic function, and art and literature are to be judged according to how this function is fulfilled. Thus not only literature originates in social factors, but its sole ground and cause of being is social and economic. Literature is, accordingly, a tool of propaganda to be used in the onward march of society. The doctrine of art for art's sake has no relevance in this theory.

Marxist literary theory accounts for much of the nineteenth century poetry (and part of the modern) in terms of the isolation of the artist from society on account of the bourgeois machine culture. In the twentieth century T. S. Eliot is taken by the Marxists as the last decadent writer who turns away from the historico-social reality.

In Russia, George Plekhanov in his *Art and Society* and Leon Trotsky in *Literature and Revolution* developed the basic view of the separation of the artist from society. Christopher Caudwell applies

---

[1] On the modern development of Marxian ideas, see *The Triple Thinkers*, by Edmund Wilson.

the same theory to English Literature in *Illusion and Reality*.

In America Marxist theory and criticism began to appear with Michael Gold, editor of the *New Masses*, Joseph Freeman (who has edited the anthology *Proletarian Literature in the United States*), and V. F. Calverton, (editor of the *Modern Quarterly*). But one of the most important works of criticism reflecting Marxian ideas was V. L. Parrington's three-volume *The Main Currents in American Thought*. Here Parrington equates literature with thought, and thought is explained in terms of economic liberalism. To give another example of Marxian literary critics in the States, we have to refer to Bernard Smith. In his book *Forces in American Criticism* (1939) he explains the superiority of Marxian criticism over both critical expressionism and impressionism, because :

> . . . a work of literature reflects its author's adjustment to society. To determine the character and value of the work we must. . . understand and have an opinion about the social forces that produced the ideology it expresses as an attitude towards life.

Concerning the achievement of Marxian criticism in America, C. Hugh Holman (in "Defence of Art : Criticism since 1930" in *Developments in American Criticism* ed. Stovall) says :

> The Marxist movement in American criticism has been vigorous, ingenious, and religiously consistent ; but it has produced little that is significant either in artistic theory or in practice.

This could be generalized to apply to every form of Marxist literary theory whether in England or America or Europe. Marxism and the forms of social criticism more closely related to it have never had any real concern with literature and literary problems." (*Literary Criticism : A Short History*, W. K. Wimsatt and Cleanth Brooks). Further, in the same book, we have the conclusion that :

In the crudity both of its determinism and of its inconsistent propagandism, the socio-realistic tradition of literary criticism has on the whole contributed little to an understanding of the relation which universality bears to individuality in artistic expression.

Impressionism

Impressionism as a movement in art and literature does not, like other 'isms' in art, begin with a deliberate philosophical revolt. To say this is not the same thing as denying that it has an important theoretical basis. But in the case of impressionism, the theory in conformity with which it interprets reality finds articulation in the impressionistic objects of art directly, and it is seldom specially formulated in a philosophy. One had better, therefore, directly go to the great impressionists themselves after a brief analysis of impressionism.

It is a modern movement in art and literature which originated in France in the last quarter of the nineteenth century. Generally, it aims to cast off the trammels of artistic tradition, and look out at nature, in a fresh and original manner. It employs general effects, vigorous structure, and deals with shape, form and colour.

As a branch of criticism in art and literature it seeks merely to record what Anatole France calls "the adventures of the soul among the masterpieces". Thus in criticism it might appear to be a product of Romantic individualism and modern self-consciousness, although, in art and literature, impressionism seems to be the very opposite of Romanticism. Impressionistic criticism centres on individual responses, and on personal sensitiveness.

Viewed thus as an artistic literary and critical movement, it is the product of the special intellectual and social milieu of the modern times, and focuses an area of contemporary sensibility. Concerning the relation between the highly industrialised character of the modern society and impressionism, Arnold Hauser writes :

The enormous technical developments that take place must not induce us to overlook the feeling of crisis that was in the air. The crisis itself must rather be seen as an incentive to new technical achievements and improvements in methods of production. Certain signs of the atmosphere of this crisis make themselves felt in all the manifestations of technical activity. It is above all the furious speed of the development and the way the pace is forced that seems pathological, particularly, when compared with the rate of progress in earlier periods in the history of art and culture. For the rapid development of technology not only accelerates the change of fashion, but also the shifting emphasis in the criterion of aesthetic taste; it often brings about a senseless and fruitless mania for innovation, a restless striving for the new for the mere sake of novelty.... Modern technology thus introduces an unprecedented dynamism in the whole attitude to life and it is above all this new feeling of speed and change that finds expression in impressionism. (*A Social History of Art, Vol. II, pp. 870-871*).

About the new points of departure which impressionism introduces into the history of art, Arnold Hauser writes :

The most striking phenomenon connected with the progress of technology is the development of cultural centres into large cities in the modern sense ; these form the soil in which the new art is rooted. Impressionism is an urban art, and not only because it discovers the landscape quality of the city and brings painting back from the country into the town, but because it sees the world through the eyes of the townsman and reacts to external impressions with the overstrained nerves of modern technical man. It is an urban style, because it describes the changeability, the nervous rhythm, the sudden, sharp but always ephemeral impressions of city life. And precisely as such, it implies an enormous expansion of sensual perception, a new sharpening of sensibility, a new irritability, and, with the Gothic and romanticism, it signifies one of the most important turning points in the history of Western art. In the dialectical process represented by the history of painting, the alternation of the static and the dynamic, of design and colour, abstract order and organic life, impressionism forms the climax of the development in which recognition is given to the dynamic and organic elements of experience and which completely dissolves the static world-view of the Middle Ages (*Ibid., pp. 871-872, Vol. II, op.cit.*).

Impressionism brings in a new attitude to time. To arrest a moment of experience in time and give it permanence through the medium of art is their aim. Rossetti said that his sonnets are moments made eternity. About the theoretical principles on which impressionism bases itself, A. Hauser sums up :

> A world, the phenomena of which are in a state of constant flux and transition, produces the impression of continuum in which everything coalesces and in which there are no other differences but the various approaches and points of view of the beholder. An art in accordance with such a world will stress not merely the momentary and transitory nature of phenomena, but will seek the criterion of truth in the 'hic et nunc' of the individual. It will consider chance the principle of all being, and the truth of the moment as invalidating all other truths. The primacy of the moment, of change and chance implies, in terms of aesthetics, the dominion of the passing mood over the permanent qualities of life, that is to say, the prevalence of a relation to things the property of which is to be non-committal as well as changeable. The reduction of the artistic representation to the mood of the moment is, at the same time, the expression of a fundamentally passive outlook on life, an aquiescence in the role of the spectator, of the receptive and the contemplative subject, a stand-point of aloofness, waiting, non-involvement—in short, the aesthetic attitude purely and simply. Impressionism is the climax of self-centred aesthetic culture and signifies the ultimate consequence of the romantic renunciation of practical, active life *(Ibid., p. 873, Vol. II, op.cit.)*.

The important connection between impressionist painting and impressionist literature is a peculiar attitude to reality based on a doctrine of the temporal process as flux rather than permanence. This attitude to time brings together philosophers and writers of differing schools and times to a common area of interest.

Recent scientific discoveries too had their impact on impressionist conception of beauty. In so far as this concept of beauty alone is taken into account they are very similar to the naturalists, and present an opposition to Pre-Raphaelitism. Paul G. Konody, sometime art critic of the *London Observer* and *The Daily Mail*, says in an article in the 14th edition of the *Encyclopaedia Britannica (Vol. 12)* :

Parallel with this technical innovation came the impressionists' revolt, led by Manet (the painter) against the academic canons of beauty. It was inspired by passionate interest in actuality, that is to say in contemporary life and manners and closely akin to the literary movement led by Flaubert, the Goncourts and Zola.

This brings impressionism directly in relation to Walter Pater, one of the successful practitioners in the literature and criticism of impressionism. A search for the experience of the moment, to look upon life as a succession of significant experiences, and the endeavour to communicate effectively the impact of significant and meaningful moments, all underlie Pater's impressionism, and his writings. In this he was influenced by Plato, Protagoras and Heraclitus. Setting forth the doctrine of Heraclitus emphasising the importance of the moment he writes (*Plato and Platonism*, London : Macmillan and Co. Ltd., 1910).

> All things give way : nothing remaineth...
> Perpetual motion, alike in things and in men's thought about them.

> The sad, self-conscious, philosophy of Heraclitus, like one, knowing beyond his years, in his barely adolescent world which he is so eager to instruct, makes no pretence to be able to restrain that. Was not the very essence of thought itself also such perpetual motion? A baffling transition from the dead past, alive one moment since, to a present, itself deceased in turn ere we can say, it is here ? A keen analyst of the facts of nature and mind, a master presumably of all the knowledge that then there was, a vigorous definer of thoughts, he does but refer the superficial movement of all persons and things around him to deeper and still more masterful currents of universal change, stealthily withdrawing the apparently solid earth itself from beneath one's feet. The principle of disintegration, the incoherency of fire or flood (for Heraclitus there are but very lively instances of movements, subtler yet more wasteful still) are inherent in the primary elements alike of matter and of the soul (*pp. 14-15*).

He continues :

> But the principle of lapse, of waste, was, in fact, in one's self.

No one has ever passed twice over the same stream. Nay, the passenger himself is without identity. Upon the same stream at the same moment we do, and do not, embark ; for we are, and are not... And this rapid change, if it did not make all knowledge impossible, made it wholly relative, of a kind, that is to say, valueless in the judgment of Plato. Man as the individual, at this particular vanishing point of time and place, becomes "the measure of all things" (*pp. 15-16 op.cit.*).

Concerning the Doctrine of Flux, which is at the basis of all modern theories of development and change and from which impressionism borrows its theoretical support Pater observes :

Nay, the idea of development (that, too, a thing of growth, developed in the progress of reflexion) is at last invading one by one, as one secret of their explanation, all the products of mind, the very mind itself, the abstract reason ; our certainty, for instance, that two and two make four. Gradually we have come to think, or to feel, that primary certitude. Political constitutions, again, as we now see so clearly, are "not made", cannot be made but "grow". Races, laws, art have their origins and end, are themselves ripples on the great river of organic life ; and language is changing on our very lips (*pp. 20-21*).

Pater attempts an impressionistic criticism of Wordsworth. He observes, as the impressionist painters do, a very intimate sense of the expressiveness of outward things in Wordsworth's poetry. He writes :

A very intimate sense of the expressiveness of outward things, which ponders, listens, penetrates, where the earlier, less developed consciousness passed lightly by, is an important element in the general temper of our modern poetry. Critics of literary history have again and again remarked upon it; it is a characteristic which reveals itself in many different forms, but is strongest and most sympathetic in what is strongest and most serious in modern literature ; it is exemplified by writers as unlike Wordsworth as the French romanticist poets" (Walter Pater, *Essays from the Guardian*, London. Macmillan and Co. Ltd., 1910, pp. 95-96).

Marius the Epicurean is an attempt by Pater to compose a novel, or a fictional portrait, on the impressionist principles. It presents a character evolving under the impact of significant experiences to seek that which is the only laudable aim of life according to the hero of the novel. Pater writes in *Marius the Epicurean* :

He caught a lesson from what was then said, still somewhat beyond his years, a lesson in the skilled cultivation of life, of experience, of opportunity, which seemed to be the aim of the young priest's recommendations. The sum of them, through various forgotten intervals of argument, as might really have happened in a dream, was the precept, repeated many times under slightly varied aspects, of diligent promotion of the capacity of the eye, inasmuch as in the eye would lie for him the determining influence of life : he was of the number of those who, in the words of a poet who came long after, must be "made perfect by the love of visible beauty" (p. 32. Vol. 1).

The above is a piece of advice given by a priest to Marius in the novel. The gist of the teaching is to be made perfect in all things by the experience of beauty in all things. This impressionistic religion of beauty is further explained by Pater :

To keep the eye clear by a sort of exquisite personal alacrity and cleanliness, extending even to his dwelling place ; to discriminate, even more and more fastidiously, select form and colour in things from what was less select ; to meditate much on beautiful visible objects, on objects, more especially, connected with the period of youth...; to avoid jealously, in his way through the world, everything repugnant to sight ; and should any circumstances tempt him to a general converse in the range of such objects, to disentangle himself from that circumstance at any cost of place, money or opportunity ; such were, in brief outline, the duties recognized, the rights demanded, in this new formula of life (*Marius the Epicurean*, p. 33).

Impressionism has been more prominent in literary criticism than in creative writing. The impressionist critical method varies from the autobiographical method of Thomas de Quincy and Swinburne to the variety of criticism about which J. E. Spingarn speaks of (quoting from Anatole France) as "the adventures of soul among the masterpieces of the world." Writing about this kind of criticism David Daiches observes (in *Critical Approaches to Literature*) :

> Mere impressionism, the simple setting forth of an autobiographical response to take the place of critical assessment, is certainly not a valuable critical method. But if literature is a form of communication, then testimony as to the effectiveness of that communication by reader with a wide and deep experience of different kinds can be taken to, in some sense, evaluation. Can a case be made for the proper exploitation of the critic's reactions to a work as a means of assisting critical evaluation of it? Many modern critics would deny that such a case can be made, and point out that the critic's duty is to show how the work lives, what its form and structure and essential life really are, and show this by pointing to qualities objectively present in the work itself; the critic, they would maintain, is concerned with the *means* rather than with the end, with how the communication is achieved rather than with effect of the achieved communication on the reader. Autobiography on the critic's part, he would urge, is not criticism (p. 269).

He defends to some extent the usefulness of impressionist criticism :

> If practical criticism were solely a matter of evaluation, of giving the author so many marks for each aspect of his work, then the case for any impressionist criticism would be weak. But it is also the function of the critic to increase understanding and appreciation, to bring the reader to see and appreciate what the work really is—to teach him to read it, even—and in achieving this kind of end cannot be allowed a judicious use of impressionist devices, even of autobiographical gestures? The only way of answering this is to pose a further question: Has an impressionist approach ever been successfully employed in illuminating and evaluating a work? Critics like Lamb, Hazlitt and De Quincey used this approach fairly, frequently and in varying degree of purity. Such a remark as Hazlitt's "I can take mine ease in mine inn with Signor Orlando Friscobaldo as the oldest

aquaintance I have, Ben Jonson, learned Chapman, Master Webster and Master Heywood" is certainly not critical in any strict sense of the term, but it does help to show the kind of atmosphere which certain works create and thus to draw the reader's attention to the proper way of reading the work. Lamb on restoration comedy talks similarly . . . . De Quincey, in his famous 'On the Knocking at the Gate in Macbeth', combines autobiographical with more objective remarks and illustrates how a composite method can be used in practical criticism, to establish an impressive series of points (*op.cit.* pp. 269-270).

A. C. Swinburne, pleading for sobering critical sternness with sympathetic consideration for the object of critical statement writes :

Reserving always as unquestionable and indisputable the primal and instinctive truths of aesthetics as of ethics, of art as of character, of poetry as of conduct, we are bound under penalty of preposterous failure, of self-convicted and self-conscious injustice, to take into full account the circumstances of time and accident which affected for better or for worse the subjects of our moral or critical sentence. The best and the greatest are not above or beyond the need of such consideration ; and some due allowance of it, not sufficient to disturb the balance of our judgment or derange the verdict of our conscience, should possibly be extended to the meanest and worst (A. C. Swinburne : *Miscellaneous*, London, Chatto & Windus ; 1911 Pt. (IX-X) in the Preface).

Joseph Conrad, one of the great names in modern fiction, discusses the essentially impressionist characteristic of the view of fiction. He writes in the preface to *The Nigger of the Narcissus :*

Fiction—if it at all aspires to be art—appeals to temperament. And in truth it must be, like painting, like music, like all art, the appeal of one temperament to all other innumerable temperaments whose subtle and resistless power endows passing events with their true meaning, and creates the moral, the emotional atmosphere of the place and time. Such an appeal to be effective must be an impression conveyed through the sense ;

and, in fact, it cannot be made in any other way, because temperament, whether individual or collective, is not amenable to persuasion. All art, therefore, appeals primarily to the senses, and the artistic aim when expressing itself in written words must also make its appeal through the senses, if its high desire is to reach the secret spring of responsive emotions. It must strenuously aspire to the plasticity of sculpture, the colour of painting, and to the magic suggestiveness of music—which is the art of arts (Quoted in *The Great Critics*, compiled and edited by J. H. Smith and Winfield Parks, New York, 1951, page 914).

Literary impressionism finds its most outspoken exponent in Anatole France. He explicitly articulates an impressionistic critical theory in *The Literary Life* :

As I understand criticism it is, like philosophy and history, a kind of novel for the use of discreet and curious mind. And every novel, rightly understood, is an autobiography. The good critic is he who relates the adventures of his soul among masterpieces.

He continues :

There is no such thing as objective criticism any more than there is objective art, and all who flatter themselves that they put aught but themselves into their work are dupes of the most fallacious illusion. The truth is that one never gets out of one self. That is one of our greatest miseries. What would we not give to see, if not for a minute, the sky and the earth with the many faceted eye of a fly, or to understand nature with the rude and simple brain of an ape ? But just that is forbidden for us. We cannot, like Tiresias, be men and remember having been women. We are locked into our persons as into a lasting prison. The best we can do, it seems to me, is gracefully to recognize this terrible situation and to admit that we speak of ourselves every time that we have the strength to be silent.

To be quite frank, the critic ought to say :

Gentlemen, I am going to talk about myself on the subject of Shakespeare, or Racine or Pascal, or Goethe—subjects that offer me a beautiful opportunity (Quoted in *The Great Critics*, New York, 1953 pp. 916-917).

In the above assertions of Anatole France we notice the metamorphosis which impressionism has undergone in its evolution from painting to literary criticism. In criticism, at the hands of Anatole France and his followers, impressionism becomes synonymous with pure subjectivity. The same emphasis on aesthetic subjectivity, nay, on the subjectivity of human experience in general, Walter Pater writes in "The Conclusion" to *The Renaissance* (1873, First Edition) :

At first sight experience seems to us under a flood of external objects, pressing upon us with a sharp and importunate reality, calling us out of ourselves in a thousand forms of action. But when reflection begins to play upon those objects they are dissipated under its influence; the cohesive force seems suspended like some trick of magic ; each object is loosed into a group of impression—colour, odour, texture—in the mind of the observer. And if we continue to dwell in thought on this word, not of objects in the solidity with which language invests them, but of impressions, unstable, flickering, inconsistent, which burn and are extinguished with our consciousness of them it contracts still further: the whole scope of observation is dwarfed into the narrow chamber of the individual mind. Experience, already reduced to a group of impressions, is ringed round for each one of us by that wall of personality through which no real voice has ever pierced on its way to us, from us to that which we can only conjecture, be without. Every one of those impressions is the impression of the individual in his isolation, each mind keeping as a solitary prisoner its own dream of a world (Quoted in *The Great Critics*, New York, 1953, pp. 895-896).

But impressionism in criticism and creation has had its day, and with the writings of T. S. Eliot, T. E. Hulme, Ezra Pound, and the Imagists in general (in short, with the beginning of the new tendencies in the 1920's) we have a devastating attack on the literary and critical impressionists. T. S. Eliot dilating on the essential absurdity of the impressionist position writes in *The Sacred Wood*, attacking Arthur Symons as an 'aesthetic' or 'impressionistic' critic :

> Mr. Symons represents the other tendency; he is a representative of what is always called 'aesthetic criticism' or 'impressionistic criticism'. And it is this form of criticism which I propose to examine at once. Mr. Symons, the critical successor of Pater, and partly of Swinburne ... is the 'impressionistic critic,' He, or anyone, would be said to expose a sensitive and cultivated mind,—cultivated, that is, by the accumulation of a considerable variety of impressions from all the arts and several languages —before 'object'; and his criticism, if any one's, would be said to exhibit to us, like the plate, the faithful record of the impressions, more numerous or more refined than our own, upon a mind more sensitive than our own (page 3).

In the next few lines, Eliot, by a subtle process of logic, demolishes the impressionist argument by pointing out that the impressions of the impressionists are no longer pure impressions, but an admixture of interpretation, translation of impressions into images, metaphors, etc., and analysis. In Eliot's own words :

> A record, we observe, which is also an interpretation, a translation ; for it must itself impose impressions upon us, and these impressions are as much created as transmitted by the criticism. I do not say at once that this is Mr. Symons ; but it is the 'impressionistic' critic, and the impressionistic critic is supposed to be Mr. Symons (page 3).

T. S. Eliot calls such a sentimental critic who trusts in inward responses an imperfect critic, and says :

> The sentimental person, in whom a work of art arouses all sorts of emotions which have nothing to do with that work of art whatever, but are accidents of personal association, is an incomplete artist.

Impressionism is no longer an important force in our time.

Symbolism

Symbolism assumed the status and importance of a literary movement with a definite set of doctrines in the last quarter of the nineteenth century in France, and in the first decades of the present century in England. Although, it might thus appear to be a movement of late origin, there are critics who maintain that art, at all times, in one sense or other, had been symbolic. There are a few philosophers, too, who, besides giving support to this critical opinion, emphatically maintain that all human achievements—science, language, myth, culture, religion, and civilisation—are all symbolic forms.

The origin of aesthetic symbolism as a deliberately self-conscious movement in the last century and the vogue of the philosophy of symbolism in the present century have to be viewed as parallel phenomena, both arising as a reaction against the nineteenth-century attitude to art and thought. One of the principal components of this attitude was naturalism, both artistic and philosophical, and it is very fruitful to consider symbolism as a philosophical and artistic protest against naturalism. But it has to be borne in mind that while this is a convenient approach, it has the defect of having over-simplified, what, in essence, is a complex phenomenon.

Literary symbolism has both a philosophical and metaphysical basis in so far as it repudiates the merely naturalistic interpretation of reality, and presents an alternative conception communicable only through symbols. Thus it poses technical problems of artistic communication, metaphysical problems of the nature of ultimate reality, and epistomological problems relating to the human apprehension of that reality. This three-fold complexity is inherent in any definition of symbolism which one may come across at random.

"Symbolism was an artistic movement flourishing at the end of the nineteenth century, in reaction to faith in nature, and endeavouring to represent spiritual values by means of abstract signs." (*Dictionary of Philosophy*, Ed. by D. Runes, London, George Routledge and Sons Ltd., 1945, p. 308). *A New English Dictionary* (Vol. IX, Part II) speaks of Symbolism as "a symbolic meaning attributed to natural objects", and of a symbolist as "one who aims at symbolizing ideas rather than representing the form or aspect of actual objects", or "one who aims at representing ideas and emotions by indirect suggestion rather than by direct expression, and attach a symbolic meaning to particular objects, words and sound". The focus of our attention in discussing Symbolism should be on such terms of the difinitions as "reaction to faith in beauty of nature", "spiritual values", "symbolizing by indirect suggestions", and "symbolic meaning". The implications of these terms and other related concepts have been examined in detail by recent philosophers and a new philosophy of symbolic forms has come into being. Ernest Cassirer and Susanne K. Langer are two of the most important names to be remembered in this centext.

Symbolist philosophers like Cassirer have been deeply interested in art and poetry, and symbolist poets, like Yeats, concerned with philosophical problems. The conception of art as symbolic is as old as Plotinus at least. Schlegel declared that the essence of all art is symbolic. Carlyle in England, and Goethe in Germany, gave currency to the symbolistic conception of art.

We should note that in all their writings it is the universe of Newton and Darwin, and the implications of a materialistic and mechanistic world-view that they are repudiating. The mechanistic world-view arising out of Newtionism and the biological materialism arising out of Darwinism have both led to the rejection of the supernatural. Instead of a metaphyical view of reality they presented a dialectical one. Blake, a romantic symbolist in the eighteenth century, and Carlyle, an idealist symbolist in the nineteenth century, had entered the lists against naturalism, materialism and all other self-sufficient systems. However, it was Ernest Cassirer (1874-1925) who systematized all these reactions into a coherent philosophy of symbolic forms and his views therefore deserve a little more detailed examination.

Cassirer carried on elaborate researches into Symbolism. He found that the Symbolist Movement had always many sided associations, now with anthropology and human scholarship, now with mathematical logic, and logical positivism, and now with psychology, religion and ethics. This led him to conclude that "symbolforming" is the most essential character of man and "symbols" have a primary place in the progressive emergence of man's self-consciousness. Man has to face the polar opposites of the realm of the spirit and the realm of matter. Man is neither an exclusive idealist; nor an exclusive materialist. He can by the aid of symbols participate in the realms of both, and thus symbols are the mediating tools of man. Man is able to live in an "in-between realm" of deposited meanings and distanced images by the aid of symbols. The faculty of symbol-formation, and not reason, is for Cassirer what makes man distinctly human. A symbol for Cassirer is an ideal object halfway between the material and spiritual world. It is thus always ambiguous because of its polarity and it is the chief tool by which man cuts himself free from nature and reinstates himself in the universe of intelligible forms and functions. As a result of this view, Cassirer looks upon all expression of the creative spirit of man, art, myth, language, religion, science and civilization as symbolic forms.

The conception of the "symbol" as that which embodies, and capable of evoking, indefinite suggestiveness constituted the common meeting point between Symbolist philosophers and poets.

The word "symbolism", as it is obvious, is derived from the word "symbol", and the letter has multivalent significations. It is used by some writers as synonymous with sign, or a conventional sign which functions as such in virtue of a convention explicit or implicit. It is something which stands for or represents or denotes something else (not by exact resemblance) but by vague suggestion or by accidental or conventional relation. In aesthetics it is considered as an object which apart from its own immediate and proper significance suggests also another, especially a more ideal content which it cannot perfectly embody. The symbolism, attributed to an object, could be natural as light is taken to be the symbol of truth or merely traditional as cross is taken to represent sacrifice.

The symbol thus became a convenient artistic tool to embody the peculiar sensibilities of a group of French poets, of whom Baudelaire is considered to be the first important representative and Mallarme its conclusion and crown.

All the Symbolist poets, whether of the French or of the Anglo-American tradition, believe that single events and individual persons are petty, transient, and unimportant. They cannot be made subjects worthy of art unless they are shown to be symbols of eternal truths. This belief shows the influence of Platonism which maintains that everything in the world is merely a poor copy of its perfect pattern in heaven, and could be understood by those who know that perfect pattern, and these for Plato were speculative philosophers, while the Symbolists held that imagina-

tive artist alone can see significance in trivial daily things and apprehend the celestial pattern. We may take Baudelaire in France
in the last century and W. B. Yeats in England in the present century as typical representatives of symbolism and a brief examination of their methods will illustrate the symbolistic poetic art.

One is initially baffled by the morbidity and the Satanism of
the poems of Baudelaire (*Fleurs du Mal*, and *Tableaux Parisiens*).
Baudelaire believed that the symbolical images of his poems ac-
costed the ineffable, and the images from the external world cor-
responded to his own inner life, so that his poems were also
portraits of himself, and the meaning of these poems is in the
interaction between the symbol and the spiritual or the subjective
state symbolized.

In the most disturbing poems of *Tableaux Parisiens* he presents
with horror, compassion and equanimity the swarming streets of
Paris, the garbage carts, rags, sewers, and the mud, and in so
doing he was not presenting as a naturalist, catalogues of the in-
fernal aspects of Paris. According to Baudelaire, the artist must
far from copying nature select significant images, heighten them
and use them to project his vision. In certain almost supernatural
states of the human soul the depth of life is revealed in ordinary
everyday happenings. Ordinary life then becomes the "symbol"
(Baudelaire : *Journaux Intimes*).

Mallarme further developed these doctrines into a literary
theory. For the Symbolists, if words are to do their special job of
suggesting the ineffable, they had to be relieved of their normal
meanings, removed from their familier contexts until purified.
Then they could provoke reveries, resonances, and suggestions.
Poems thus built by meticulous crafts from words deprived of
syntax could suggest things too fugitive for expression, and meanings at once precise and multiple. Poems so composed are in one
sense absolute, far from meaning, from time, chance, life, passion
and matter. A symphonic relationship among the parts of the
poems takes the place of a comprehensible relationship with
external things. It is much the same thing which Mallarme implied when he said that the poem "is a mystery to which the reader
must hunt the key." Abandoning the hope of single interpretation,
he must discover the main images, observe the effect upon them of
peripheral images and guess the idea generated by their interaction.

Although Symbolism entered the theatre by 1895, through Maeterlinck and Villiers, there was a falling away from the symbolist ideal. Among the English Symbolists we have George Moore, Oscar Wilde, Arthur Symons, Ernest Dowson, Edmund Gosse, and W. B. Yeats. Wilde's book *Salome* is thoroughly symbolic. Arthur Symons was the most note-worthy populariser of Symbolism in England.

About these English Symbolists, except Yeats, much need not be said because as compared to the French they were small figures. Their achievements too are not very great. They were content merely with making poems exotic and they are not symbolistic according to the strict definitions of Mallarme. They are the products of the marriage of exhausted English Romanticism and French Decadence. This fact, in particular, makes Edmund Wilson consider (inaccurately) Symbolism as a second wave of the earlier Romantic revolt (in *Axel's Castle*).

Arthur Symons considered W. B. Yeats as the chief representative of English symbolism. But Yeats belongs to an independent and parallel tradition coming down from Blake and Shelley. Besides these, Yeats was influenced in his development by the Symbolist Theosophy, the occultism of the Rosicrucians and the Hermetical Society, and the Upanishadic doctrines of India. He came to poetry with a definite set of convictions to express which he found the symbol, the only medium. One of these important convictions was that contemporary man must be free from the shackles of his conventional habits of thought, which in our era has become scientific, pragmatic, and sociological. Yeats, like Eliot felt that there had been a dissociation of sensibility or as Professor Vivian de Sola Pinto terms it a "schism in the soul" which was leading to "standardization and uniformity" as far as human personality was concerned. In the words of Prof. Pinto :

Standardization and uniformity have been noted by Arnold Toynbee as marks of the period of 'schism in the soul' which heralds the decay of civilization....A new kind of poetry was needed to express that 'schism in the soul', which is the most significant fact in the modern world and at the same time to attempt the supremely difficult task of overcoming it and creating a new spiritual integration, thus defying at any rate on the imaginative plane, the process of standardization which was proceeding rapidly in an industrialised society (V. S. de Pinto, *Crisis in English Poetry*, 1951, London, pp. 11-12).

Yeats' poetic endeavour was devoted to this specific task mentioned by Prof. Pinto. He brings out a philosophy of life, art, and civilization in his prose work, *A Vision* (1925). The symbol was the means, as it was for Blake, through which he could restore on the imaginative plane the organic unity of life. A symbol for him was a unified, meaningful, complex, and revelatory thing. He uses a collection of symbolic cluster in his major poems; the symbol of the city of 'Byzantium' in his *Byzantium* poems, the symbol of the 'Tower' in the volume of poems with that name and the symbol of 'Rose' in the earlier lyrics. That Yeats was able to suggest a deeper meaning of life and a sense of unity in the midst of division and fragmentation through literary symbolism is his strongest claim to the title of a great poet.

Much the same social, philosophical and metaphysical factors have been operative in the Symbolists like T. S. Eliot, Edith Sitwell, and Dylan Thomas. Some criticism and comments on Symbolism are given below.

Joseph T. Shipley, dealing with the birth of the Symbolist Movement, writes :

Influences from various lands aided the French in their development. The social sympathy of England was reinforced by the Russian Chorus. The positivism of Comte was countered by the progress of Renan towards intellectual idealism...Wagner was calling for an art that should move...from without, inward; from within, upward. Geothe and Browning viewed the works of art as sign-post for an inner journeying. Heine declared : 'In matters of art I am a supernaturalist".

He continues :

Here is the birth of Symbolism. Symbols, of course, are as old as man. Language itself is a symbol; and every art is another tongue; and every artist proffers but his coined token. But we are now told that every sensible phenomenon may yield the central core of all philosophy. Mallarme, the most deliberate of the school, strove to make every phrase 'a plastic image, the ex-

RECORDS — PRODUCER & NUMBER

call number

author / composer / etc.   format

title

TO OBTAIN MATERIAL, BRING SLIP TO MEDIA CENTER
LORETTE WILMOT LIBRARY

808.1
wsu

820.9
Pal

801
Ste

808.3
Ald

critic essay

pression of a thought, the stir of a feeling, and the draught of a philosophy'. Object and essence, the view and the vision : here is a blending indeed !

He comments on the nature of Symbolistic art :

As the most fundamental characteristic of the Romantics was the direct presentation of the personal feeling, we must expect their successors' subjectivity to be accompanied by a deliberate attempt to remove any signs of the artist's emotion. To the Romantic, a poem is a heart-cry, or a tear. Even with Gautier, it is nearer to an itemized account ; and many today consider that a work of art should be modelled upon a stock-taking or a laboratory experiment. Again, the symbolist bridges the chasm between the instant emotion and the ultimate calm. The ego and things, man and nature, are, in the Romantic, opposed ; in the Parnassian, severed—and the ego withdrawn, in the symbolist, fused. Mallarme arrives at this unity through the force of a rigorous logic ; Baudelaire forges it in the white heat of passion. Suffering, soul-wringing anguish marred the life of Baudelaire, as his diaries deeply attest. His normal state was akin to the chaos of madness ; it was only when he was inspired (as Plato would say, possessed) that his spirit through the pressure grew clear and radiant as diamond. Then the torture of his days, the wind from the wing of imbecility, the knell of a wretched doom, were chaliced in loving attention and crystallized in deathless form (p. 163).

And again :

In the poerty of the symbolist, words and music were one. Baudelaire announced the intimate union : 'Poetry joins music by a prosody whose roots plunge deeper into the human soul than any classical theory indicates. Looking back in the great symbolist period (1885-1895) during which decade the partial bibliography of Remy de Gourmont lists one hundred and thirty magazines of the school), Valery goes so far as to say : What has been baptized symbolism is very simply, the determination of several groups of poets (otherwise enemies) to recapture their endowment from music. We are nourished on music, and our literary heads dream only of winning from language the same effects which pure sounds produce on the nervous system.

What the symbolist hearkens is the music of spheres. He seeks to express the eternal and essential analogy between a moment of the continuance of the ego and a moment of the continuance of things (p. 169).

About Symbolism, in general, Prof. C. M. Bowra (in *The Heritage of Symbolism*) observes :

A poetical movement is recognised in its exponents, and the chief poets of symbolism are Baudelaire, Verlaine and Mallarme. Baudelaire was the first to exalt the use of symbols; Verlaine used them instinctively, and Mallarme erected a metaphysic to explain and justify them. In his theory and practice Mallarme was the conclusion and crown of the Symbolist Movement. In spite of its many shapes symbolism was united by a single creed which determined the character of its poetry.

Seen in restrospect the Symbolist Movement of the nineteenth century in France was fundamentally mystical. It protested with noble eloquence against the scientific art of an age which had lost much of its belief in traditional religion and hoped to find a substitute in the search for truth.

Against scientific Realism the Symbolists protested, and their protest was mystical in that it was made on behalf of an ideal world which was, in their judgment, more real than that of the sense....It was a religion of Ideal Beauty, of 'le Beau' and of the 'Ideal'.

Prof. Bowra compares the latter-day Symbolists with the earlier religious Symbolists :

A doctrine of this character has much in common with that of orthodox religious poets. Just as Mallarme tried to capture in verse an ideal beauty, so Dante had created his image by the accepted symbols of the Christian Heaven and Hell, so Mallarme too had to use symbols. He and his followers are rightly called Symbolists, because they attempted to convey a supernatural experience in the language of visible things, and therefore almost every word is a symbol and is used not for its common purpose but for the associations which it evokes of a reality beyond the senses. His methods are not new. It may be seen in the apocalyptic poems of William Blake, and mystical literature is almost inconceivable without it. But whereas most earlier Symbolists had been concerned with the facts of religious devotion, Mallarme was concerned with a special aesthetic experience which he interpreted as a saint might his visions of God...."

The essence of Symbolism is its insistence on a world of ideal beauty, and its conviction that this is realised through art. The ecstasies which religion claims for the devout through prayer and contemplation are claimed by the Symbolists for the poet through the exercise of his craft.... For the undivided attention which the enraptured worshipper gives to the object of his prayers and the sense of timeless contentment which he finds through them are not entirely different from the pure aesthetic state which seems to obliterate distinctions of time and place of self and not-self, of sorrow and joy.

Prof. Bowra points out their defects :

Symbolism, then, was in origin a mystical kind of poetry whose technique depended on its metaphysics and whose first popularity was due to the importance that it gave to poet's self and to the element of music in his art. It made converts and spread to many lands. But behind this golden promise lurked defects, not indeed fatal or fundamental but still insidious. By the simple act of cutting himself off from vulgar emotions and concentrating on private visions the Symbolist severed himself from a large part of life and his work became the activity of a cultivated few. This fastidiousness drove a wedge between poetry and ordinary life. The public finding itself despised and feeling that the new poetry was beyond its comprehension, turned to cruder authors. And the poets, cut off from the public, were forced back on themselves and deprived of the strength which may be found in streets and crowds (pp. 1-15).

Jean Moreas describes Symbolism as follows :

Enemy of explanation, of declamation, of false sensibility, of objective description, symbolist poetry tries to clothe the Idea in a palpable form, which, nevertheless, is not an end itself, but which, while serving to express the Idea, remains subject to it. The Idea in its turn does not let itself be seen without sumptuous trains of exterior analogies; for the essential character of symbolic art consists in never going to the conception of the Idea in itself. Thus in this art, pictures of natures, actions of men, concrete phenomena are not therefore there for their own sake, but as simple appearances destined to represent their esoteric affinities with primordial ideas (*Les Premieres Armes du Symbolism, 1889*).

About the high functions of symbols, Thomas Carlyle writes :

In the symbol proper, what we can call a symbol, there is ever more or less distinctly and directly, some embodiment and revelation of the infinite : the infinite is made to blend itself with the finite, to stand visible, and as it were, attainable there. By symbols, accordingly, is man guided and commanded, made happy, made wretched. He everywhere finds himself encompassed with Symbols, recognised as such or not recognised : the Universe is but one vast Symbol of God ; if thou wilt have it, what is man himself but a Symbol of God ; is not all that he does symbolical ; a revelation to sense of the mystic god-given force that is in him ; a 'Gospel of Freedom', which he, the "Messias of Nature", preaches, as he can, by act and by act and word ? Not a Hut he builds but is the visible embodiment of a Thought ; but hears visible record to invisible things ; but is, in the transcendental sense, symbolical as well as real" (*Sartor Resartus*, Book III, Chapter III).

We find the same conception of the Symbol in Blake :

To see a World in a Grain of Sand
And Heaven in Wild Flower,
Hold Infinity in the Palm of your Hand
And Eternity in an Hour.

W. B. Yeats maintains that : "All symbolic art should arise out of real belief". (*Discoveries*, 1906). In William Blake, and his

"*Illustrations to the Divine Comedy*", Yeats distinguishes between allegory and symbolism :

I find that I love symbolism, which is often the only fitting speech for some mystery of disembodied life. I am for the most part bored by allegory, which is made, as Blake says, by the daughters of memory and with no wizard frenzy.

It is easy to see how this idea of the exalted function of the symbol and symbolism has been employed by recent philosophers too. Karl Jaspers (in *Way to Wisdom*, 1951, New Haven, Yale University Press) speaks of the metaphysical symbol :

Through metaphysics we obtain an intimation of the comprehensive in transcendence. We understand this metaphysics as symbol...its content is manifested to us only if we perceive the reality in the symbol (pp. 25-36).

Ernest Cassirer (in *Language and Myth*, translated by Susanne K. Langer, Dover Publications, Inc.) observes :

For all mental processes fail to grasp reality itself, and in order to represent it, to hold it at all, they (men) are driven to use symbols. But all symbolism harbours the curse of vagueness; it is bound to obscure what it seeks to reveal. (p. 7).

In the *Philosophy of Symbolic Forms* (Vol. II, p. 120) he writes :

The characteristic and peculiar achievement of each symbolic form—the form of language as well as that of myth or of theoretical cognition is not simply to receive a given material of impressions possessing already certain determination, quality and structure, in order to graft on it, from the outside, so to speak, another form out of the energy of consciousness itself.

And again :

When one characterises language, myth, art, as 'symbolic forms' then there seems to lie in that expression the presupposition that all of them, as definite modes of the spirit, point back to a last primary layer of reality, which is seen through them only, like through a strange medium" (pp. 296-297).

Dealing with languages as one of the symbolic forms he says :

The function of language is not to copy reality, but to symbolize it (*Philosophy of Symbolic Forms*, Vol. 1).

Susanne K. Langer in *Feeling and Form* (Routledge and Keegan Paul Ltd., 1953) defines art itself in terms of symbol : "Art is the creation of forms symbolic of human feeling" (p. 40).

Wilbur Marshall Urban (*Language and Reality* : London, 1939) discusses the apprehension of reality through the symbolic agency :

The essential function of the symbol—and this as the expansion of any symbol shows— is to give us insight into, or knowledge of certain aspects of reality. We may, if we will, call this "perspected" in contrast to "asserted" reality—although, as I have already shown, assertions are always implicit—nevertheless, it still remains true that when the symbol is expanded, the insight given by the symbol finds expression in assertions which have significance for discursive knowledge (p. 491).

In the opinion of Urban :

The complete interpretation of a poetic symbol leads ultimately to the interpretation of poetry itself as a mode of apprehending that reality. To determine the existential or ontological implications of a symbol is to determine the ontological implications of the language of which the symbol is a part. Otherwise expressed, the language of poetry 'says something' about reality (p. 492). The symbolist movement is one of the most powerful currents of influence on the art and thought of our times.

BIBLIOGRAPY

General

ABRAMS, M. H., *The Mirror and the Lamp*, 1953.

ALLEN, G. W., and H. H. CLARK, *Literary Criticism : Pope to Croce*, 1962.

ATKINS, J. W. H., *English Literary Criticism : the Medieval Phase*, 1961.

AUERBACH, ERICH, *Mimesis*, tr. by W. R. Trask, 1953.

BATE, W. J. ED., *Criticism : The Major Texts*, 1948.

BROWN, C. A., *The Achievement of American Criticism : Representative Selections from Three Hundred Years of American Criticism*, 1954.

CRANE, R. S., and OTHERS, *Critics and Criticism, Ancient and Modern*, 1952.

ELIOT, T. S., *The Use of Poetry and the Use of Criticism : Studies in the Relation of Criticism to Poetry in England*, 1933.

FOERSTER, NORMAN, *American Criticism : A Study in Literary Theory from Poe to the Present*, 1962.

GILBERT, A. H., *Literary Criticism : Plato to Dryden*, 1962.

GLICKSBERG, C. I., *American Literary Criticism*, 1952.

LEVIN, HARRY, ED., *Perspectives of Criticism*, 1950.

O' CONNOR, WILLIAM V., *An Age of Criticism, 1900-1950*, 1952.

PRITCHARD, J. P., *Criticism in America*, 1956.

SAINTSBURY, GEORGE, *A History of Criticism and Literary Taste in Europe*, 3 vols., 4th edition, 1949.

SCOTT-JAMES, R. A., *The Making of Literature*, 1936.

SHIPLEY, J. T., *Quest for Literature : A Survey of Literary Criticism and the Theories of the Literary Forms*, 1931.

SHIPLEY, J. T., ED., *Dictionary of World Literature : Criticism ...Forms... Technique*, 1943.

SMITH, J. H., and E. W. PARKS, EDS., *The Great Critics : An Anthology of Literary Criticism*, 1951.

STALLMAN, R. W., *Critiques and Essays in Criticism, 1920-1948, Representing the Achievement of Modern British and American Critics*, 1951.

WARREN, A. H., JR., *English Poetic Theory, 1825-1865*, 1950.

WEBER, EUGEN, ED., *Paths to the Present : Aspects of European Thought from Romantic Criticism to Existentialism*, 1960.

WELLEK, RENE, *A History of Modern Criticism, 1955-1965*, 4 vols.

WELLEK, RENE, and AUSTIN WARREN, *Theory of Literature*, 1956.

WEST, R. B. JR., *Essays in Modern Literary Criticism*, 1952.

WIMSATT, W. K., JR., and CLEANTH BROOKS, *Literary Criticism : A Short History*, 1957.

ZABEL, M. D., ED., *Literary Opinion in America : Essays Illustrating the Status, Methods and Problems of Criticism in the United States in the Twentieth Century*, 1951.

Plato

ATKINS, JOHN, W. H., *Literary Criticism in Antiquity : A Sketch of its Development*, 2 vols., 1934.

COLLINGWOOD, R. G., *The Principles of Art*, 1938.

GRUBE, G. M. A., *Plato's Thought*, 1935.

PLATO, *Dialogues*, tr. by Lane Cooper, 1938.

PLATO, *Dialogues*, tr. by Benjamin Jowett, 1892.

PLATO, *Dialogues*, Loeb Classics Series, 1917-1935.

SHOREY, PAUL, *What Plato Said*, 1933.

TAYLOR, A. E., *Plato*, 1929.

Aristotle

BUTCHER, S. H., *Aristotle's Theory of Poetry and Fine Art*, Dover Publications, 1959.

BYWATER, INGRAM, *Aristotle on the Art of Poetry*, Oxford, 1959.

COLLINGWOOD, R. G., *The Principles of Art*, Oxford, 1955.

COOPER, LANE, *Aristotle on the Art of Poetry*, New York, 1946.

DIXON, D. M., *On Tragedy*, London, 1924.

ELSE, *Aristotle's Poetics : The Argument*, Harvard, 1957.

FERGUSSON, FRANCIS, *Aristotle's Poetics*, 'Introduction', ; New York, 1957.

FYFE, W. H., *Aristotle, The Poetics*, 1927.

FYFE, HAMILTON, *Aristotle's Art of Poetry : A Greek View of Poetry and Drama*, 'Introduction', Oxford, 1961.

HERRICK, M. T., *The Poetics of Aristotle in England*, 1930.

HUMPHRY, HOUSE, *Aristotle's Poetics*, London, 1961.

KITTO, H. D. F., *Greek Tragedy*, London, 1961.

LUCAS, D. W., *The Greek Tragic Poets*, London, 1959.

WARRY, J. G., *Greek Aesthetic Theory*, London 1962.

Renaissance Criticism and Sir Philip Sidney

ATKINS, JOHN, W. H., *English Literary Criticism : The Renaissance*, 1951.

BALDWIN, C. S., *Renaissance Literary Theory and Practice*, edited with introduction by D. L. Clark, 1939.

SMITH, G. G., ED., *Elizabethan Essays*, 2 vols., 1937.

SPINGARN, J. E., *A History of Literary Criticism in the Renaissance*, 1908.

SPINGARN, J. E., ED., *Critical Essays of the Seventeenth Century*, 3 vols., 1908.

John Dryden

ARNOLD, THOMAS, ED., *Dryden's Essay of Dramatic Poesy*, 1903.

ATKINS, J. W. H., *English Literary Criticism: 17th and 18th Centuries*, 1951.

BREDVOLD, L. I., *The Intellectual Milieu of John Dryden*, 1934.

ELIOT, T. S., *Homage to Dryden*, 1924.

HUNTLEY, F. L., *On Dryden's "Essay of Dramatic Poesy"*, 1951.

KER, W. P., ED., *The Essays of John Dryden*, 2 vols., 1926.

SMITH, D. N., *John Dryden*, 1950.

VERNON, HALL, *A Short History of Literary Criticism*, 1964.

Wordsworth

BANERJEE, SRIKUMAR, *Critical Theories and Poetic Practice in the "Lyrical Ballads"*, 1931.

BARSTOW, M. L., *Wordsworth : Theory of Poetic Diction*, 1917.

BEATTY, ARTHUR, *William Wordsworth : His Doctrine and Art in Their Historical Relations*, 1922.

SMITH, N. C., ED., *Wordsworth's Literary Criticism*, 1906.

WORDSWORTH, W., *Lyrical Ballads : A Reprint*, edited with introduction by H. Littledale, 1911.

WORDSWORTH, W., *Prose Works*, edited by William Knight, 2 vols., 1896.

Coleridge

BEER, J. B., *Coleridge, The Visionary*, 1959.

COLERIDGE, S. T., *Biographia Literaria*, edited by J. A. Symons, 1908.

COLERIDGE, S. T., *Literary Life and Opinions*, edited by J. A. Symons, New York, 1908.

COLERIDGE, S. T., *Lectures and Essays on Shakespeare and Some Other Old Poets and Dramatists*, 1907.

COLERIDGE, S. T., *Letters of Coleridge*, edited by E.H. Coleridge, 2 vols., 1895.

COLERIDGE, S. T., *Miscellanies, Aesthetic and Literary*, collected and edited by A. J. George, Boston, 1895.

FOGLE, R. H., *The Idea of Coleridge's Criticism*.

RICHARDS, I. A., *Coleridge on Imagination*, 2nd edition, 1950.

SHERWOOD, MARGARET, *Coleridge's Imaginative Conception of the Imagination*, 1937.

Matthew Arnold

ARNOLD, MATTHEW, *Essays in Criticism*, First and Second Series, Complete, 1902.

ARNOLD, MATTHEW, *Essays in Criticism*, 3rd Series, 1910.

ARNOLD, MATTHEW, *Essays Letters and Reviews*, collected by Fraser Neiman, 1960.

BUCKLEY, VINCENT, *Poetry and Morality*, 1959.

DAWSON, W. H., *Matthew Arnold and His Relation to the Thought of Our Time*, 1904.

GARROD, H. W., *Poetry and the Criticism of Life*, 1931.

HARVEY, C. H., *Matthew Arnold, A Critic of the Victorian Period*, 1931.

T. S. Eliot

BROMBERT, V. H., *The Criticism of T. S. Eliot : Problems of an "Impersonal" Theory of Poetry*, 1949.

BUCKLEY, VINCENT, *Poetry and Morality*, 1959.

ELIOT, T. S., *Essays: Ancient and Modern*, 1936.

ELIOT, T. S., *The Frontiers of Criticism*, 1956.

ELIOT, T. S., *Selected Essays*, 1950.

ELIOT, T. S., *The Use of Poetry and the Use of Criticism*, 1933.

ELIOT, T. S., *On Poetry and Poets*, 1957.

GEORGE, A. G., *T. S. Eliot : His Mind and Art*, 1962.

Naturalism

BALFOUR, A. J., *The Foundation of Belief*, 1901.

BALFOUR, A. J., *Theism and Humanism*, 1915.

BERGSON, H., *Creative Evolution*, 1912.

BROAD, C. D., *The Mind and its Place in Nature*.

COLLINGWOOD, R. G., *The Idea of Nature*, 1945.

KRUTCH, J. W., *The Modern Temper*, 1929.

OTTO, RUDOLF, *Naturalism and Religion*, 1907.

PERRY, R. B., *Present Philosophical Tendencies*, 1912.

SANTAYANA, G., *The Life of Reason*, 5 vols., 1922.

WARD, JAMES, *Naturalism and Agnosticism*, 1915.

WHITEHEAD, A. N., *Science and the Modern World*.

WHITEHEAD, A. N., *The Concept of Nature*, 1925.

Marxism

BURGUM, E. B., *The Novel and the World's Dilemma*, 1947.

FARRELL, JAMES, T., *A Note on Literary Criticism*, 1936.

KLINGENDER, F. D., *Marxism and Modern Art*, 1943.

LIPSHITZ, MIKHAIL, *The Philosophy of Art of Karl Marx*, 1938.

PLEKHANOV, GOERGI, *Art and Society*, translated from the Russian, 1936.

TROTSKY, LEON, *Literature and Revolution*, 1925.

WILSON, EDMUND, *The Triple Thinkers*.

Impressionism

HAUSER, ARNOLD, *A Social History of Art*.

ELIOT, T. S., *The Sacred Wood*.

FRANCE, ANATOLE, *The Literary Life*.

PATER, W., Essays from the "Guardian".

PATER, W., *Marius the Epicurean*.

PATER, W., *The Renaissance.*
PATER, W., *Plato and Platonism.*
SWINBURNE, A. C., *Miscellanies.*
WOOLF, VIRGINIA, *The Common Reader.*

Symbolism

BAUDELAIRE, *Intimate Journals.*
BOWRA, C. M., *The Heritage of Symbolism,* 1954.
CASSIRER, ERNEST, *An Essay on Man.*
CASSIRER, ERNEST, *The Myth of State.*
CASSIRER, ERNEST, *The Philosophy of Symbolic Forms.*
CASSIRER, ERNEST, *Language and Myth.*
LANGER, SUSANNE, *Feeling and Form,* 1953.
OGDEN and RICHARDS, *Meaning of Meaning.*
RAYMOND, MARCEL, *From Baudelaire to Surrealism,* 1950.
SYMONS, ARTHUR, *The Symbolist Movement in Literature,* 1899.
URBAN, WILBUR MARSHALL, *Language and Reality,* 1953.
YEATS, W. B., *A Vision,* 1925.

Modern Criticism

BELL, CLIVE, *Art.*
BLACKMUR, R. P., *Language as Gesture,* 1953.
BURKE, KENNETH, *The Philosophy of Literary Form : Studies in Symbolic Action,* 1957.
DAICHES, DAVID, *Critical Approaches to Literature,* 1956.
DAICHES, DAVID, *The Present Age.*
FOSTER, R. J., *The New Romantics : A Reappraisal of the New Criticism,* 1962.
FRYE, NORTHROP, *Anatomy of Criticism,* 1957.
GOLDBERG, GERALD J., and N. M., EDS., *The Modern Critical Spectrum,* 1962.
HARDISON, O. B., *Modern Continental Literary Criticism,* 1962.
HOWE, IRVING, *Modern Literary Criticism,* 1958.
HULME, T. E., *Speculations,* 1925.
HYMAN, S. E., *The Armed Vision,* 1948.
KRIEGER, MURRAY, *New Apologists for Poetry,* 1956.
LEAVIS, F. R., *New Bearings in English Poetry.*
LEAVIS, F. R., *Revaluation.*
LEAVIS, F. R., *The Great Tradition.*
LEAVIS, F. R., *The Common Pursuit.*
MOORE, G. E., *Principia Ethica.*
PERRY, R. B., *Present Philosophical Tendencies,* 1912.
RANSOM, J. C., *New Criticism,* 1941.
RICHARDS, I. A., *Science and Poetry.*
RICHARDS, I. A., *Principles of Criticism.*
RICHARDS, I. A., *Practical Criticism.*

SPITZER, LEO, *Linguistics and Literary History*, 1948.

STALLMAN, R. W., *Critiques and Essays in Criticism*, 1949.

STALLMAN, R. W., *The Critic's Notebook*.

WHEELRIGHT, PHILIP, *Metaphor and Reality*, 1962.

WINTERS, YVOR, *In Defence of Reason*.

WINTERS, YVOR, *The Function of Reason*.

ZABEL, M. D., *Literary Opinion in America*, Revised Edition, 1951.